THE CINEMA OF JAPAN AND KOREA

First published in Great Britain in 2004 by
Wallflower Press
4th Floor, 26 Shacklewell Lane, London, E8 2EZ
www.wallflowerpress.co.uk

A catalogue for this book is available from the British Library

ISBN 1-904764-11-8 (paperback)
ISBN 1-904764-12-6 (hardback)

Printed in Turin, Italy by Grafiche Dessi s.r.l.

THE CINEMA OF
JAPAN & KOREA

EDITED BY

JUSTIN BOWYER

 **WALLFLOWER PRESS** LONDON & NEW YORK

24 FRAMES is a major new series focusing on national and regional cinemas from around the world. Rather than offering a 'best of' selection, the feature films and documentaries selected in each volume serve to highlight the specific elements of that territory's cinema, elucidating the historical and industrial context of production, the key genres and modes of representation, and foregrounding the work of the most important directors and their exemplary films. In taking an explicitly text-centred approach, the titles in this list offer 24 diverse entry-points into each national and regional cinema, and thus contribute to the appreciation of the rich traditions of global cinema.

Series Editors: Yoram Allon & Ian Haydn Smith

OTHER TITLES IN THE **24 FRAMES** SERIES:

THE CINEMA OF LATIN AMERICA *edited by Alberto Elena and Marina Díaz López*

THE CINEMA OF THE LOW COUNTRIES *edited by Ernest Mathijs*

THE CINEMA OF ITALY *edited by Giorgio Bertellini*

FORTHCOMING TITLES:

THE CINEMA OF CENTRAL EUROPE *edited by Peter Hames*

THE CINEMA OF SCANDINAVIA *edited by Tytti Soila*

THE CINEMA OF BRITAIN & IRELAND *edited by Brian McFarlane*

THE CINEMA OF SPAIN & PORTUGAL *edited by Alberto Mira*

THE CINEMA OF FRANCE *edited by Phil Powrie*

CONTENTS

NOTES ON CONTRIBUTORS

SAMARA LEA ALLSOP has a Bachelor of Arts (Hons) in Visual Culture and European History from Monash University as well as holding a second Bachelor of Arts (AsSt) in Asian Studies from Murdoch University. She also has a Graduate Certificate in Information Management and Systems and is currently writing a book on Thai contemporary cinema.

ANTHONY ANTONIOU is a freelance film journalist who lives and works in London. He has written extensively for a number of online and print publications on a broad variety of topics, most notably classic and contemporary American narrative cinema, cult movies and genre filmmaking. He is currently working on a book exploring the history of Blaxploitation.

CHRIS BERRY teaches Film Studies at the University of California, Berkeley. His work on Korean culture includes the website *The House of Kim Kiyoung* (www.knua.ac.kr/cinema/index.html), which he compiled with Kim Soyoung, 'What's Big about the Big Film? 'De-Westernising' the Blockbuster in Korea and China', in Julian Stringer (ed.) *Size Matters: Blockbusters in the 1990s* (Routledge, 2003) and 'Syncretism and Synchronicity: Queer 'n' Asian Cyberspace in 1990s Taiwan and Korea', (co-authored with Fran Martin) in Fran Martin and Audrey Yue (eds) *Mobile Cultures: New Media and Queer Asia* (Duke University Press, 2002). He has also written widely on Chinese cinema.

STEPHANIE DEBOER is a PhD candidate in Critical Studies at the School of Cinema-Television, University of Southern California. She holds an MA degree from the departments of Comparative Literature and East Asian Languages and Cultures at Indiana University, Bloomington, where she completed a thesis on modernist writers in Tokyo and Shanghai and their relationship to cinema. She is now writing a dissertation on more recent transnational interfaces among Japanese and Chinese language media, particularly as they relate to questions of gender, space and memory.

ADRIEN GOMBEAUD graduated in Chinese from the Institute of Oriental Languages in Paris, France. He is the author of the thesis *The organization of Space in Korean Cinema from the 1980s to the Present Day* and often writes for *Positif*, amongst other French publications. He is the director of publication of *tan'gun* – a review on Korean culture and society published twice a year in Paris by the Independant Research Centre on Korea.

ANDREW GROSSMAN is the editor of *Queer Asian Cinema: Shadows in the Shade*, the first critical anthology about gay, lesbian and transsexual Asian cinema. He is also co-author of the short monograph *An Actionist Starts to Sing*; a collaboration with Austrian film-maker Otto Muehl. His writings on Asian cinema will appear in the forthcoming anthologies *Chinese Cinema: Diaspora, Text and Identity* (Temple University Press) and *New Korean Cinema* (Edinburgh University Press). He is a regular contributor to *Bright Lights Film Journal, Scope: The Film Journal of the University of Nottingham* and *American Book Review*.

ADAM HARZELL manages the Korean Film Bibliography on the Korean Film webpage, www.koreanfilm.org, where he also contributes film reviews, essays and reviews of books on Korean Film. He has also been published in the online journal, *The Film Journal*.

SOYOUNG KIM is chair of the Cinema Studies Department at the Korean National University of Arts' School of Film and Multimedia. She is a graduate of Sogang University and the Korean Institute of Film Arts in Korea, and is completing a PhD in Cinema Studies at New York University. She served as editor of *Cine-Feminism: Reading the Popular Films* (1994, Seoul) and has written extensively on Korean cinema and the Korean film industry. A noted film critic in Korea, Kim has served on the juries of three film festivals and on the editorial boards of two leading Korean film journals.

HAN JU KWAK majored in philosophy in Seoul National University, Korea, and worked in journalism for fourteen years. He moved to the United States to study film in 1996. He is a doctoral candidate at the School of Cinema and Television, University of Southern California, currently completing his doctoral dissertation on the emergence of 1990s South Korean popular cinema in light of Korea's socio-cultural change. His recent essays appeared in Im Kwon Taek (ed.) *The Making of Korean National Cinema* (Wayne State University Press, 2002) and *Multiple Modernities: Cinemas and Popular Media in Transcultural East Asia* (Temple University Press, 2003). He has also edited a book on cult cinema and co-translated Francois Truffaut's *Hitchcock* into Korean.

ANTHONY LEONG has been a film critic on a part-time basis for six years. In addition to running his own film review and essay site, MediaCircus.net, he has had his articles published in a number of magazines and books. He is a regular contributor to the American magazine *Asian Cult Cinema* and Australia's science fiction and fantasy magazine *Frontier*. He is a recent 'convert' to Korean cinema, and is in the process of writing a book on the subject.

TOM MES is the author of *Agitator: The Cinema of Takashi Miike* (FAB Press, 2003), the first in-depth study of the complete work of the director of *Audition*. Mes is also the founder and co-editor (with Jasper Sharp) of MidnightEye.com, the world's leading English-language publication on contemporary Japanese cinema. His work has appeared in such magazines as *Fangoria* (USA), *IdN* (Hong Kong), *Impact* (UK), *Japan Magazine* (Holland) and *Skrien* (Holland), while his writing on Takashi Miike has been published in England, the USA, Canada, France and Russia. Mes also has a background in animation, having worked as director of scriptwriting and storyboarding for the BAFTA-nominated Dutch animation studio ExtraTainment. He now resides in Paris, France.

MARIA ROBERTA NOVIELLI specialised in Japanese cinema at Nihon University (Tokyo) and now teaches Japanese Cinema and Literature at the Department of Asian Studies of the University Ca' Foscari, Venice. She is a contributor to numerous Italian magazines, including *Cineforum* and *Panoramiche*, the author of *Storia del cinema Giapponese* (*History of Japanese Cinema*, Marsilio, 2001), the first history of Japanese cinema written in Italy. In addition she has cooperated with various Italian film festivals organising retrospectives on Japanese film directors.

DARCY PAQUET studied Russian Language and Literature at Carleton College and Slavic Linguistics/ Applied Linguistics at Indiana University before moving to Seoul in 1997. After teaching English language for several years at Korea University, he began working as English Editor at the Korean Film Commission (KOFIC), a government-supported promotional organisation. In April 1999 he launched the website Koreanfilm.org. He is also the Korea Correspondent for *Screen International*, serves as programme advisor for the Far East Film Festival in Udine, Italy and together with his wife Yeon Hyeon-sook, translates subtitles for Korean films. Articles by Darcy are forthcoming in the anthologies *Made in Korea: Cinema and Society* (Indiana University Press), edited by Frances Gateward and *New Korean Cinema* (Edinburgh University Press), edited by Chi-Yun Shin and Julian Stringer.

PETER HARRY RIS has been teaching film history and aesthetics at Concordia University, Montreal, Canada since 1989. He was Chair of the Mel Hoppenheim School of Cinema (formerly Department of Cinema) for six of these years. He was the principal writer for, and edited *Guide to the Cinema(s) of Canada* (Greenwood Press, 2001) and (co-edited with Timothy Barnard) *South American Cinema: A Critical Filmography, 1915–1994* (University of Texas Press, 1998). He has written extensively on Chinese and Korean cinemas, including the first article on Korean cinema to be published in a Canadian film journal, *Sequences*, in 1997.

JASPER SHARP is the co-founder of the Japanese cinema website MidnightEye.com. His writing on Japanese film and culture has appeared in publications in Britain, Holland, Malaysia and Russia. He is currently based in Tokyo, and is working on a book on contemporary Japanese film.

MAGNUS STANKE spent his teenage years issuing a variety of fanzies, making Super-8 shorts and attempting to write the first German biography of Clint Eastwood. Settling in London after a period of globetrotting he studied at Goldsmith's College, University of London before taking his BA in Hispanic Studies and Drama, also at University of London. He has written several feature screenplays and recently directed a short film, *Of Tadpole and Other Human Beings*. As a reviewer he has worked for numerous film festivals including the London Film Festival, the London Gay and Lesbian Film Festival and the Latin American Film Festival.

DONATO TOTARO received his PhD in Film and Television from the University of Warwick, UK, and is a lecturer in Film Studies at Concordia University, Montreal, Canada. Since 1997 he has been the editor of the online film journal *Offscreen* (www.offscreen.com), a wide-ranging journal which specialises in international and alternative cinemas. He has published extensively on recent Asian cinema, the cinema of Andrei Tarkovsky and the horror genre and is a regular contributor to the US horror magazine *Fangoria*. He is currently preparing a manuscript entitled *Time and the Long Take in Narrative Cinema*.

STEVE YATES read Film Studies and English at Kent University before taking an MA in Film and TV Studies at Westminster University. Since then he has worked briefly for Renaissance Films as a Film Development Officer and is now a freelance journalist. In November 2002 he sat on the Jury for FIPRESCI at the Bratislava International Film Festival. He received his certificate of registration as a Line Producer from the Hollywood Film Institute.

What are 24 frames on a strip of film able to capture? It only amounts to one second of moving image. How about 24 films? What can they tell us about national cinemas? *The Cinema of Japan and Korea*, though, another title in the *24 Frames* series by Wallflower Press, provides us with insights into both Japanese cinema, one of the most prominent of national cinemas, and Korean cinema, a lesser-known but burgeoning national cinema in the world film scene.

Japanese cinema has long been considered by film scholars as an anomaly within world cinema. The popularity of *benshi* – an oratory performer for silent films who explained the story and sometimes enacted dialogue – in the early Japanese cinema, or the unique film styles of *auteurs* from the Japanese studio era, such as Yasujiro Ozu or Kenji Mizoguchi, has led film scholars to claim that Japanese film aesthetics fundamentally departs from that of Hollywood cinema. If the film style of Hollywood had been devised to efface the storytelling process, that of Japanese cinema calls attention to itself, foregrounding the very storytelling process, in the way that Noël Burch once characterised Japanese cinema as 'presentational', as opposed to the very 'representational' Hollywood cinema.

The essays on Japanese cinema in this volume invite us to closely examine the dialectic unfolding within its history. Like any other national cinema, it has incorporated film techniques and aesthetics from beyond its borders, including Hollywood. *A Page of Madness* (1926), considered to be one of the first Japanese avant-garde films, well demonstrates the filmic exchanges that took place between Japanese and West European avant-garde filmmakers. In contrast, many films covered in this collection turn their gaze inwards, foregrounding the political circumstances at work within and around the Japanese film industry. Stephanie DeBoer discusses how colonial policy influenced the industry, resulting in propaganda films such as *Sayon's Bell* (1943). Samara Lea Allsop provides us with an allegorical reading of *Godzilla* (1954) by underlining the political significance and implications of this post-war popular science fiction film. We are also given an opportunity to (re)trace the genealogy of Japanese *auteurs*, both old and new. How do contemporary Japanese filmmakers, such as Takeshi Kitano (*Violent Cop*, 1989), continue and/or depart from the *auteurs* of the Japanese studio system, such as Akira Kurosawa (*Stray Dog*, 1949), Mizoguchi (*The Life of Oharu*, 1952) or Seijun Sujuki (*Branded to Kill*, 1967) in terms of their thematic preoccupations and film styles? And how did veteran director Kinji Fukasaku, who directed numerous *yakuza* films in the 1970s, make such a remarkable comeback with the violent high-school drama *Battle Royale* (2000)? Lastly, in his essay on *Perfect Blue* (1997), Jasper Sharp looks at the phenomenon of Anime and questions its relationship with the comic book (*manga*) industry.

Korean cinema may just be, as Anthony Leong suggested in 2002, the next Hong Kong cinema. This volume offers a wonderful introduction to it. The commercial viability of Korean cinema has been tested in both the domestic and international market. *Shiri* (1999) and *Joint Security Area* (2000) – two Korean blockbuster films coming out of a trend that began in the late 1990s – attracted larger audiences at the domestic box office than *Titanic* and *Gladiator*. And in 2004, the box-office race among Korean blockbuster films was re-ignited with Korean War epics such as *Shimi Island* (Kang Woo-suk) and *Tageuki* (Kang Je-kyu). Korean films, however, have not only enjoyed box-office success, but have also gained international recognition on the film festival circuit. In 2002, Im Kwon-taek was named best director at Cannes for his film *Chiwhason* and Lee Chang-dong received the best director award at the Venice Film Festival for *Oasis*. In 2004, *Samaria* won Kim Ki-duk the Silver Berlin Bear award at the Berlin Film Festival, whilst Park Chan-wook – director of *Joint Security Area* and *Sympathy for Mr. Vengeance* (2002) – took home the Grand Prix for *Old Boy* at the Cannes Film Festival. The essays in this anthology will certainly help alleviate the paucity of literature on a cinema that continues to grow more and more interesting.

One of the causes of the industrial boom in Korean cinema can be attributed to the emergence of a new generation of filmmakers: the 386 Generation, a term borrowed from computer chip technology, which refers to the generation who were born in the 1960s and educated in college in the 1980s, one of the most politically traumatic periods in Korean history. The 386 Generation directors are film literate, educated in film schools or academies, at home or abroad, and, as a group, are characteristically self-conscious of film style. Another welcome outcome of this industrial change can be found in the increasing prevalence of female directors, including Byun Yong-joo (*My Own Breathing*, 1999), Lee Jeong-hyang (*Art Museum By the Zoo*, 1998; *The Way Home*, 2002) and Jeong Jae-eun (*Take Care of My Cat*, 2001). These directors challenge both the gender bias deeply rooted in Korean society and socio-economic issues, such as the disintegration of urban family, with their own distinct sensibilities.

Peter Harry Ris' two essays, on *Hurrah! For Freedom* (1946) and *The Guest and My Mother* (1961), not only offer us close readings of two important films, but also provide us with an historical overview of Korean cinema before and after the Korean War. In a discussion of the widely-hailed Korean film classic *Aimless Bullet* (1961), Darcy Paquet offers an interesting account of director Yu Hyun-mok's realistic, as well as modernist, portrayal of the post-war experience of one extended family. Meanwhile, *Killer Butterfly* (1978), as discussed by Chris Berry, provides a fascinating link with more contemporary Korean directors who are challenging norms: the traditionalist Im Kwon-taek (*Sopyonje*, 1993), the modernist Hong Sang-soo (*The Power of Kwangwon Province*, 1998), the stylist Lee Myeong-se (*Nowhere to Hide*, 1999) and one of the most contentious film directors in Korea, Kim Ki-duk (*The Isle*, 2000).

The essays collected within this volume cover a wide spectrum of methodologies and subject matter. They are historical as well as comparative, scholarly as well as journalistic; and they concern both the thematic and stylistic aspects of films. The contributing authors constantly question and attempt to disentangle conflicts between film aesthetics and ethics or politics. Films such as *In the Realm of the Senses* (1976), *Battle Royale* and *The Isle* are claimed to be provocative, yet they are also unsettling. There is no systematic way to determine whether the unsettling quality of these films merely serves the purpose of sensationalism or can be aesthetically justified within the work in question. Likewise, it is up to the reader to decide whether they would agree with the interpretations provided. Nevertheless, to question oneself regarding such issues will only further one's understanding of not only the intricate issues embedded in film ethics, but also the films themselves. This volume raises, and goes some way to answering, many questions and, to its merit, poses even more.

Jinhee Choi

Assistant Professor, Film Studies, Carleton University, Canada

June 2004

INTRODUCTION

If imitation truly is the sincerest form of flattery then an unparalleled degree of flattery is currently being bestowed upon South East Asian cinema by Western – and particularly, of course, Hollywood – filmmakers. In recent years, American film production has busied itself absorbing the styles and trends of Hong Kong cinema and is now turning its attention to the surrounding film cultures. Miramax have snapped up the rights to Jo Jin-gyu's *Jopog Manura* (*My Wife is a Gangster*) whilst Gore Verbinski's *The Ring* (*Ringu*) terrified global audiences, despite being a pedestrian, if chillingly effective, remake of Hideo Nakata's *Ringu* (1998). Dozens of other remake and re-release deals continue to be brokered.

Of course imitation can, and often does, result in a pale reflection. Take the Chinese example of Yuen Woo-ping's *Siunin Wong Fei-Hung Tsi Titmalau* (*Iron Monkey*, 1993) or Korea's *Whasango* (*Volcano High*, Kim Tae-gyun, 2001) compared to the rather lacklustre wire work and fight choreography on display in McG's *Charlie's Angels* (2000) and its sequel. Yet at their best, these – anything but cheap – imitations can also lead to fresh discoveries by Western audiences who choose to look beyond their own boundaries and to the film cultures of the original releases. The 2004 DVD re-release of *Iron Monkey* made much of Yuen Woo-ping's recent foray into American features: 'From the action director of *Kill Bill* and *The Matrix Trilogy*.' One can only hope that those left disappointed by the Wachowski Brothers' inability to sustain the momentum of the first *Matrix* film will indeed turn towards these superior, though all-too-often neglected, Asian originals.

A fuller understanding of the sensibilities and preoccupations of these 'other' cinemas is always welcome and it is hoped that this book will, to some extent, fulfil this function and help further push open the door that has been left ajar by Hollywood. Historically, cinema was introduced into Japan and Korea within a few short years of each other. Edison's Kinetoscope made its first appearance in Japan in 1886, closely followed in 1887 by the Lumière Brothers' Cinematograph, with representatives of the latter company visiting the country by 1898 in order to film on location. The first recorded public screening of a film in Korea took place just five years later in 1903, followed by a decade of rapid expansion of the numbers of theatres opened for screenings. The majority of films screened were either of European or American origin and it was not until 1919 that the first domestic production, a *kinodrama* which combined live performance and projected backdrops, was presented. Meanwhile, the popularity of the moving image in Japan had increased dramatically during the Russian–Japanese war (1904–05), with a significant number of newsreels exhibited domestically.

1923 saw the production of Korea's first true silent film and three years later, Na Un-Kyu, at 25, produced, directed and starred in Korea's first major film, *Arirang* (1926), a politically subversive tale of Japanese imprisonment and torture, which set the standard for the cinematic representation of resistance against the imperial Japanese army. Despite the success of Korea's first sound production in 1935, the invasion of China by Japan effectively transformed Korean cinema into a wing of the Japanese propaganda machine. Tragically, few fragments of early Korean film remain today, the majority of work having been destroyed during the Korean War. The earliest surviving example, Choe In-gyu's 1946 *Jayu Manse* (*Hurrah! For Freedom*, aka *Victory of Freedom*) is discussed in this volume by Peter Harry Ris, whose chapter also serves as a broad overview of early Korean cinematic history and helps to set the stage for the subsequent films discussed.

Korean cinema enjoyed a revival in the late 1950s, with production rising from a mere eight domestic features to over 100 in less than five years. This new-found confidence and exponential increase in cinema attendance led, in the early 1960s, to the appearance of many of Korea's most significant and famed directors, including Kim Ki-young, Shin Sang-ok and Yu Hyon-mok. Kim's *Salinnabileul Ggotneun Yeoja* (*Killer Butterfly*, 1978), Shin's *Sarangbang Sonnim-Kwa Omoni* (*The Guest and My Mother*, aka *The Houseguest and My Mother*, 1961) and Yu's *Obaltan* (*Aimless Bullet*, 1961) are featured in this collection.

This renaissance of the 1960s was short lived, with government censorship blocking both creativity and true artistic expression and despite the Korean Motion Picture Promotion Corporation (KMPPC) being formed in 1973 in an effort to reinvigorate the industry it was not until the early 1980s that Korea would witness a turnaround in its cinematic fortunes. Although Im Kwon-taek was a long-established director with more than seventy films to his credit, it was his 1981 feature, *Mandala*, that finally saw him recognised as one of the country's most significant filmmakers. His later and arguably most acclaimed feature, *Sopyeonje* (*Sopyonje*, 1993), is discussed in this book by Han Ju Kwak, who rightly describes Im as a 'towering, magistrate presence in Korean cinema'.

The late 1980s saw two hugely significant developments in Korean film production. Firstly, an easing of the stringent censorship laws (with Park Kwang-soo one of the first to take advantage of this development with his production of *Chilsu and Mansu* (1988)) and secondly, a lifting of the import restrictions on foreign features. This latter development resulted in Korean audiences and filmmakers, enjoying exposure to a wider array of world cinema releases.

Of the Korean films included in this book, the majority are relatively contemporary releases; with five of the films hailing from the last ten years and of these, four from the period 1999–2000. Whilst this may seem disproportionate, it is hoped that the remaining chapters will more than adequately serve as a broader historical overview of Korean national cinema. That so many of the Korean films selected are recent is in large part due to the recognition of what may be termed the 'Korean Blockbuster', and which loosely began with the release of *The Contact* (*Cheob-Sok*, 1999) and *Swiri* (*Shiri*, 1999), the latter successfully marketed to Western audiences as a blend of *Die Hard* (John McTiernan, 1988) and *La Femme Nikita* (Luc Besson, 1990).

Similarly, and as part of what Anthony Leong describes in his chapter as belonging to the 'Korean New Wave', Lee Myeong-se's 1999 *Injong Sajong Bolgeot Eobda* (*Nowhere to Hide*) exemplifies the refreshing and brave new direction of Korean national cinema. As Leong points out, nature abhors a vacuum and the decline in international interest in Hong Kong cinema – which arguably began when many of the finest exponents of action films, chief amongst them John Woo and his frequent muse Yun-Fat Chow, moved to Hollywood – resulted in one such artistic void. And South Korea's own remarkable transformation as an international player has provided a more than adequate source of vitality and entertainment for those who hunger of Hong Kong cinema's glory days.

Another film covered here, which stands alongside *Nowhere to Hide*, is Pak Chan-wook's *Kongdong Kongbi Guyok* (*Joint Security Area*, aka *JSA*, 2000), made as a direct response to the success of the previous year's blockbusters, yet possessing far more in the way of culturally specific sensibilities and themes. *Joint Security Area* works as both a superficial narrative and a stunningly realised and powerful story of division and hope for unification – themes common in Korean cinema, but rarely so well presented. Adrien Gombeaud's chapter attempts to unravel and understand the iconography and imagery of the film, in particular, the symbolic importance of the concept of division, a notion clearly understood by Korean audiences.

There is, somewhat regrettably but necessary due to space restrictions, only one entry in this volume covering a documentary film. Byun Yongjoo's remarkable *Sumgyol* (*My Own Breathing*) completed the director's trilogy of films on the so-called Korean 'comfort women' – those forced into sexual slavery during the Japanese colonisation of Korea. The chapter contextualises the film within the framework of the trilogy as a whole and examines the unique relationship between the director and her 'stars'; a relationship which demonstrably blurs the lines between the two, inadvertently calling into question the very nature of documentary film-making.

The earliest Japanese film covered in this volume is Kinugasa Teinosuke's silent masterpiece, *A Page of Madness* (1926), which boasted a dizzying array of cinematic techniques in terms of both framing, camera movement and editing. It is a remarkable early example of Japanese cinema 'finding its own feet'; taking alternative routes from the imported American movies that were so popular at the time, and making a significant impact in terms of pushing the boundaries of the cinematic medium. What made this film even more intriguing was the fact that it was believed lost for over two decades, until the original negatives were discovered by chance, in a rice barrel, in 1971.

Of all the Japanese directors included here, none are more renowned internationally that Akira Kurosawa. Although his life and works have been covered comprehensively elsewhere, it was felt that one of his films should be included in order to look at his unique relationship with Western audiences. With so much criticism already existing in print (most noticably Stuart Galbraith's extraordinary *The Emperor and the Wolf*) Magnus Stanke presents an overview of the influences that resulted in one of the director's most impressive non-period films, *Stray Dog* (*Nora Inu*, 1949), looking at Kurosawa's relationship with his frequent on-screen collaborator, Toshiro Mifune.

As with America's preoccupation with representing – or mythologising – criminal life in films ranging from the rawness of *Little Caesar* (Mervyn LeRoy, 1931) and *Scarface* (Howard Hawks, 1932) to the sophistication of the *Godfather* trilogy (Francis Ford Coppola 1972, 1974 and 1990), so the Japanese have enjoyed a long cinematic tradition charting the role in society of their own criminal underworld, the *yakuza*. And like its American counterpart, the Japanese genre evolved over time, from Kurosawa's sun-drenched noir through to more recent, blood-splattered epics, from the stables of Takeshi Kitano and Takashi Miike. Somewhere between these worlds is Suzuki Seijun's 1966 feature, *Branded to Kill*. A powerful evocation of the genre's preoccupations, it remains a perfect glimpse into the workings of a truly renegade director, whose refusal to follow studio demands with this production all but ended his career. Separated by the best part of a quarter century (and although not strictly a straight *yakuza* film) Kitano Takeshi's directorial debut, *Violent Cop* (1989), was as much the work of a maverick as Suzuki and other trailblazing directors. In his chapter on the film, Donato Totaro discusses the career of Kitano – whose fame is almost impossible to comprehend outside of Japan and whose persona is that of a polymath celebrity, equally at home on television or writing magazine columns and poetry as he is acting and directing – and traces his cinematic trajectory through both his *yakuza* and non-*yakuza* features.

Another genre that proved a mainstay of the Japanese film industry has been the softcore pornographic *pink* film or *pinku eiga*, whose importance – commercially and in terms of their frequent subversive political subtext – cannot be ignored. The most internationally recognised and celebrated example is Nagisa Oshima's controversial 1976 art-house crossover *Ai No Corrida* (*In the Realm of the Senses*), which was released at a time when European critics were championing such serious erotica as Bernardo Bertolucci *Last Tango in Paris* (1972) and Liliana Cavani's *The Night Porter* (1974). Although Oshima is now more widely associated, at least to Western audiences, with the 1983 David Bowie vehicle *Merry Christmas, Mr Lawrence* (which featured the international debut of 'Beat' Takeshi Kitano) or possibly even with 1999's homo-erotic *samurai* drama *Gohatto* (*Taboo*, 1999), it was with *Ai No Corrida* that he made his international name. Beyond its taboo-breaking story structure, the film is also significant in its re-telling of one of Japan's most infamous incidents, based on Sada Abe's castration and murder of her lover in 1936. Her story has been told many times and filmed on numerous occasions, before and after Oshima's film. However, his bold working remains the most significant, emotionally powerful and controversial rendition.

A third Japanese genre, or art form, discussed here is the increasingly popular anime film. Until recently, the genre has often been misunderstood outside of Japan, particularly by European audiences, who associate it with fantastical subject matters, particularly science fiction. However the films are almost as likely to cover socio-realistic subject matters or psycho-dramas as they are giant robots and post-apocalyptic mayhem. It would have been natural to choose one of the most acclaimed international successes, Katsuhiro Ôtomo's *Akira* (1988), as representative of anime film. However, Kon Satoshi's 1997 masterpiece, *Perfect Blue*, offers a dynamic and daring blend of hyper-kinetic animation and psychological thriller, transcending expectations and genre stereotypes. For those unacquainted with anime, it is a film that will both provoke debate and challenge preconceptions.

The most recent Japanese film featured here is Kinji Fukasaku's brilliantly-rendered vision of an anarchic near-future, *Battle Royale* (2002). Although the veteran director – who sadly died at the age of 72 whilst this volume was being prepared – was famed for his violent *yakuza* films, such as *Jingi Naki Tatakai* (*Battles Without Honor and Humanity*, 1973) and *Jingi No Hakaba* (*Graveyard of Honour*, 1975), *Battle Royale* belatedly brought him widespread international fame. The film's depictions of seemingly amoral carnage as a class of high-school students are banished to an island where they are forced to kill or be killed, caused considerable controversy at screenings around the world. And yet, Fukasaku imbues his film with a surprising degree of humanity, humour and warmth, in addition to the uninterrupted satirical swipes at institutionalised government and its lack of understanding of younger generations.

Shinya Tsukamoto's mesmerising and delirious *Tetsuo 2* (*Tetsuo 2: Body Hammer*, 1992) is arguably more of a remoulding or revisiting of his earlier *Tetsuo* (*The Iron Man*, 1988) than a legitimate sequel. As such, both films are discussed in detail here. Tsukamoto operates on the very fringes of Japanese film production; his features (and shorts) are highly personal affairs and he can undoubtedly be described as a true *auteur* – writing, editing, shooting, designing and directing each film with an intensely individual eye. Yet his work is almost invariably discussed in relationship to the early productions of both David Cronenberg and David Lynch. Both *Tetsuo* films can loosely be described as belonging to the science fiction sub-genre of cyber-punk, although his other, non-genre films share many of the same preoccupations – particularly urban alienation – and as such both reinforce and paradoxically explode many Western preconceptions of Japanese society and an individual's relationship with technological advance.

As a counter-point to Tsukamoto's films Nam Gee-woong's *Daehakno-yeseo Maechoon-hadaka Tomaksalhae Danghan Yeogosaeng Ajik Daehakno-ye Issda* (*Teenage Hooker Became Killing Machine in Daehakno*, 2000) is included here as both a perfect example of digital cinema's continuing democratisation of world film production and as an exemplary instance of brave new directions within Korean national cinema. Like Tsukamoto, Nam seems deeply influenced by cyber-punk, Cronenberg and Lynch, and is similarly concerned with alienation within contemporary urban society. His work is also at the cutting edge of experimentation, mixing unique visual approaches with the ocassional and brazen pilfering of sequences from Western films.

Collectively it is hoped that these chapters will function as both an introduction to and exploration of individual bodies of work and to a wider collective understanding of how these two national cinemas have evolved. And whilst it is perhaps enough to appreciate their individual merits as works of creative endeavour, it is further hoped that a greater understanding of how these films influence global audiences and 'feed into' international cinema through an osmotic process will be achieved.

Inevitably, writing on two national cinemas – any two national cinemas – in a single volume is inherently problematic and the decision to do so at best raises a number of unique questions and sets of difficulties. When this work was first under discussion, several questions were raised. Why not a book on each country? Would the chapters of a combined work be equally divided between Japan and Korea? And which films and directors would be covered by the book? The *24 Frames* series from Wallflower Press, 18 volumes in all, will feature a number of 'collective' editions, ranging from 'dual' territories such as *Britain and Ireland, Spain and Portugal* and *Australia and New Zealand*, to more recognisable regional cinemas such as *Latin America, Scandinavia, Central Europe* and *The Low Countries*. Each have their own problematic selection of films or criteria of inclusion yet each contribute, in differing ways, to popular and academic discourses of national and regional cinema. In this case, it is true to say that at the time of writing Japanese film has a greater following amongst Western audiences than Korean film. Equally, it may be hoped that any discussion on national cinema could be enhanced by a wider discourse covering complimentary regional cinemas. Clearly a simple geographic grouping is an insufficient justification, but the complex relationship between Korea and Japan provides a fascinating and inextricably linked 'pair' of national cinematic identities, which are at once complementary and, paradoxically, conflicting. Whilst both Japanese and Korean films and filmmakers demonstrate their own unique preoccupations, narrative traditions, structures and cultural sensibilities, it is inevitable – due in the most part to their historical bindings – that a considerable amount of shared ground can be explored. With the films presented here in chronological order, it is possible to begin to detect both the similarities and intrinsic differences between these two cinemas. It is also anticipated that those familiar only with Japanese cinema may find in this book a potential point of entry to their own discovery of Korean cinema.

As to the division of the 24 available chapters between Korea and Japan, it is true to say that no particular formula was intentionally employed. Certainly, an editorial policy which stuck doggedly to the notion of a 50/50 split was deemed inappropriate and potentially misleading to the readership. However, it was hoped from the outset that the balance would be as equal as possible and that strong arguments for the inclusion of particular films/directors might be made to achieve roughly equal coverage. The process of deciding which films and directors were finally chosen was begun with a 'short' list of between seventy and eighty titles. This list was, certainly more by accident than design, already split on a near-equal footing between Japanese and Korean films. These titles were circulated for discussion amongst a wide range of international writers and experts (to all of whom we are enormously indebted and many of whom would ultimately contribute chapters) over the course of several months. Slowly, the list was whiled down to 13 Japanese and 11 Korean films.

The titles presented here are not strictly intended to be a 'best of', either in terms of national cinema or indeed from amongst a particular director's oeuvre. There are many hundreds of films from both Japan and Korea that could be said to be 'worthy' of consideration and discussion here. What has been attempted is a selection of 24 films which best represent the diversity of each country's cinema in terms of form, style historicity and narrative. It is also impossible to prevent a degree of subjectivity in the final decision-making process, although it is hoped that the films selected either represent an appropriate introduction to the respective countries' national cinematic history or as an overture to the wider body of work of a specific director. Occasionally, this in itself can be problematic. Take for example Takashi Miike, arguably one of the most prolific (and significant) director's of his or any other generation, whose output of work averages five films per year and whose films invariably provoke heated debate and fierce controversy. The choice for inclusion here was *Audition* (2000), which is hardly representative of many of his most frequently-explored themes and preoccupations, yet serves as an appropriate entry point to his body of work; not least because of its international festival success having provided many with their first glimpse of the director's unique genius. *Audition* is, initially at least, less of a kinetic assault on the senses than either his previous or subsequent films; yet the violence, when finally delivered, is amongst the most brutal he has meted out – to both character and audience.

This book is the result of collaborations from around the world – including, of course, Japan and Korea. For this reason it must be understood that the opinions expressed are filtered through – and hopefully enhanced by – individual nationalistic viewpoints, as well as critical. Though this may result in a lack of homogeneity throughout, it is hoped that the volume will be more rewarding for it.

Inevitably, a collection such as this cannot please everyone, particularly in reference to the editorial choices that have been made in regard to the directors and films under discussion. There are notable absences from Japan: Hideo Nakata for example, whose influential *Ringu* (*Ring*, 1998) and *Ringu 2* (*Ring 2*, 1999) reinvigorated interest in supernatural narratives and resulted in a plethora of similarly-themed films. Likewise, and perhaps even more significantly, there are no films by either Yasujiro Ozu or Shomei Imamura – and again both space and a degree of editorial choice play a part here in the attempt to best represent a true cross-section from the diversity of the national cinemas. There are comparable 'omissions' with the films and directors from Korea – such is the nature of a collected work where difficult, sometimes painful, editorial decisions must be taken. But to re-emphasise, the titles included here are not intended to represent a 'best of' list or to be viewed as in any way exhaustive. Collectively, they serve as in introduction to the wider themes of the countries' broad national cinematic identities.

Ultimately this book is a celebration of two often intertwined and interrelated national cinemas. Both have a grand heritage and an enormous gift to offer world audiences and if this book can go some way towards making an initial introduction or whetting a collective appetite to explore further or view a greater diversity of films, then its job is done.

Each essay includes references to those works specifically discussed but a comprehensive bibliography appears at the end of the book. A final note on the romanisation of both Japanese and Korean names and words – this is a notoriously problematic issue but we have decided to use the most commonly-accepted Western versions throughout.

Justin Bowyer

KURUTTA IPPEJI A PAGE OF MADNESS

KINUGASA TEINOSUKE, JAPAN, 1926

The evolution of cinema is invariably described within the context of developments in Europe and America. The standard wisdom has it that the rest have followed where the West has led in the adoption of the technical innovations, dramatic conventions and narrative forms of what has become commonly known as the dominant art form of the twentieth century.

From this perspective, Kinugasa Teinosuke's silent masterpiece *Kurutta Ippeji* (*A Page of Madness*, 1926) appears to have emerged from a cinematic void. A cryptic yet mesmerising mood-piece set within the claustrophobic confines of a lunatic asylum, it is a long way from the creaky stage-bound adaptations of *Kabuki* theatre or *jidai geki* – historical action adventures with which Japan's motion picture industry began. In many respects it is also far in advance of the type of films being made anywhere else in the world at the time.

Utilising the entire spectrum of cinematic techniques of the time (tracking shots, superimpositions, whip pans, optical distortions and associative cross-cutting), from the very outset the film comes across as a series of striking and hypnotic images, seemingly devoid of meaning or metaphor and possessing a visual density that could rival any modern-day music video. As Vlada Petric states in an article published in 1983, 'The fact remains that historically Kinugasa made the first full feature film whose plot development is radically subverted, whilst its cinematic structure includes virtually every film device known at the time. These devices, moreover, are used not for their own sake but to convey complex psychological content without the aid of titles.'

All of this went unnoticed at the time. Despite some favourable reviews, the film made little lasting impact upon its initial release in Tokyo in autumn 1926, and was originally not screened abroad. For over 30 years it was believed to be lost; destroyed in a fire in 1950 at the studios in Kyoto where it was made. Then in 1971 the director discovered the original negative languishing in a rice barrel in the potting shed of his country home. A new print was immediately struck with an accompanying soundtrack supervised by Kinugasa himself. When, soon after, he brought the film to Europe for its first-ever screenings abroad, it stunned contemporary reviewers with its dreamlike continuity and the dazzling audacity of its technique. Even now, almost eight decades on, Kinugasa's film seems remarkably fresh and when seen on the big screen, is a truly dazzling experience.

Stripped down to its basics, the plot is simplicity itself: the story of a retired sailor (Inoue Masao) who has taken a job as a janitor in a lunatic asylum to look after his insane wife (Yoshie Nakagawa), though a synopsis gives little indication as to the impact of this stunning invocation of the world as viewed by the mentally ill. From the outset as the rapid montage of the opening storm sequences dissolves into the surrealistic fantasy of the sailor's wife dressed in an exotic costume dancing in front of an art-deco-inspired backdrop dominated by a large spinning ball flanked by ornate fountains, *A Page of Madness* overwhelms its audience with a barrage of startling imagery.

Until its reappearance on the world stage, the only substantial information on the film in English was in Joseph L. Anderson and Donald Richie's seminal book on Japanese Cinema, *The Japanese Film: Art and Industry*, first published in 1959 and written at a time when the film was unavailable for viewing. The film's rediscovery opened up fresh new debate as to the context within which it was produced, issues of the film's genesis, its influences (both domestic and foreign) and its initial reception by Japanese audiences. Did its roots lie within developments in film theory in Europe, or was it shaped by cultural forces closer to home? Was it conceived as a kickback against the staid condition of the nation's industry of the day, or is it best viewed as a freeform technical experiment?

From the very first moment cinema arrived in Japan in 1896, developments in film narrative diverged rapidly from what was happening elsewhere. Up until 1915, domestic production had been dominated by filmed adaptations of *Kabuki* plays, and their theatrical conventions resulted in their theatrical portrayal on film – long, unbroken shots filmed from the fixed low-angle perspective of a spectator seated in front of the stage. This close affiliation with Japanese theatre had its disadvantages, one of which was that the male-only field of *Kabuki* effectively kept women from screens until the early 1920s, their parts being played by male *oyama* (or *onnagata*) actors specialising in female roles. Moreover, as these adapted plays were originally around five or six hours long, the cost of mounting these as cinematic spectacles meant they had to be considerably condensed to a more manageable size, necessitating a continuous narrated exposition of the plot to explain the missing parts.

These early screenings thus came to be taken over by a character known as the *benshi*, who presided over the entirety of the event acting as a type of master of ceremonies, responsible not only for warming up the audiences and keeping them entertained between screenings, but also, as the bulk of the films being shown in Japan at this point were imported from overseas, explaining to these ever-curious early audiences (newly exposed to the West with the dawn of the *Meiji* Period) exactly what was unfolding onscreen.

Though recent research has revealed that the *benshi* had their equivalents in other countries (early French film programmes were also compered, for example), their main precedents stemmed from the traditional theatrical forms of *Kabuki*, *Noh* and especially the *gidayu* chanters of *Bunraku* doll theatre. And so the *benshi*'s narrated *katsuben* commentary is often looked upon as a tradition unique to Japan; a mixed-media performance in which audiences were more likely to be drawn to a particular commentator than to the film itself. They became a powerful force in the rapidly expanding film industry, effectively delaying the development of synchronised sound for years. As endemic an element of Japanese cinema as they were, however, there were still a handful of industry figures with their eyes fixed upon what was going on elsewhere in the world.

One such person was the future director of *A Page of Madness*, Kinugasa Teinosuke, who had witnessed these early developments at incredibly close quarters. Born in 1896, the son of a tobacco merchant, Kinugasa finished his studies at 17 and ran off to Osaka to join an itinerant troupe of actors who specialised in *Shimpa* theatre, a less-stylised contemporary offshoot of *Kabuki*, changing his family surname from Kogame in order to avoid embarrassment to his mother. Immediately Kinugasa was assigned the role of *oyama* by the troupe's director. His stage debut came in April 1914 and within three years he had become sufficiently popular to attract the attention of Japan's oldest existing film studio, Nikkatsu. Nikkatsu's premiere *oyama* star, Tachibana, had fallen ill, and so in 1917 Kinugasa was invited to Tokyo for his first screen appearance in Oguchi Chu's *Nanairo no Yubiwa* (*The Seven-Coloured Ring*).

Kinugasa rapidly established himself as one of the top actors in his field, appearing in around ninety films between 1917 and 1919. One notable role came in Tanaka Eizo's *Ikeru Shikabane* (*The Living Corpse*, 1917), a Tolstoy adaptation in which he played the young Russian love interest, apparently looking, according to Anderson and Richie, 'very much like a woman in his dress, wig and make-up, except for the fact that since the film was shot in muddy November he wore heavy workmen's boots throughout'.

However the tide was turning and the *oyama*'s part in the rapidly changing development of a national cinema was coming to an end. Yaeko Mizutani's starring role in Ryoha Hatanaka's *Kantsubaki* (*Winter Camellia*, 1921) really opened the floodgates, and when Nikkatsu broke the mould and began to hire actresses for its films on a regular basis,

Kinugasa led a dozen or so of the studio's most important *oyama* out on strike in angry protest.

Meanwhile Kinugasa was already exploring other avenues within the film industry. In 1921 he wrote and co-directed *Imoto no Shi* (*The Death of My Sister*) for Nikkatsu in which he also played the leading lady. A tragic melodrama about a girl who, after being raped by her brother's best friend, throws herself beneath a passing train, the film was a great enough success to lead to further work for the studio. *Niwa no Kotori* (*Two Little Birds*, 1922) and *Hibana* (*Spark*, 1922) followed, after which Kinugasa joined the Makino Motion Picture Company in Kyoto (founded by ex-Nikkatsu star and early pioneer of silent cinema, Shozo Makino).

Over the next few years, Kinugasa kept up a steady output of around two films a month (a typically prolific rate for a director of the time), all of which made Makino's company a good deal of money whilst allowing the director to become more fully-versed in filmmaking technique. However, he soon realised that in order to gain the complete degree of artistic freedom he desired, it would be necessary to produce his own work.

In 1925 Kinugasa formed the Kinugasa Motion Picture Company (Kinugasa Eiga Renmei) and the following year turned his attention towards creating his thirty-fifth film as a director. Utilising the most modest of budgets, from the very outset *A Page of Madness* was a triumph of inventiveness over harsh financial reality. Money was so tight that most of the cast and crew (around fifty people) agreed to work without payment and slept on the sets. The actors, some of them (including Inoue) major stars of the day, even helped out making props or pushing the camera dolly. Kinugasa shot in Shochiku's temporarily empty Shimokama studios, which with only eight lights at his disposal proved to be too dark; consequently the walls of the sets were painted silver in order to boost the available light.

That *A Page of Madness* had such little influence on immediate developments in Japanese cinema is no doubt attributable to the fact it reached so few people. Despite Anderson and Richie's assertion that the film 'was at once a big success' upon its release on 24 September 1926, the commonly received wisdom is that it was a commercial failure. At a time when the studios dominated all aspects of the market from finance through to distribution, the expense in producing and distributing a film outside of the established system was near prohibitive. As a result Kinugasa's film, Japan's first independent feature, played in a severely limited number of venues. Kinugasa had almost bankrupted himself making it, and returned immediately to commercial filmmaking with a slew of productions for Shochiku, all falling under the aegis of the popular *jidai geki* (*samurai*-period swashbucklers).

A Page of Madness's deliberate flouting of cinema's theatrical foundations, particularly in terms of its narrative drive, must have seemed shockingly alien to its early audiences, though met with favour in at least some quarters. One contemporary reviewer, Akira Iwasaki wrote, 'The beauty portrayed on the screen by him is not theatrical. It is not fictional, nor is it pictorial. It is a cinematic beauty, a kind of beauty which is different from that of the conventional art forms. I must say without any hesitation that the director has rightly treated the cinema essentially as a novel type of visual art.'

Such an idea was not exactly new. Kinugasa's experiments in form, at a time when film-makers the world over were struggling for articulacy in establishing the syntax of a universal film language already had its antecedents in Europe; in German Expressionism, the French avant-garde and Soviet theories of montage. In Japan, however, the director's most immediate sources of inspiration lay outside the world of film.

During the 1920s, the hub of the cultural and artistic world were still seen as being firmly located within Europe – in Paris, Berlin, Vienna and London. The horrors of World War One had sent shock waves throughout the world and given rise to a whole new generation eager to rebuilt society upon thoroughly different foundations. Though Japan had not been deeply involved in the conflict, its aftermath saw the country opening itself up considerably to new Western ideas, be they political, economic or artistic. Newly-born movements such as Constructivism, Expressionism and Futurism were already being enthusiastically embraced and re-interpreted to fit the ideals of a burgeoning avant-garde in Japan as eager to demolish traditional modes of expression as their European counterparts, whether in drama, dance, the plastic arts or literature.

In 1925, Kinugasa directed *Nichirin* (*The Sun*) from a short novel by the young writer Riichi Yokomitsu, as part of a series of four films for Rengo Eiga Geijutsuka (United Film Artists Company), a short-lived affiliate of Makino's company. The film, which has survived only in partial form, was a re-working of Flaubert's *Salambo* populated with characters from Japanese mythology, and fell into censorship problems upon its original release due to its depiction of the 'Age of the Gods'. It was later drastically re-edited and re-released in 1930 under the new title *Josei no Kagayaki*.

It was through this that Kinugasa became involved with the group of up-and-coming writers known as the *Shinkankaku School*, or Neo-Sensualists. The Shinkankaku writers' brand of modernist fiction favoured the use of vivid imagery and jarring simile in order to evoke the world in terms of the sensations of the characters rather than straightforward description. The group eagerly kept abreast with the recent artistic developments in Europe, and appeared to have little interest or respect for ancient literary traditions. Indeed Riichi, best known for his two translated short stories, *Time* and *Machine*, was later to write that this period was, as James Peterson describes, 'a war of utter rebellion against the Japanese language'.

However, it was another member of the group, Yasunari Kawabata (1899–1972) who was to prove the most decisive influence for *A Page of Madness*. Widely referred to as Japan's greatest novelist and best known abroad for his novel *Yukiguni* (*Snow Country*), Kawabata's first great literary success occurred with the publication of *Izu no Odoriko* (*The Izu Dancer*) in 1926, itself later adapted as a silent film in 1933 by Heinosuke Gosho. During his Nobel Prize-winning acceptance speech in 1968, he praised Japanese tradition and culture, especially its oneness with nature, though during his Shinkankaku period Kawabata's apparently richly traditional style at least found a point of reference with the ideas of the European avant-garde before he turned away from his models.

Kawabata's translator, Edward G. Seidensticker, compares his prose to the ancient Haiku masters, who seek 'to convey a sudden awareness of beauty by the mating of opposite or incongruous terms'. This description could just as easily be applied to the haunting dreamlike visuals of *A Page of Madness*, for whose script Kawabata is often given sole credit. However, Kinugasa later played down the novelist's involvement, stating that whilst the original idea stemmed from Kawabata, the film itself was scripted during shooting and the screenplay published by Kawabata immediately after the film was released. In 1965, Kinugasa stressed that 'The story was of less importance than the technical research … I utilised in this film almost all of the techniques of the avant-garde.' The sheer complexity of the resulting film would seem to bear out this account that the story predominantly took shape in the editing room.

Though the literary connection is well established, in later interviews, Kinugasa would often answer disingenuously when questioned about direct cinematic influences (indeed many of the myths surrounding the film can be attributed to the fact that Kinugasa was prone to a certain degree of self-aggrandisement when talking about his work, and often contradicted previous interviews). With the new availability of foreign pictures from Europe and America which had begun to be imported in earnest after World War One, new ideas about what cinema should or should not be had already begun to make serious inroads into both filmmaking *and* intellectual circles. A number of the films of the French avant-garde had already been released in Japan in 1924 and Kinugasa was most certainly aware of them. Later he cited *Das Kabinett des Dr Caligari* (*The Cabinet of Dr Caligari*, Robert Wiene, 1919) as a specific influence, although ten years later, soon after *A Page of Madness*'s first screenings abroad, he told Max Tessier, 'I never had time to watch films at that time, but I discussed them a lot with young intellectuals and artists. Meanwhile, I don't believe that I had been especially interested by what was going on in Europe.' Whilst the approach of trying to pinpoint a single source of influence for the film may be a little reductive given the artistic environment in which it was conceived, it is nonetheless impossible to ignore what was going on in Europe at the time.

At first glance, Wiene's landmark of expressionism, *The Cabinet of Dr Caligari*, is the most obvious comparison, with its similarities in both location and emphasis on mood. However, viewing the two films alongside one another reveals a fundamental difference in approach. German Expressionism, an established movement in painting, theatre and literature, aimed at depicting the inner vision and emotions of the artist rather than any more naturalistic portrayal of the world. In its first cinematic application, Wiene emphasised the insanity of his scenario by use of distorted sets, exaggerated make-up and non-naturalistic lighting, though in terms of visual style the approach was wholly theatrical. In contrast, *A Page of Madness*'s evocation of insanity lies not within the actuality of what is filmed, but in the cinematic language used to portray this bewildering world. Rather than opt for the viewpoint of any one person, the narrative disorientates the viewer by altering its perspective between the characters of the wife, the janitor, the doctor and the cages full of asylum denizens; shifting between flashbacks, dreams, hallucinations and what may or may not be the present-tense dynamic. This cinematic 'impressionism' was firmly associated with the avant-garde in France with films such as Germaine Dulac's *La Souriante Madame Beudet* (1923), Abel Gance's *La Roue* (1923) and René Clair's more overtly surreal *Paris Qui Dort* (1924).

According to Swiss film historian Mariann Lewinsky, one particularly decisive influence was F. W. Murnau's *Der Letzte Mann* (*The Last Laugh*, 1925), which had been released a month before Kinugasa started filming *A Page of Madness* and had elicited a lot of debate in contemporary Japanese film magazines as being the first silent film to abandon intertitles, an approach shared by his film. In a published poll at the time, the director cited it as his favourite film of all time, having seen it five times, and several similarities in shots and images between the two films are apparent. Noël Burch goes one step further with the groundless conjecture that Kinugasa also eliminated the use of a *benshi*, though Lewinsky's book contains a *benshi* script for the film, and she also asserts that it was only with the co-operation of the most famous *benshi* of the time, Musei Tokugawa, that the film was able to be screened at the Musashino-kan in Tokyo, a cinema that specialised in Western films. Screenings of the film since its rediscovery have not been accompanied by such narration (it has been shown accompanied by a diverse range of live musical accompaniments, ranging from free-form jazz, electronica and indie-rock) and the film certainly does not suffer without it. Still, whatever Kinugasa's intentions, the fact remains that the *benshi* were a vital component of any film screening at the time of its original release, and it seems unlikely that the film would have been able to be shown without one.

A particular form of cinema from abroad that Kinugasa was certainly shielded from were the Soviet films of the directors Sergei Eisenstein, Dziga Vertov and Vsevolod Pudovkin. Though Japan had entered a period of increased liberalisation in the immediate aftermath of World War One, communism was considered a dangerous threat to the established order. Due to their subversive political content *Stachke* (*The Strike*) and *Bronenosets Potemkin* (*Battleship Potemkin*), both released in the Soviet Union in 1925, were quickly confiscated by the authorities in Japan.

However, *A Page of Madness* certainly displays an awareness and understanding of the theories of montage initiated by Lev Kuleshov, who stated that individual shots acquire meaning in relation to their succeeding or preceding shots. Eisenstein was later to evolve this theory, with an emphasis on what he termed as 'intellectual montage', and the 'production of meaning' by juxtaposing unrelated, often abstract images to create a dissonance leading the viewer to a certain awareness or insight.

Kinugasa's debt to Soviet cinema, if only through reading Eisenstein's translated essays, was acknowledged two years later after the release of *Jujiro* (*Crossroads*, 1928), made in conjunction with Shochiku. Described as a *jidai geki* without swords, Kinugasa's second independent production stressed the psychological aspects of his self-penned tale in a dark, angst-ridden piece more directly inspired by the techniques of German Expressionism. The director barely waited until it had finished its theatrical run before leaving Tokyo and hopping aboard the Trans-Siberian Express with a print of the film in his hands. Upon arriving in Moscow, he made the acquaintance of his idols Pudovkin, then in the process of making *Potomok Chingiskhana* (*Storm over Asia*, 1928), and Eisenstein, who granted him a sneak preview of his latest work, *Oktyabr* (*October*, 1927). The two directors discussed film technique at great length before Kinugasa continued on to Berlin, where he managed to sell his film. Thus *Crossroads*, re-titled *The Shadows of Yoshinara*, became the first Japanese film to be to be widely screened outside of Japan; going on to play in Paris, London and New York. Selling it had earned Kinugasa enough to stay in Europe for a further two years during which time he applied himself to studying the emerging techniques for synchronised sound film production.

Returning from his pilgrimage, his experimental phase seemingly worked out of his system, Kinugasa kept up a steady output over the next decades, creating a respectable number of domestic commercial successes. These include the first *jidai geki* talkie, *Ikinokotta Shinsengumi* (*The Surviving Shinsengumi*, 1932); the first sound version of the oft-filmed tale *Chushingara* (*The Loyal Forty-Seven Ronin*, 1932); and a three-part serial in 1935, *Yukinojo Henge* (*Yukinojo's Revenge*) scripted by the director from his own experiences working as an *oyama* actor onstage, and later remade in 1963 by Kon Ichikawa with Kazuo Hasegawa reprising the lead role in a version known abroad as *An Actor's Revenge*. Kinugasa's final taste of success outside Japan occurred when his first experiments with colour, *Jigokumon* (*Gate of Hell*, 1953), earned him the Grand Prix at the 1954 Cannes Film Festival and an Academy Award for the new Best Foreign Film category in the same year. Kinugasa's last film as director was the Russian co-production, *Chiisai Tobosha* (*The Little Runaway*), in 1967.

The veteran director died in 1982, undoubtedly heartened in his winter years by the rediscovery of *A Page of Madness*. Critics remarked upon the director's new lease of life when he arrived in Europe in the early 1970s, then aged 76, with a newly struck print of what he affectionately proclaimed as the favourite of all his films, his mind no doubt flooded with his memories of his first trip abroad some fifty years earlier.

Despite the enduring interest *A Page of Madness* still elicits during its periodic appearances in film museums, revival houses or on the festival circuit, its inexplicable unavailability for the home market has shielded far too many contemporary viewers from discovering the mastery of Kinugasa's technique and his cohesiveness of vision, and its significance is all too often overlooked in film history texts. Whilst the fruits of Kinugasa's early experimental period may have proved too outré to be of immediate influence on the course of Japanese cinema, *A Page of Madness* remains an outstanding achievement for being the only film of its time produced wholly outside of the studio system, and the first attempt at elevating the status of cinema within his own country to the level of 'high art'. In the annals of film history, Kinugasa's page is too often skipped. It is, however, most certainly a crucial one.

Jasper Sharp

REFERENCES

Kawabata, Y. (1984) *Snow Country*. New York: Vintage Books. Forward by E. G. Seidensticker.

Lewinsky, M. (1997) *Eine Verrückte Seite: Stummfilm und Filmische Avant-Garde in Japan*. Zurich: Chronos.

Peterson, J. (1989) 'A War of Utter Rebellion: Kinugasa's A Page of Madness and the Japanese Avant-Garde of the 1920s', *Cinema Journal*, 29, 1.

Petric, V. (1983) 'A Page of Madness: A Neglected Masterpiece of the Silent Cinema', *Film Criticism* 8, 1, 86–106.

Kinugasa, T. (1998) *Classic Japanese Screenplays: A Crazy Page and Crossroads* (trans. by D. A. Rajakaruna). Sri Lanka: Kandy Offset Printers.

SAYON NO KANE SAYON'S BELL

HIROSHI SHIMIZU, JAPAN, 1943

Any examination of the 1943 film *Sayon No Kane* (*Sayon's Bell*) must contend with the question of how director Hiroshi Shimizu's celebrated modern 'realist' and location-driven style was utilised for colonialist purposes. What this imperative suggests is Japanese cinema's implicit relationship with empire. Coinciding with the often-cited correspondence between the 'birth of cinema' and the global intensification of European imperialisms between the late nineteenth century and World War One, Japan's own entry into the imperialist camp was intricately linked with the spread of early film technologies throughout Asia.

In 1895, the Sino-Japanese war ended with a ceding to Japan of its first colony, in Taiwan. Japan's occupation of Taipei thus set the stage for Japanese capitalists to import to the city one of the first kinescopes recorded as existing in Asia, in 1896, to follow in 1900 with Taipei's first public screening of a motion picture – film technologies that would later be utilised to imagine Taiwan as an exotic backwater (and later, front line) to the Japanese empire, as well as incorporated into local colonialist policies of assimilation and imperialisation that lasted up to the end of Japan's occupation of the island in 1945. Of course, such imperialist expansion only further suggests the difficulty of delineating the boundaries of Japanese cinema. A film set in Taiwan and co-produced by Japan's Shochiku Film Studios, the Manchurian Motion Picture Association and the colonial Government of Taiwan, *Sayon's Bell* is equally central to histories of both Japanese and Taiwanese film. As Longyan Ye has argued in his history of Taiwanese cinema during the Japanese occupation, 'If, as Tadao Sato has indicated, "Japanese film history is part and parcel of the footsteps of imperialism", then Taiwanese film history – after its gradual sinking into the cruel and violent ranks of war – also reflects the arrogance of militarism in Taiwan.'

Ye's allusion to the contested implications of a shared film history for Taiwan and Japan suggests both the productivity and limitations of the terms that have become central to defining the location and meaning of cinema. How one defines a film as 'national' – as Japanese or the even more problematically Chinese, for example – and the place of the filmmaker in relationship to it, has become a significant subject of recent debate. While the study of 'national cinemas' has facilitated attention to the differing locations of cinema throughout the globe, its uses have often assumed its films to be constitutive of an 'imagined community' outlined by well defined territorial, linguistic or political borders. And yet, colonialist histories and experiences complicate the boundaries of such approaches to film, particularly as national cinema models have often done little to acknowledge imperialist projects or contradictions on their own screens. Recently revived discussions of Hiroshi Shimizu, for example, have rarely addressed at any length his wartime colonialist films set in Korea and Taiwan (those set in Korea, for example, include *Keijo* (*Seoul*) and *Tomodachi* (*Friend*), both made in 1940). It is here where Japanese cinema also reveals itself to have been produced through another related critical tradition – that of the auteur as its representative sign. As a so-called 'forgotten Japanese master', Hiroshi Shimizu has recently been revived as a filmmaker who, despite a wide range of 'undisciplined' and 'popular' productions, transcended his studio constraints to develop a body of films reflecting an innovatively modern and realist style. In this concern, for both quality and consistency of film style, auteurist approaches to the cinema have functioned as a significant gatekeeper to Shimizu's inclusion into the canon of Japanese (national) filmmaking, treating his colonialist films in a similar manner to his popular ones – as unrepresentative of a coherent cultural context or oeuvre.

Imperialist concerns are arguably central to the very construction of national cinema. This link becomes apparent when we examine the 'realist' and so-called 'all location' style that has largely worked to establish Shimizu as an auteur – a style purporting the unmediated depiction of everyday life through a central concern for location and landscape – and its centrality to the depiction of Japanese empire in *Sayon's Bell*. Here, it is significant that one central component of colonialist films is also their concern with location and place. As Priya Jaikumar has suggested in a different context, 'place is always an important part of the imperial narrative, in that the coherence of narrative is predicated on the continuation of the colonial place as an unproblematic backdrop'. This observation is equally relevant to Japanese imperialist films. 'Continental' films (*tairiku eiga*) of the early 1940s, for example, positioned the Chinese mainland landscape as an idyllic, exotic or penetrable backdrop upon which Chinese/Japanese wartime relations could be depicted as a romance between a Chinese woman and a Japanese man. The regular appearance of Li Xianglan – a Japanese national also advertised as a Chinese star in *Sayon's Bell* – presented such romantic fantasies through an ideal pan-Asian geography that figured place and the consenting work within it as exotic and female. Hiroshi Shimizu's particular concern for location similarly demands attention to imperial imagination – a recognition of realism's complicity with empire as *Sayon's Bell's* interweaving narration of gender, family and ethnicity sustained the production of the places of Japanese empire.

The narrative of *Sayon's Bell* is based upon an account that circulated throughout imperial Japan and Taiwan in the late 1930s and early 1940s about a Taiwanese girl, Sayon, and her dedication to the Japanese empire, even as a beloved Japanese official from her remote village was called up to join the imperial army to contribute to an intensified offensive against mainland China in 1938. Despite the dangerous conditions of a heavy downpour, Sayon is depicted in the film as insisting on sending the official off and accompanying him on his departing journey through the winding mountain paths. While crossing a narrow and wet bridge, the girl loses her footing and falls helpless into a raging stream, leaving behind no trace of herself but a report of the luggage she had carried. Three years after this reported incident, in 1941, the eighteenth imperial governor of Taiwan issued a bell to Sayon's village in remembrance of her patriotic and innocent sacrifice in the service of the empire.

This story, re-told and re-circulated in the interests of promoting the Japanese empire, reveals not only the importance of gender to mapping its contours but also the primacy of the family and its children as a metaphor for the narration of national and imperial interests. Shimizu's translation of this imperial tale to the screen maintained these configurations through his film's central concern with place, locating Taiwan as a backdrop that bore a particular, if negotiated, relationship to the Japanese empire. *Sayon's Bell* opens with a long sequence of textual intertitles that begins from a simple description of its setting – the 'summery and beautiful island of Taiwan'. The titles that follow then work to locate this tropically idyllic landscape through a narrative mapping of Taiwan as an untenable yet exotic vanguard to the empire. On the one hand, Taiwan is the southern front line of the Japanese imperial 'Greater East Asian Co-prosperity Sphere' – a phrase Japan introduced in 1940 that promoted interracial solidarity and community among the peoples of Asia, founded on the notions of cooperation and interdependence and, especially after the outbreak of the Pacific War in 1941, resistance to the powers of the West. That this idealised Asian community was to be administered under the benevolent leadership of Japan is, in these intertitles, expressed through an inscription of family into the narration of this place and its people. Here, the exemplary *takasago* people (a late colonial term generically indicating the 'tribal peoples' of Taiwan) are positioned along a progressive trajectory of assimilation – as subjects of the empire who had once been 'uncivilised' outsiders, but had since come to be true 'children' of the empire through their valiant fight at its front lines.

The process of assimilation was central to Japanese imperial interests in Taiwan – one that found a strategic rhetorical target in the island's *takasago* cultures. The 'celebrated' aboriginal participation in the empire, which was constructed around them, worked to incorporate the occupied island into Japan's 'Greater East Asian' imperial family, yet at the same time indicated that their position would be under the differentiated status of ethnicised children. Leo Ching has convincingly argued for the specificity of later Japanese policies of assimilation in Taiwan. As opposed to earlier, more general policies of *dôka* (literally, the creation of equivalence through assimilation), the process of *kôminka* after the late 1930s was a 'political and cultural intensification required to transform colonised peoples into loyal imperial subjects in preparation for war'. Restricting the use of Taiwanese language and customs with the intent of annihilating the colonised's identity and culture, the newness of *kôminka* lay in 'its inauguration and internalisation of "Japanisation" as exclusively a problematic of the colonised, viewed as an incomplete "imperial subject"'. In response, a spirit of voluntary work for the empire – often prominently represented in inscription into its imperial army – became one way the imperial subject was imagined to negotiate such differences in identity.

Sayon's Bell's idealised textual narration of the colonialist map as colonial subjectivity is followed by an extended sequence of documentary-like scenes that bring the viewer ever closer to the main setting of the film – an idyllic southern countryside of hills, sparkling rivers, bucolic oxen and peasants working in fields and traversing over roads. The camera, first lingering on the still image of a road's surface, then pushes forward into the landscape in a series of shots that travel along its increasingly remote path, finally resting on the distant view of a rural village in the valley below. Our first view of this community is an extreme long-shot of neat rows of peasants simultaneously bowing to the raising of the Japanese *hinomaru* flag. Yet such a linking of even this distant community to the expanding network of the Japanese empire is followed by a brief ethnographic study of the exotica of daily life in the village – barefoot feet walking along dirt paths, a mother nursing her child, crying babies carried on backs and villagers labouring in fields, all of which is interspersed with scenes of the intricate process of producing local clothing, from close-ups of thread being spun to hands weaving and cloth being hung out to dry. Shimizu's own comments about the production of *Sayon's Bell* interestingly paralleled these scenes and their treatment of location. Wishing to conceive of the film's progression in relation to its Taiwanese location, Shimizu claimed that its true inspiration came from the customs, stories and 'beautiful and dreamlike clothing' of the villagers, which provided the backdrop for the Japanese actors that were featured most prominently in the narrative that followed. Documentary footage was, in this way, central to the promotion of the film, claiming it was closely linked to the daily patterns of rural (if exoticised and imperial) life in Taiwan.

This attention to the detailed activities of everyday life was a reflection of the realist style central to Hiroshi Shimizu's recognition as a Japanese auteur. Films such as *Arigatosan* (*Mr Thank You*, 1938) were praised in the 1930s for their deep understanding of the nature of filmic realism as a tool for approaching the actualities of a rapidly modernising Japan. Described by its studio as a 'location film', *Mr Thank You* presented landscapes not from the confined views of a studio set, but rather from the actual interior of a bus being driven from city to countryside that allowed for a continuous display of moving rural landscape – a seemingly unspoiled and remote space filmed under the guise of a modern, 'realist' and unmediated record of daily life. Indeed, as Mitsuyo Wada-Marciano has argued, realism formed a 'contentious discourse' in the flux of 1930s and wartime Japan, as it displayed a 'tug between modernity and nationalism in the process of creating Japanese popular culture'. Expanding upon critical readings of the centrality of landscape to Japanese literature's construction of the modern Japanese subject, Wada-Marciano describes Hiroshi Shimizu's elaborate use of domestic locale:

> Shimizu's use of country vistas likewise located a regional, even backward cultural identity … represent[ing] for the mainstream urban audience … a carnivalesque procession of 'exotic' and 'native' culture. The films offered a nativised space, reifying the disparity between mainstream and regional cultures in order to secure a modern identity. The spectator, thus, had the benefit of realism's twin pleasures: vicariously gazing at primitive locals on the one hand, and self-satisfaction at being sufficiently modern on the other.

Shimuzu's *Mr Thank You* presents a slightly more complex regional landscape, as its roads are produced through classed characters and labourers who have a range of levels of access to the city. Yet the simultaneous workings of national and modernising discourses that Wada-Marciano identifies in these 'local' views of Japan easily found a place in the links between modernisation and imperialism within the Japanese colonialist project of the 1940s. Film in particular was a suitable device to aid, simultaneously, the colonial processes of modernisation and assimilation in Taiwan. Shochiku studios already had a strong presence on the island, and had taken advantage of its close ties to Japan's imperial command of commodity capital to influence local filmmaking. More significant to this chapter, however, is the question of visuality – the ways in which the project of modernisation is inscribed into the metropolitan and imperialist gaze of *Sayon's Bell*. As the opening sequence displays its documentary footage of local peasants tied to their rural Taiwanese landscapes, the film presents 'for the mainstream urban', and thus imperial, audience a 'carnivalesque procession of "exotic" and "native" culture' – a 'nativised space' that, rather than reify, more aptly negotiates the disparity between colonising and colonised cultures in order to secure a simultaneously modern and imperialist identity. Indeed, the distance necessary to construct this identity is established in the way in which the camera initially travels along the opening road of the film, penetrating deeper into the mountains and seemingly further away from the civilising auspices of the Japanese empire.

Films characterised by Shimizu's 'realist' and location-driven style often downplay the technologies of modern life (telephones, automobiles, and so forth) and their relationship to the local and nativised countryside. Yet what is significant to the narration of place in *Sayon's Bell* – in its naturalised (if exotic) details of everyday life in rural Taiwan – is the way in which even the daily, seemingly innocuous activities of walking are inscribed into the workings of the Japanese empire. A peasant's bare feet plodding over a dirt-packed road, even the production of indigenous cloth, can only be understood within imperialist concerns, given the ways in which the film's first intertitles present the context from which the manual labour follows. This rendering of everyday activities is also dependent upon a landscape inscribed with an imperial teleology – of modernisation, assimilation and participation in the empire, no matter the distance from its metropolitan centre. The film's structuring of empire building is made explicit in the third and final montage of its opening sequence. Here, the Japanese village officer's benevolent work on behalf of the remote community is carefully documented in scenes where he is presented as doctor, teacher, military leader and, most importantly, public works officer directing the construction of a bridge that connects the village to the distant mountain paths that ultimately lead to the rest of Japan's empire. In the film's background is the constant activity of the villagers – even the 'old timers' – eagerly trudging out to the land surrounding the village in a daily stream of pickaxes and shovels, which pull and turn over its surface in preparation for seemingly essential work in support of imperial construction. Less an idyllic and timeless paradise, the backdrop of *Sayon's Bell* remains, as in other imperialist narratives, complicit in the imperative that 'work must change the place' and reproduce it for the purposes of empire.

That the social categories produced in relation to this landscape are equally about the (re)production of imperial identity through the repetitions of work, is strongly suggested by the throng of village children in *Sayon's Bell* who accompany the young Sayon through her narrative. Shimizu's image as a humanist children's director remained with him long into his post-war career. Yet this cinema, which utilised children and their views of the world as a focal point for social insight, here revealed itself as being dependent upon a particular conception of landscape – as central to Shimizu's 'realistic' depiction of pure, idyllic and innocent locale. *Sayon's Bell*'s frequent feature of these children frolicking over the lush hills and valleys of Taiwan is paralleled with scenes of them caring for younger children and tending to the village while their elders are out working the land. Such innocent play is also, in a significant scene, closely intertwined with their maintenance of fluency in the Japanese language through the model tutelage of Sayon. Walking down a dirt road after a frantic and innocently comedic search over the countryside for a lost baby, Sayon utilises this respite in the film's action to instruct her younger charges on the proper Japanese words for the days of the week. Indeed, the dialogue and intertitles of *Sayon's Bell* were produced and filmed entirely in Japanese. While this benefitted the almost all-Japanese cast (save, of course, for the 'native' villagers who provided the film's 'backdrop'), it was also in keeping with later colonial and educational policies that enforced the learning and use of the Japanese language for all Taiwanese subjects of the empire – a policy strikingly inscribed into the rhythms of idyllic village life in this scene. Children are thus utilised throughout the film's narrative in the task of supporting both modernisation and policies of assimilation and imperialisation. In a location so inscribed in work and progress, it is only fitting that they – an latent metaphor for children of the empire – should work for its maintenance as well.

In the final scene of the film, the children of *Sayon's Bell* run to the shores of a lake to which the now tragically deceased Sayon had often accompanied them. As they repeatedly call out her name, their voices echo out over an ever-widening view of their surroundings until the camera rests on a full-screen of its lush green outline – a static scene of landscape against which a bell ('Sayon's bell') solemnly tolls in the distance.

Li Xianglan, the popular star who was loaned out from the Manchurian Motion Picture Association to play the role of Sayon, is often said to denote an ambiguous figure during the early 1940s. A Japanese national advertised as a Chinese star in war-time melodramas linked with Japan, the image of this star (also known as Yoshiko Yamaguchi or the Japanisation of her Chinese name, Ri Kôran) has been more recently revived in debates of hybridity and Japanese popular culture. Within the context of the Japanese empire, it was the very ambivalence of Li Xianglan's star persona that played a central role in the popular construction of its pan-Asian and militaristic ideals. Yet while her *qipao* clad – and thus 'Chinese' – image often worked to represent imperial ideals as a patriotic and national romance, her figuring of Sayon, costumed in the 'ethnic' clothing woven and spun by the aboriginal people of *Sayon's Bell*, indicated a childlike and fast disappearing 'primitivity' strategically negotiated through the repetitions of imperial work and military inscription. This final toll of Sayon's bell utilises the ambiguities of loss – and the after-effects of violent spectacle – to re-inscribe place and locale into the very production of empire by way of the redeeming and interweaving contours of gender, family and ethnicity that were central to mapping its naturalised landscape into the Greater East Asia Co-prosperity Sphere.

In her description of the ways in which these tropes were inscribed into the daily activities of empire, Jennifer Robertson has examined the Japanese imperial project through what she terms 'cross-ethnicking' – theatrical revues and 'soldier show' entertainment of the time that 'invited a vicarious, fantastical experience of foreign travel and exotic romance, while at the same time sounding a call to cultural arms and the shared work of empire'. Similar activities of the empire are paralleled in *Sayon's Bell's* repeated return to an aboriginal dance performed by Sayon and her fellow villagers around a bonfire set against the primordial sounds of local voices and drumbeats. A rhythmic extension of the local costume and locale of the opening sequences of the film, this patterned, if expressly exoticised, ritual of everyday life is celebrated every time a new villager is conscripted into the imperial army. Idealising primitivity in the service of the empire and its military, such scenes suggest the ways in which, by strategically assuming a hybrid character itself, Japanese national cultural practices worked to inscribe into its very reproduction the daily activities and places of its empire. For *Sayon's Bell*, this was an ambivalence performed and worked through the realist aesthetics of location.

Stephanie DeBoer

REFERENCES

Jaikumar, P. (2001) '"Place" and the Modernist Redemption of Empire in *Black Narcissus* (1947)', *Cinema Journal*, 40, 2, 57–77.

Robertson, J. (1998) *Takarazuka: Sexual Politics and Popular Culture in Japan*. Berkeley: University of California Press.

Sato, T. (1996) '*Shimizu Hiroshi*.' *Nihon eiga no kyojintachi I [Masters of Japanese Cinema I]*. Tokyo: Gakuyo shobo, 139–83.

Ye Longyan (1998) *Rizhi shiqi Taiwan dianying shi [Taiwanese movies during the Japanese colonization]*. Taibei: Yushan.

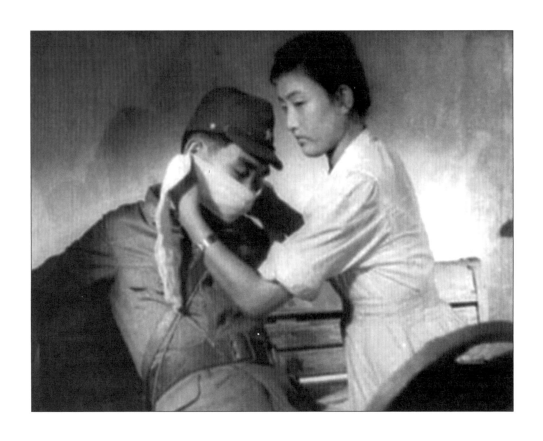

JAYU MANSE HURRAH! FOR FREEDOM

CHOE IN-GYU, KOREA, 1946

Historically, Korean cinema has been virtually invisible to the rest of the world, and, to some extent, to its own people. According to Adriano Aprà, only three films made in Korea before 1946 have survived, and all of those are, strictly speaking, Japanese films, having been made during World War Two by occupation forces. In fact, the oldest surviving Korean-made film is *Jayu Manse* (*Hurrah! For Freedom*, aka *Victory of Freedom,* aka *Long Live Liberty*), and the complete loss of Korean cinema pre-1946 could well be the most tragic loss in world cinema history. It follows that nothing has survived from the period 1926–35, known as the 'Golden Era of Silent Films'. It is estimated that 80 per cent of all the silent films that were made in the world have been lost. In many countries of Europe and the United States, where a concern for the preservation of film began in the 1930s and 1940s, the statistics are much better. The Swedish Cinemataket in Stockholm was the first film archive to be founded in 1933. But, the (South) Korean Film Archive in Seoul was not established until 1974, while the North Korean film archive in Pyongyang had begun in 1961. By then, virtually all of the films made before and during the Korean War had disappeared. There was, of course, no reason for the Japanese government to save films made in Korea during the years of their occupation, and the civil war, as Aprà has written, was, in both North and South Korea, 'impartial in its destructions'.

There are various accounts as to when films were first projected in Korea (by American and British travellers between 1897 and 1900) but historians all agree with surviving newspaper accounts that French short films were shown to the general public on the premises of the Hansung Electric Company in Seoul on 23 June 1903. The first film theatres opened in Seoul in 1906, but the first permanent theatres (which showed only films) were not established until 1909, the same year that Korea became a Japanese colony. Surprisingly, perhaps, there is no evidence of any fiction films being made in Korea before this date, and, less surprisingly given the repressive colonial regime, no films were made by Korean nationals until 1919. On 27 October of that year, *Uirijok Gutu* (*The Righteous Revenge*, aka *Loyal Revenge*), a 'kino drama' (*yeonsoegeuk*) – a stage play with film inserts – directed by Kim Do-san and produced by Park Sung-pil was premiered at the Dangsongsa Theatre. This is generally regarded as being the first Korean-made film, although the film segments (approximately 1000ft, or 10 minutes long) were shot by a Japanese cameraman, and in 1966 the South Korean government declared 27 October 1919 to be the 'Day of Cinema', commemorating the true beginnings of a national cinema. There is disagreement on which of two 1923 films, *Wolha-ui Maengse* (*The Plighted Love Under the Moon*), written and directed by Baek-nam Yun but produced by the Japanese colonial government to encourage the 'salvation of Korea', and *Gukkyong* (*The National Borders*, aka *The Border*) directed by Kim Do-san, constitutes the first *real* Korean feature film. Until recently, it was assumed that *The National Borders* was never finished, but film scholars Kim Chongweon and Cho Heuimun both wrote in 1993 of the discovery of an advertisement of its premiere on January 11 1923, pre-dating the first screening of *The Plighted Love Under the Moon* by almost two months. Young-Il Lee's account was typical of earlier histories: 'Kim Do-san, director/producer of the first kino-drama was killed in an automobile accident in 1923 while filming one such kino-drama. It is said that his last work, *Gukkyong* (*The National Borders*) was not a kino-drama but a complete motion picture.' Clearly, it would be preferable to recognise as 'Korean' a film that was immediately banned by the colonial government the day after its only screening 'on the basis of its "undesirable" political content' (*The National Borders*) rather than a work of Japanese propaganda (*The Plighted Love Under the Moon*) and, no doubt, in the future Korean film historians will favour the new history'.

Included in the 'complete loss' is the recognised masterpiece of Korean cinema, *Arirang* (1926), directed by Na Un-gyu, which has been called the first Nationalistic film. Na was only 24 when he made this, his first film, and had been jailed for two years previously for his radicalism and involvement in the Korean 'independence movement'. In *Arirang*, he found a way to clandestinely criticise Japanese oppression by having his protagonist, a student, kill a rural landowner for attempting to rape his sister. The main subject of the film is one of class, not national, struggle and yet Korean audiences easily identified themselves with oppressed characters and imagined the oppressors as being Japanese. Na was saved from having the film censored by the Japanese authorities by having his young 'hero' suffer from mental illness, and by the use of allegory; the brutal oppressor is not *actually* Japanese. The film was hugely influential for other Korean filmmakers and has been remade a number of times since. The years 1927, with 14 films being made and 1928, with 13, were the peak years for Korean film production under Japanese occupation (1930, with 12 films, was the only other year when Korean production hit double figures). Na made another film in 1926, three in 1927 and two in 1928, the second of which, *Sarang-ul Chajasu* (*Searching for Love*) is considered to be 'nationalist', and was heavily censored by the authorities. 1928 was also the year in which the first film was made by the more overtly political group, KAPF (Korean Art Proletariat Foundation, or, more correctly, Korean Artista Proletariat Federatè in Esperanto), *Yurang* (*Wandering*) being the first Korean 'tendency' film. At most, only seven films were finished by the group (all directed by Kim Yu-yong and Kang Ho) and only four were released, none with commercial success. Their last film, *Jihachon* (*The Underground Village*) was banned before it could be released, and all of those involved in its production were arrested. Government censorship had become progressively more stringent through the 1920s, and the banning of *The Underground Village* marked the end of any recognisably anti-Japanese cinema until the appearance of *Jayu Manse* in 1946. Surely, had any of these truly 'Korean' films from this 'experimental' phase of national cinema survived, we would find many of them to be pioneering examples of clandestine political cinema, prefiguring that of Eastern Europe (notably Poland and Hungary) beginning in the 1950s, where filmmakers could not overtly criticise their own, or Soviet, governmental forces, yet did so by suggestion. Indeed, a later tendency of more subtle, allegorical filmmaking under stricter Japanese control where violence was not tolerated at all, developed in the 1930s. These were films of 'enlightenment', where a person would typically leave his/her home, often a village, to return later, in order to teach others to be better people.

Tragically then, not only are the first 25 years of Korean film history completely lost, but an entire movement, too. What has survived is a written text of *Arirang*. As in Japan, with the *benshi* narrator, from 1910 on Korean silent films have been accompanied by a single individual 'talking' all of the roles for the audience; a *byun-sa*. No doubt influenced by the *benshi*, through the filtering effects of Japanese occupation, the *byun-sa* storyteller nonetheless derives from the Korean indigenous theatrical tradition of *pansori*, where a single musician/poet/singer performs opera, alone on stage. According to Hee-moon Cho, a professor in Korean Film History at Sang-Myung University, the division of Seoul by the Hangang River into Korean residences on the north side (Northern Village) and Japanese occupiers on the south side (Southern Village) was matched by film performances during the 1910s and 1920s, which would be narrated by Korean-speaking *byun-sas* in the north and Japanese-speaking ones in the south. Cho notes that some 60 *byun-sas* operated in Seoul at this time, one quarter of which were Japanese (and three or four, female). As in Japan, 'talkies' were late to arrive in Korea. The first fully synchronised sound film did not appear until 1935 and silent films, which were not, of course, strictly speaking 'silent', remained popular for a long time after this. Gradually, the *byun-sas* moved away from the capital, to rural areas where they would continue to operate until the 1960s. One such storyteller/narrator, Shin-chool, who began working as a *byun-sa* at the age of 12, in 1942, is not only still living, but also continues to give performances, standing on stage in front of the film, as he used to 60 years ago. Although there is no evidence to support this, it is certainly possible that, under certain circumstances, a *byun-sa* could have narrated a film as if the villainous characters were Japanese. It is certainly very likely that films with Japanese titles would be read to the audience in the Korean language. The colonial government systematically tried to eliminate the Korean people's sense of national identity and included in this programme was the introduction of the Japanese language in schools and the concomitant elimination of Korean, and the forced change of Korean family names into a standard Japanese style. And one can certainly understand that, with the ready availability of Korean-speaking *byun-sas* and heavy government censorship of spoken Korean on a film's soundtrack, the silent form persisted longer in Korea than in almost any other country (with the possible exception of Thailand where silent films were still being made in the 1960s).

Only one Korean silent film is still extant, *Geomsa-wa Yeoseonsaeng* (*A Prosecutor and the Lady Teacher*), directed by Dae-ryong Yun and made quite late, in 1948, during the next phase of Korean (cinema) history; from the liberation (15 August 1945) to the end of the Korean War (1953). In 'Two Restorations in Seoul' by Bae Jong-keang it is noted that this film is *mostly* complete, but is only 40 minutes long. He talks of the restoration being extremely difficult for the Korean Film Archive (KFA) because the only surviving print (of the only surviving silent film) which was obtained from a 'gentleman who was the original "narrator" of the film' was badly damaged and very fragile. It can be assumed that this 'gentleman' is none other than Shin-chool. As it is, this era is not much better served, cinematically, than that of the Japanese occupation. Only five films have survived, none of which were made during the war. *The Guinness Book of Movie Facts and Feats* lists 59 films made from 1946–49, but claims that an unknown number were made after this, during the Korean War. Fortunately, the first of all the 'liberation' films, and the oldest extant Korean film (rather than a 'film made in Korea'), *Hurrah! For Freedom*, has survived, be it in fragmented form.

During the last two years of World War Two, no films were made in Korea by a private company and essentially all of the films made by the Chosun Film Company under strict instructions from the Office of the Governors General and the Chosun Military Headquarters were for Japanese propaganda. Two of these films, *Taeyang-ui Aidul* (*Children of the Sun*, 1944) and *Sarangui Maengse* (*Promise of Love*, aka *Love and Pledge*, 1945), were made by In-gyu Choe, the director of *Hurrah! For Freedom*. Perhaps the understandably anti-Japanese 'liberation' stance of *Hurrah! For Freedom* comes from Choe's own reaction to his being 'used' as a promoter of Japanese anti-Korean propaganda, but in any event, the argument over who was and who was not a 'nationalist' or 'political' Korean director is a very complex one. Even Un-gyu Na, the best-known 'nationalist' Korean film director prior to World War Two, made pro-Japanese films. There were not too many options if one wanted to continue making films. Hangjin Lee has written that in the 1930s, 'Korean film-makers turned to literary films as a reaction to the government's control, viewing them as a way to escape from the forced production of pro-Japanese films on one side and to avoid conventional melodramas on the other'.

Hurrah! For Freedom takes place during the last days of World War Two. Hanjung (Jon Jang-gun) is fighting for Korean independence and is involved in a clandestine operation. Together with a fellow resistance worker, he is wanted by the Japanese police. Climbing a cliff, his accomplice is shot and falls to his death. Hanjung is wounded and hides in a house occupied by a mother and daughter. Hyeja (Hwang Yeo-heui), the daughter of the household is sick, but nevertheless nurses Hanjung to a rapid recovery. Their close relationship leads to their falling in love. They do not want to separate, but Hanjung must continue his struggle and hence they must part. But, before he is able to leave, the police arrive and arrest them both. There is a violent struggle and they escape together. However, the Japanese catch up with him and, again, he engages in a desperate fight. He is badly wounded but dies a hero to the Korean people only days before his country's liberation.

I was fortunate to have seen *Hurrah! For Freedom* at a small retrospective in Montreal in 1994, but when I viewed it, the print was in a terrible condition. Only 50 minutes of the original feature (of unknown length) now remains. It was made on 16mm and the surviving print was also in this gauge. As the 35mm travelling print contained English sub-titles, it can be supposed that the surviving material had been discovered outside of Korea. Initially, the film is silent. Given the chaotic politico-economic conditions, and the shortage of filmmaking equipment, it may well be that the sound, including dialogue, was post-synched. The surviving film is so fragmented, that it is not possible to reconstruct the story with any surety. For example, immediately following the first chase sequence, we see Hanjung escaping together with a female resistance fighter. He is trying to save her life by getting her to leave him, and he slaps her face in this effort. They are both shot, and we presume he is dead. In retrospect we assume that the woman must be Hyeja, and that the action is the story's conclusion, but it is unclear if the sequence is a flash-forward or a misplaced reel. The latter interpretation seems likely, especially because the film ends suddenly as they are being shot at. In any event the film is full of action and extremely powerful on an emotional level. A good use is made of close-ups, and extrapolating from the evidence of this film, it is probable that Choe was a truly 'stylish' director. Critically the Japanese are depicted as being extremely brutal and one can easily imagine that *Hurrah! For Freedom* would have enjoyed great popularity with Korean audiences, many of whom had been denied any pro-Korean, anti-Japanese images their whole lives. Indeed, with its nationalist, revolutionary rhetoric, the film reportedly greatly impressed the leader of the nationalist, anti-communist Chinese, Chang Kai-shek.

Peter Harry Ris

REFERENCE

Bae, J. (1996) 'Two Restorations in Seoul', *Journal of Film Preservation*, 52, 51–3.

NORA INU STRAY DOG

AKIRA KUROSAWA, JAPAN, 1949

Akira Kurosawa's life covered most of the twentieth century. In that time (from 1910 to 1998) Japan underwent more radical changes than in almost any other other century. The director's historical films are often those that received most attention in the West, be it the films themselves, including *Shinchin No Samurai* (*Seven Samurai*, 1954), *Kimonosu-Jo* (*Throne of Blood*, 1957), *Kakushi Toride No San-Akunin* (*The Hidden Fortress*, 1958), *Yojimbo* (1961), remakes such as *The Magnificient Seven* (1960) and *A Fistful of Dollars* (1964), or the *Star Wars* (1976–ongoing) and *Godfather* (1972–1990) sagas, which were inspired by them. While his contemporary features are no less significant, their comprehension outside of a Japanese cultural context is more difficult. This is never more true than in the case of *Nora Inu* (*Stray Dog*, 1949), which consolidated the collaboration between the director and his star, Toshiro Mifune. More than just a base for their later work, it is an accomplished work in its own right.

Following the drawn-out war in the Pacific (begining with the Japanese invasion of China in 1931 and ending with the nuclear attacks on Hiroshima and Nagasaki in 1945), Japan was far from the highly industrialised nation it is today. Its military leaders had run the country into defeat, devastation and the brink of self-destruction. Most of the country's industry had been destroyed and political control rested with a foreign occupying power, with the Emperor renouncing his divinity. *Stray Dog* is set against the backdrop of these political, social and cultural upheavals.

The story itself is relatively simple. Murakami, a young policeman (played by Mifune) reports the theft of his pistol. It was stolen from him on a crowded bus and giving chase, the perpetrator managed to escape. Murakami is reprimanded and ordered to find the gun. Accepting advice from a former *geisha* Ogin (Sengoku Noriko), Murakami enters the *yakuza*-run twilight zone of Tokyo, becoming one of its many restless inhabitants. He apprehends a woman who leads him to a gun dealer, slowly gaining ground on the thief. When a man is killed and a robbery committed using his gun, Murakami's guilt consumes him and he offers his resignation. Instead, he is assigned to inspector Sato (Shimura Takashi). The older policeman takes his younger colleague under his wing and together they delve deeper into Tokyo's crime world. They discover that the culprit, Yusa, is not dissimilar to Murakami; both were former soldiers who chose to live on opposite sides of the law after being discharged. Murakami increasingly identifies with the criminal but Sato reminds him that their shared past and any problems Yusa has encountered since cannot excuse theft, robbery and murder. Closing in on the criminal, they visit his family and girlfriend, suspicious that they are witholding information. Finally catching up with him, in a state of panic, Yusa kills another man and wounds Sato. Finally, his girlfriend decides to help Murakami, telling him the location where Yusa is hiding. In a wordless finale Murakami catches up with Yusa who has only three rounds left. One bullet hits Murakami, causing only a minor injury. After a prolonged fight in an overgrown wasteland, Yusa surrenders. The last scene shows Murakami at Sato's hospital bed. The wiser detective commends his protogee, who has matured into a more experienced officer.

Stray Dog is one of Kurosawa's finest early films, displaying a confidence in film technique and storytelling. His superiority over many of his peers may have come from his experience working in the film industry during the war, when many other prospective filmmakers were drafted into the armed forces. He escaped conscription through his father's doctor, who exempted him from military service as a favour to his father, a strict authoritarian who was the descendant of a *samurai* warrior. In 1936 he joined what was to become Toho studio as assistant director. As the more experienced assistants above him were constantly being called up to one front or another, Kurosawa rapidly rose through the ranks. His talent for writing screenplays quickly also helped him and, by the early 1940s, he was directing films and showing evidence of the greater work to come.

Stray Dog was Kurosawa's tenth film as director and the eigth time he had worked with the actor Shimura Takashi, here playing Sato (Shimura would continue to appear in the director's films, most notably playing the leads in *Ikiru* (*To Live*, 1952) and in *Seven Samurai*). It was also the the third time he had worked with Toshiro Mifune, the actor he would become most associated with. Mifune had, after appearing in only two other films, exploded on to the screen when Kurosawa directed him for the first time in *Yoidore Tenshi* (*Drunken Angel*, 1948). Their professional partnership was so important that most film historians divide Kurosawa's career into three stages: the years before (1941–47), the years with (1948–65) and the years after Mifune (1966–98).

In *Drunken Angel* Kurosawa gave Mifune free reign in his portrayal of a tuberculosis-infected *yakuza* thug whose redemption arrives too late. Japanese audiences were hungry for new values and faces; they could not resist the charms of the ruggedly handsome young actor.

Much to the director's chagrin he was an overnight success, setting a seductive and persuasively bad example of how not to behave. Shimura, who played a flawed doctor opposite Mifune and whose function was to counter-balance Mifune's impact, was bound to fail at making decency look as interesting as Mifune's deviousness. The trio then worked together on *Shizukanaru Ketto* (*The Silent Duel*, 1949), a mostly forgotten film. It is important for highlighting the increasing control Kurosawa held over Mifune's performance, although the film has widely been considered a failure artistically and if their next collaboration was anything to go by, they learned their lesson well. In *Stray Dog*, Mifune is mesmerising.

In the opening shots if the film, Mifune is dressed in a white suit and wears a white cap. The colour is a metaphor for his naïvité and innocence and makes him an easy target for the pickpockets who set the story in motion. The learning arc the narrative places him on, and the experience he acquires on this journey are reflected in his changing attire, particularly in his donning his old war uniform. In the surroundings of Tokyo's black markets he remembers who he is – a former soldier who has seen people turn bad under the pressures of war. Sato says at one point, 'A stray dog turns easily into a mad dog.' Under Sato's tuition, Murakami begins to understand that he has made the right decision by not going the way of Yusa. Moreover, he realises that he had made that choice from the moment he left the army and joined the police. From the outset, he is more worried about what harm will come of the loss of his pistol than about being suspended for his mistake.

An important factor in understanding the film and the culture in which it was made was that the concept of individuality as a trait of virtue emerged only shortly after the end of the war in the Pacific. It was not a tradition that the feudal system or the repressive military regime had encouraged. On the contrary, individuality had always been associated with lack of morality in Japanese society. Kurosawa's values represented those of a more progressive Japan, welcoming some of the changes imposed by the occupying forces. Many of the heroes (and even the few heroines) of his films, from *Waga Seishun Ni Kuinashi* (*No Regrets for Our Youth*, 1946) and *Ikiru* to *Yojimbo* and Akahige (*Red Beard*, 1965) can be seen as celebrations of individuality. This freedom to celebrate individuality was the result of another progression – the relaxation of strict censorship codes.

One of the themes running through Kurosawa's life as well as his films is his fascination with the duality of human nature. There is never just good or bad. In his autobiography he described the beginings of this fascination in connection with the anti-Korean riots that broke out after the 1923 Tokyo earthquakes. Mobs of Japanese blamed the Korean population for the disaster and the scenes of bloody revenge were witnessed by a young Kurosawa. Later, in 1945, just before a radio proclamation by the Emperor, he observed how his compatriots prepared themselves for the anticipated call to mass suicide in the face of military defeat. When the Emperor asked the country to accept the peace treaty, the same people who had just prepared their *seppuku* joyously celebrated the end of the war. Murakami can be seen as a symbol of Kurosawa's positive message for his fellow Japanese: do not give in to self-destructive instincts but go out and work for better days.

The climax of the film, featuring a prolonged chase and fight between Murakami and Yusa, underlines Kurosawa's blurring of the lines between good and bad. Both men roll through the dirt together, soiling their suits and almost making them indistinguishable from each other. Their identification with each other becomes total as they are transformed into two sides of the same coin. In the years to come Kurosawa would create numerous ambigious characters, whom Mifune often played. Some of the best examples featured in *Rashomon* (1951), *Seven Samurai* and *Warui Yatsu Hodo Yoku Nemuru* (*The Bad Sleep Well*, 1960). Only in the last shot of *Tengoku to Jigoku* (*High and Low*, 1963) did Kurosawa return to such a dramatic comparison between 'good' and 'bad', when he superimposed the kidnapper's (Yamazaki Tsutomu) reflection on Mifune's face.

Another theme of Kurosawa's that appears in *Stray Dog* is the inclusion of a mentor/pupil relationship. Shimura's and Mifune's characters pick up where they left off in *Drunken Angel*, although unlike that film, Murakami learns before it is too late. Far from purely educative and beneficial, Kurosawa highlighted that this relationship could be fraught with problems and, ultimately, may do more harm than good. In *Stray Dog* Sato observes that Murakami has not learnt yet to distance himself enough from his work to remain cold-blooded. This implies that the younger policeman will have to give up a part of his humanity in order to function as a good policeman. In later films the director created inversions and parodies of the theme, like the monk (Chiaki Minoru) in *Rashomon* who begins to doubt the very nature of truth, the dying civil servant (Shimura) in *To Live* whose mentors include a young woman (Odagiri Miki) and a beatnik writer (Ito Yunosuke), or the two peasants (Chiaki Minoru and Fujiwara Kamatari) in *The Hidden Fortress* who refuse to learn from their mistakes.

Kurosawa, who was 38 while directing *Stray Dog*, was in the process of becoming a *sensei* himself after serving various apprenticeships. He often named his brother Heigo as the person who introduced him to the cinema and who had tried to help him conquer fear by not looking away from the legions of charred bodies after the earthquake. In his days as assistant director his mentor was film director Yamamoto Kajiro who encouraged him to write and direct. By 1948 he took Toshiro Mifune under his wing, an actor who, other than a six-month stint at the Toho studios, had never received any formal acting training. Under Kurosawa's tuition (not to mention Shimura's, with whom the actor would appear in more than 20 films) Mifune became the single most recognisable Japanese star (at least until the arrival of 'Beat' Takeshi Kitano) and a formidable actor.

From a Western point of view it is almost impossible to discuss Kurosawa or any of his films – be it their content or style – without mentioning the osmosis of Eastern and Western cultures that permeates his work. Besides the European and American silent films which he proudly quotes in his memoirs the director was also profoundly influenced by theatre and literature from around the world. Among his 'Western' (from a Japanese point of view Russia belongs to the West) adaptations are Shakespeare's *Macbeth* (*Throne of Blood*), *King Lear* (*Ran*, 1985), Gorky's *Lower Depths* (*Donzoko/The Lower Depths*, 1957), Dostoyevsky's *The Idiot* (*Hakuchi*, 1951), Ed McBain's *King's Ransom* (*Tengoku To Jigoku/High and Low*, 1963) and Dashiell Hammett's *Red Harvest* (*Yojimbo*). The literary inspiration for *Stray Dog* came from the works of French novelist Georges Simenon whose speciality were detective novels that were as interested in depicting the social millieu of its protagonists as they were in the thriller plot. Cinematically the US occupation meant that an onslaught of non-Japanese films reached Tokyo in relatively little time. The look of *Stray Dog* is certainly informed by *film noir* features (underworld, high contrast black-and-white photography) as well as Italian Neorealism. The film bears striking similarities in both style and content to Vittorio de Sica's *Ladri di Biciclette (Bicycle Thieves*, 1948). Here a post-war Rome is the backdrop to the story of a commom man whose bicyle is stolen at the beginning of the film. He spends the rest of the film looking for his only means of transport. Not unlike de Sica, Kurosawa shot much of the film on location, as opposed to the more controlled environment of the studio. This was not the director's first foray into a form of documented reality. Two of his earlier films, *Ichiban Utsukushiku* (*The Most Beautiful*, 1944) and *Subrashiki Nichiyobi* (*One Wonderful Sunday*, 1947) already featured similar visual charactaristics. In *Stray Dog*, the most obvious example is when Murakami mingles with the poor and the underworld at the beginning of his investigation. In terms of post-war realism it is highly interesting to also compare *Stray Dog* with *To Live*. Though only made three years later it already shows a rejuvenated Tokyo, both economically and, as it had returned to self-rule in 1951, also in terms of Japanese self-esteem. By the late 1950s Kurosawa's individual optimism had been replaced by a tendency towards pessimism about the state of Japanese corruption, reflected in *The Bad Sleep Well*.

Many stylistic devices that have come to be considered typical of Kurosawa were already clearly developed in *Stray Dog*. The director discovered cinema before sound had been introduced (in fact the popular tradition of the *benshi*, who made their living by performaing commentaries, made sure that talkies arrived later in Japan than in most other countries). His love for silent films stems from then and the tendency to feature scenes without dialogue was a constant feature in all of his work, up to the end of his career. *Stray Dog* features several sequences of purely visual storytelling. In the opening moments there is a shot of Murakami chasing a suspect on foot that is very redolent – although anything but comical – of Buster Keaton's great chase sequences. The actors run towards a camera mounted on a moving vehicle. The scenee where Murakami mingles with the people on the black markets in order to be approached by arms dealers is another example. Though it has been criticised for its length – it runs for over eight minutes in total – it succeeds in evoking both time and place, whilst also conveying Murakami's point of view. The audience's identification with Mifune's character is achieved by a complex montage of close-ups and long-shots, points-of-view and details which are joined together by a range of wipes, dissolves and cuts. We see what Murakami sees (which includes a tracking-shot pointing directly at the sun, through a straw roof; it pre-empts the more famous varitation of the same shot in *Rashomon*), witnessing his fatigue – both mental and physical – as he continues wandering the streets for hours and hours. The temperature and grime on the streets are impressively evoked in the sequence, creating a brooding atmosphere that reflected the air of menace created by Murakami's investigaton.

Another technique that was to become a hallmark of Kurosawa's style is his editing, especially his use of the screen wipe. The director had already employed this device – which was not uncommon at the time – in his first film *Sugata Sanshiro* (1942). In *Stray Dog* its use is particularly memorable in the scenes preceding the black market sequence. The story is set in motion when we learn what happened to Murakami on the bus. Kurosawa takes pleasure in showing how the police investigation functions. He would return to this passion in 1963 for *High and Low*. In order to make the sequence of events as dynamic as possible he wipe-cuts between each event, often combining the movement of the wipe with that of his characters walking on screen (i.e. from the left towards the right). His control of the device had already become quite sophisticated compared to his first film (where he still wiped vertically as well as horizontally). In *Stray Dog*, it creates an energetic effect which enhances the audience's faith in the effectiveness of the work of the police appartus. At the same time it whips up the film's tempo. In the 1950s the technique appeared increasingly in Kurosawa's work. It was used to great effect in *Seven Samurai* and *The Hidden Fortress* (the latter film inspired George Lucas' *Star War* saga so profoundly that he even borrowed the wipe-cut from Kurosawa at a time – the 1970s – when few other directors continued to use it). By the late 1950s Kurosawa had nearly abandoned dissolves for time ellipses altogether (there is just one in *Throne of Blood*). Besides the wipe-cut Kurosawa made great use of fading to and from black. However, its func-tion, in terms of film grammar, is very different to that of the screen wipe. While the latter accelerated the tempo of the narrative, fading to black slowed it down and marked the end of an act, following a plotpoint. When the next image emerges from a fade up from black the story would continue and show the consequences of the plotpoint. In *Stray Dog* the first such fade to black occurs after the premise of the story is established, just before the black market sequence.

Kurosawa's mastery of black and white was also impresssively displayed in the film. Though it might have been the only option available in late 1940s Japan, Kurosawa continued to work with the medium until 1970 and his first colour film, *Dodeskaden* (*Clickety-clack*). The choice had nothing to do with cinematic conservatism because, unlike many Hollywood direc-tors, he adapted and mastered widescreen format and stereo sound immediately after they had been introduced to the Japanese industry in the late 1950s. From *The Hidden Fortress*, all of his films (except *Dodeskaden*) embraced these technological advances. In *Stray Dog*, the use of black and white could be seen as both an economically enforced and an artistic decision. Another reason for using black and white for so long was the director's trademark employment of the telephoto lense. In the 1950s and 1960s the colour film process was not suited for the way Kurosawa employed deep focus. The depth perception is dramatically diminished which makes Kurosawa's images look very different from those of any other director. His contemporary films feature fewer telephoto shots than his historical dramas because they are mostly set in urban locations, which do not allow for the necessary distance between object and lense to achieve the given effect. However, in *Stray Dog*, there are a few short scenes that feature this technique. One occurs about 15 minutes into the narrative when Ogin, worn down by Murakami's insistance, gives him vital advice of how to get in touch with gun dealers. Ogin and Murakami are placed under a light in the centre of the frame. The end result is as surprising for the protagonist as it is for the audience at this early stage of the narrative: the upright policeman receives kindness and near-intimacy from the former *geisha* without compromising his honour.

Widescreen brought a new dynamism to the director's work, although his compositons were rarely less than masterful before. In *Stray Dog* we often see three-shots in which Murkami is positioned on the left of the frame, Sato in the centre and an interogee on the right. Murakami is usually in the background which implies that he is listening and learning; Sato is leading the interrogation and in full control of the situation and therefore framed in the centre of the shot. Physically he stands between his younger colleague and the interviewee who is positioned in the foreground. The use of triangle shots grew in significance and mastery in *Rashomon* where the composition is mixed with thematic significance even more succesfully.

Weather played an essential role in many of Kurosawa's films. As already discussed, he employed the baking heat of summer to evoke a specific atmosphere; one of claustraphobic intensity. More often than not, weather in Kurosawa's film also took on a symbolic meaning. The title credits of *Stray Dog* are superimposed on the shot of a panting dog. It evokes a hot day and introduces the mad dog metaphor of the title before the narrative even begins. In one sequence, before Sato and Murakami interrogate Yusa's girlfriend Namiki Harumi (Awaji Keiko), she appears in a revue number as dancer. This is followed by a series of shots in the dancers' changing room. The heat is conveyed by a camera that lingers for a moment on close-ups of the sweating and panting dancers. But rather than merely conveying a sense of the climate Kurosawa was building up to a finale that would not only discharge the tension of the narrative but also one where a break in the weather, resulting in a torrential downpour, symbolises a form of cleansing. Several times Sato and Murakami share a scene in which they are photographed against a forboding sky. The coming rainstorm is feared but hoped for in equal measure. When it does come it brings pain but will lead eventually to Yusa's arrest by Murakami. Wind, fog and rain (as well as heat and dust) were to become an integral part of Kurosawa's filmography. His masterful use of the elements as metaphysical omen and as naturalist ingredients have contributed and enhanced the dramatic effects and enriched the photographic texture of virtually all his films and especially masterpieces such as *Rashomon* (the rain under the gate in contrast to the sunshine in the forest), *Seven Samurai* (the final battle in the mud bath) and *Throne of Blood* (the supernatural, eerie fog).

Magnus Stanke

REFERENCES

Kurosawa, A. (1982) *Something Like an Autobiography*. New York: Alfred A. Knopf.

KENJI MIZOGUCHI, JAPAN, 1952

The world is an imperfect place, as Kenji Mizoguchi's battered heroine Oharu could tell us; yet from this truism Mizoguchi has made a very nearly perfect film. *Saikaku Ichidai Onna* (*The Life of Oharu*, 1952) is an extended, graceful tumble from fortune to penury by a girl who commits the dual crime of love and disobedience and spends the rest of her life paying for, usually at the hands of men whose misdemeanours are far, far worse. The beleaguered heroine clawed by fate is a story as old as sex itself, but Mizoguchi chooses to tell us the woes of a prostitute. A seventeenth-century tragedy, it is also a sophisticated pry into the foibles of humanity. Its themes are utterly contemporary.

Kinuyo Tanaka, as Oharu, leads us into the film – reluctantly. Her drooping shuffle moves akwardly through the darkness. She clutches a scarf, shielding herself from view. As a prostitute drags a reluctant, presumably drunk, man into a doorway, Oharu's coyness could be taken for prudery, but within one of his long, signature takes, Mizoguchi has disabused the audience of such a possibility. 'I am nothing but a spectacle of an ill-fated woman', she says to a fellow prostitute. Mizoguchi devoted his career to making spectacles, in the best sense, of ill-fated women, whether in the Edo period, when this is set (the film's flashback begins in 1686); the ensuing Meiji era, a time of great change that began in 1868; or in his own time, when there were still plenty of unfortunate females to serve as symbols and examples of the pitiful state of society, the weakness of men and the pathos of the human condition.

Oharu, at the beginning of the film, is fifty and – as she recounts wryly to her friend – has just been used as an illustration of moral decadence to a troupe of pilgrims. By the time of this scene, the film is almost over, having journeyed back through Oharu's life. As a result, the pilgrim's cruelty is more affecting because he will only be copying, on a small and ignorant scale, the illustration that Mizoguchi has made. The parallels are uncomfortably close, although the message is different: this, says the pilgrim to his protégés, is what a bad woman will do to you; this, says Mizoguchi, is what a venal, hierarchical and indifferent society will do to a good woman.

Oharu and her raddled compatriots, who have also failed to entrap a client, cluster round a fire under the temple, and the camera stays on their level to record their desperation for the free warmth. Oharu, though, is drawn away by the sound of ritual drums. She has spent her whole life looking for love, finding instead only stony indifference. In this scene, she reverses the process by sheer will: in one of the statues she conjures up the features of her first love, Katsunosuke (Toshiro Mifune), and with a girlish smile she pulls the scarf from her head and travels back to a time when she had nothing to hide.

Mizoguchi, who early in his career expressed dissatisfaction with screenwriter Yoshikata Yoda's tenth rewrite of *Osaka Elegy* (1936) because he wanted to be able to smell the characters' body odour, was a realist filmmaker – but a realist of a very eclectically Japanese kind (Yoda, incidentally, was made of stern stuff: sixteen years after this typically stringent demand he was the screenwriter on *The Life of Oharu*, as he had been on most of Mizoguchi's intervening films). Temporal and geographical space was there for him to use to his own purposes, and frequent use was made of the flashback and, more bizarrely in terms of a realist aesthetic, the supernatural.

Oharu's shield, her scarf, has been thrown off, and the film dissolves to the Imperial Palace and her young self – a being whose beauty, nobility and privileged status within the aristocratic arena are perfectly signified by the long length of flimsy gauze she wears about her head. Other contrasts are equally powerful: Oharu, who is once again shuffling diagonally across the screen, as she did at the film's start, now moves with a different gait and is followed by a maid. When she bumps into a nobleman, his conversation makes clear that she is much sought-after. The shot, as so often with Mizoguchi, is beautifully composed: as the nobleman asks about a daring poem that has been written to her, we become aware of his servant in the top left of the frame, listening with obvious horror: Katsunosuke.

Mifune's role was small but pivotal. His is the voice of sincerity, preaching liberty and practising what he preaches by luring the higher-born Oharu to an inn, where he declares his love for her. Oharu succumbs to his idealism and, in a prescient motion, swoons to the ground: her fall has begun. This choice has always been the crux of traditional Japanese *kabuki* theatre (which Mizoguchi greatly admired). Here, the heroine has chosen desire over duty, and her punishment is inevitable.

In the seventeenth-century novel by Ihara Saikaku, on which the film is based, it is love of sex that ruins the heroine. Mizoguchi replaced this theme with one much closer to his own perennial concerns ('Saikaku's book was implacable and ferocious', Yoda said, 'and we human-ised the theme.') His upbringing was impoverished and his older sister was obliged to become a *geisha*. She was lucky enough to find a devoted patron, and she shared her luck with young Kenji

– a generosity he took advantage of without compunction. Perhaps that is why the paradox of women's economic weakness and emotional strength fascinated him. Certainly, they were always central to his films, although his profound sympathy for their problems, coupled with his willingness to put their suffering on show, reflects that paradox as well as illustrating it.

When Oharu hears that her lover is dead (he is ritually executed in a shot that Japanese critic Tadao Sato has compared to a *kabuki* dance movement) she tries to kill herself, but that power, like the knife she takes up, is wrested from her grasp: the life of Oharu is not her own. This is borne out further when she is chosen as the vessel for Lord Matsudaira's future child. This entire episode clarifies Oharu's status as commodity. 'I thought you'd come to ask for money', comments the local notable, relieved that the Lord's messenger has come to buy and not to extort. Having rejected hundreds of silent, acquiescent girls he sees, through a sheaf of cloths, Oharu dancing. The cloths were draped to shield the girls from curious – presumably male – eyes. She will become a reproductive machine, and her father will be paid well for the privilege (money that he will, significantly, spend on bolts of material, intending to open a shop).

Oharu's parents realise their daughter's new owner will raise her status because of his standing and bring them benefit. But any prestige is illusory, as is seen when the Lord's wife appears. Her frailty has occasioned Oharu's purchase, but she is not too fragile to feel her humiliation and with it, a hatred of the young concubine. Oharu meets her new master at a puppet show. He inquires solicitously after her comfort, while his wife looks on; the dynamics between the two women are reflected in the puppet show on-stage, so closely that the wife eventually storms out. Mizoguchi regularly employed the use of illustration through parallels – between image and narrative. Ultimately, both women are at the mercy of this seemingly genial man, and are considered no better than the quality of face or womb. Ultimately, both – in the literal as well as the figurative sense – have become puppets.

Once she has borne the required child, Oharu is dismissed. Her furious father sells her as a courtesan to the red-light district of Shimabaru. There, she encounters the forger. Like Lord Matsudaira's wife, he highlights the flaws in the hierarchy. If she was high-born but powerless, he is a working man who uses money to buy his way through society. His tragedy is that because money is his passport, he has lost faith in everything. He knows money is fake, and that it reveals others' concerns for propriety. And so, even when he encounters someone truthful and dignified he fails to recognise their quality. Charmed by her refusal to crawl after the coins he scatters, he offers to marry Oharu. She questions his sincerity, but realises – even before the brothel's infuriated inhabitants break in to denounce him – that he has none. He is Katsunosuke's polar opposite, but will also be beheaded, for his lies, just as his predecessor was for his honesty. As he is carried off struggling, the camera pulls back to show Oharu, on the brothel's higher level, quietly watching. His offers were as worthless as his cash, and both left her unmoved.

Oharu's next protectors are the town notable, who mediated between her and Lord Matsudaira's messenger, and his wife, who has a secret so potent that she forces Oharu to sign a promise not to reveal it. She is almost bald. As the forger faked money, so she fakes beauty, and just as society's preoccupation with money aided him, the deeply ingrained artifice of seventeenth-century Japan helps her. No woman could walk naturally in their elaborate kimonos, or sit comfortably in the hand-carried transportations (when Oharu arrives at Matsudaira's, she must unfold herself from an airless box in a way that makes clear that she is passing from one prison to another). And the artful hairstyles mean that this wife can hide her disfigurement, even from her husband. These people are obsessed with appearances. When they find out about Oharu's Shimabaru past, their reactions are entirely consistent. The wife, riven with jealousy, cuts off Oharu's hair; the husband rapes her (delighted, more than anything, that he is getting something free that others paid for). For once, Oharu takes revenge – although, significantly, her reprisal is against the woman. She gets a cat to steal her hairpiece. This is a victory for sincerity (the wife really is uncovered, as is the falseness of the couple's intimacy), and vital in establishing Oharu as sinning human rather than saint. Her reward is the happiest interlude in the film – her marriage.

Yakichi (Jukichi Uno) is Katsunosuke's parallel; an honest businessman, who knows Oharu's past and loves her anyway. He also signifies the present (an economic- and development-minded Japan) while her first love symbolised a feudal past. Yet there is little difference here between past and present. Both men are killed by an intricate mesh of love and money. We have seen enough to suspect that Oharu's original love affair would not have been frowned on so much if he had been rich; Yakichi's fate is far more explicit. He is murdered for money, having gone to deliver goods and stopped to buy his wife a present on the way back. Their entire relationship, from proposal to widowhood, lasts three sequences.

Oharu's heart is so big – and the amount of kindness shown her so small – that she falls deeply in love with anyone who is genuinely good to her. Tanaka skilfully conveys the depth of her feelings. She was a seasoned actress and Mizoguchi's most frequent heroine. Perhaps her wide experience – she was a star in the 1920s, and still acting fifty years later – helped her to withstand the martinet director's methods. Mizoguchi gave collaborators great freedom to work out themselves what they wanted to do. (He said that with Tanaka and his other regular actress Isuzu Yamada there was no point in detailed explanations: 'All I can do for them is to adapt to their style of acting and find the right rhythm for their actions.') But he was fierce if he did not like the results, and although this is entirely compatible with the style of his films, where every detail is perfect but the languorous shots and lack of close-ups leave discernment to the viewer, the lack of restrictions during filmmaking must have been hard to handle. But then, he did not believe in restrictions – the stories of his excesses in order to achieve the shot he wanted, are legion. He was known to immerse an entire crew in a river or (as happened with *The Life of Oharu*) refuse to post-synchronise the sound, despite the fact that the set was next to train tracks. Yoda described how everything had to stop whenever the trains came within earshot – a nightmare with the length of Mizoguchi's takes. And the director was as hard on himself as on others – Tanaka has said: 'In *Oharu*, he had the best actors, even in the smallest roles ... to get them all together, he had to wait five years.' After the film's tremendous success – it became only the second Japanese film (after Kurosawa's *Rashomon* in 1951) to win an international award, garnering the Director's Prize at the 1953 Venice Film Festival jointly with John Ford's *The Quiet Man* (which must have pleased Mizoguchi, a Ford fan). It is worth noting that historically, this single-minded determination is hardly a common Japanese trait, prizing as it has, cooperation over individual assertion. Yet the results were far from a Western view of the world.

Kinuyo Tanaka, incidentally, made 13 films with Mizoguchi, and withstood everything, from his directing methods to a rumoured marriage proposal, but eventually she snapped. In a move entirely typical of his conflicted attitude to women, he tried to block Tanaka's efforts to direct. He failed, and she proved her independence by becoming Japan's first female director – and by never working with him again.

Oharu, now an impecunious widow, makes another attempt to leave the world and its sordid obsessions, by retreating to a Buddhist convent. But even here she is not safe from men and their various desires. Bunkichi, the servant at the notable's shop, sends her cloth and when his superior, Jihei, comes to retrieve it, the space between public and private is once again breached. Oharu removes her clothes, since she cannot pay for them. Jihei takes advantage of her and a nun catches them *in flagrante*. With bitter irony, she accuses Oharu of having deceived her; the despairing incline of Tanaka's head at these words says more than any verbal response could. In a parody of *michiyuki* – the lovers' journey in *kabuki* – Bunkichi flees with her, but proves himself unworthy when he is caught with money stolen from his master's shop. Dragged away, one of his captors turns to the powerless girl and shouts: 'Whore! Just you disappear!'

She becomes the beggar-musician she talked to earlier; invisible to the uninterested eye. Mizoguchi's composition sets this up carefully, with his heroine dwarfed at the foot of a temple, given coins by some and ignored by others. To underline her status below the social sightline, he brings in a well-attended palanquin, inside which sits her son, now a young boy. This is a visitation from the top end of the scale – only the upper class, as we have seen, are entitled to the luxurious palanquin – but not a visit. In a series of short shots (unusual for Mizoguchi, and effective in emphasising the distance between mother and child), Oharu peers round a rock as her pampered child is fed a cake (a strong contrast with his unknown mother, who has not eaten in three days), before the procession continues on its way. No-one speaks, but in a stunning piece of physical performance, Tanaka goes from longing through anger, hurt, resignation and finally despair. She turns away from the camera, as if in shame, and weeps. Mizoguchi, the essence of whose films Donald Richie described as 'the grand display of the will of a woman who endures her fate in tears', directed his cameraman, Kazuo Miyagawa, to merely watch.

The prostitutes rescue Oharu from her despair and loneliness. They have defences against the world's cruelty: laughter, resignation, and heavy makeup. Smearing their faces in white paint, they wonder how they are supposed to fool potential customers that they are fresh-faced girls of twenty. Oharu's journey through levels of artifice has reached this tawdry point: from being (or becoming) the beautiful drawing Matsudaira's messenger hung on the wall, she has been a dancer, a puppet, a musician and now an actress, paid – if she is lucky – to disguise herself and conjure up a wanton young girl.

It is a conceit of Mizoguchi and Yoda, to invite contradiction into the most surprising places. Fathers are mere purveyors of human goods and sons are no different from any of the men who despise Oharu and want her to disappear. This topsy-turviness is reflected in the *mise-en-scène*: tranquil beauty of form is placed in service to relentlessly questioning content, and the perfectly-aligned diagonals of a typical Mizoguchi composition point out of the frame to the misshapen world around us. Nothing here is conformist. Low-born men preach honour while their so-called betters commit rape, nuns are judgemental and a pilgrim – a leader of presumably virtuous young men – is equally devoid of any scrap of understanding. He pays Oharu to display her painted face as the wages of sin; yet in assuming her sinfulness he sins himself. She is not, as he tells his followers, a 'goblin cat' or a symbol of the transience of life. She is a powerful sign of endurance, and the boys would have learned much more if their leader had asked Oharu for her true story. The ultimate toppling of assumptions, after all, consists in making a prostitute a virtuous heroine and in fixing the camera's gaze on a woman who is, according to custom, supposed to be invisible.

When Oharu enters a new space, the camera starts overhead; it then cuts to the man and the woman huddled by the fire, and as he removes his coat – in preparation, we assume, for sex – the camera rises up to the boys on a raised level behind him. They are the audience and Oharu is the show. It is in understanding this that she wryly jingles the coins given to her, as she leaves. Like a dancer or a puppetmaster, she has embodied the paradox of showmanship, simultaneously displaying and hiding herself, and it is for this that she has been paid.

Japanese approaches to the concept of time and space differ to those of the West, considering them to be inseparable, and rarely is this clearer than here. Mizoguchi performs an elision – the temporal equivalent of the spatial shift described above. The young Lord was a small boy when we saw him last; when Oharu receives word that he has succeeded his father and wants to see her, he is a grown man. This shift, like the moment when the pilgrim's lodging goes from assignation-place to theatre, is skilfully blurred, implied through a moment of actual blurring: a rare point-of-view shot as the flashback comes full circle. Oharu sits in the temple, having reflected on her life – a reflection that was set off by an unusually subjective shot: her superimposition of Katsunosuke's face on the statue. As she looks again at the figures, her vision blurs and she falls to the ground, unconscious. This is conveyed with a matching subjective shot. The camera focuses on the statues, blurs out of focus twice, then switches back to the woman who, as so often before, is tumbling to the ground. These two shots – rare in Mizoguchi's oeuvre – bookend the flashback far more artfully than the actual matching shot of Oharu shuffling down the road at dawn. The message seems clear: we may no longer be inside Oharu's mind – since we are no longer reliving her memories through flashback – but the perspective is still hers. She is not in charge – Mizoguchi is – but he uses her own experience and recollections to release her. Freedom, such as it is, comes from within. So, if she wishes to elide ten years of misery, he is willing to collude.

The encounter with her son has several different elements of farce, none of which detracts from the scene's emotional power. In a shot/reverse-shot that harks back to Oharu's dismissal from the Imperial Court, she is told that by becoming a prostitute she has disgraced the Matsudaira clan; if the Court finds out there could be consequences, so she is to be shut away in retirement – but she is permitted to see her son first. The gall of the clan's attitude – no breath of culpability for kicking her out and denying her sight of her child for years, no whisper of understanding as to why an ageing woman with no support might become a prostitute – has a ludicrous element in that these noblemen have brought her out of what was effectively retirement (she was bedridden until the prospect of seeing her child gave her the strength to rise) in order to retire her. She manages to escape them and the final scene, one three-minute take, shows Oharu as a beggar woman, knocking on doors for a coin.

The first half of her story was dominated by her father, the second half by her son, as if to stress the infantilisation of women in this society. She is indignant, but she is free, and she has finally reached the ideal of *mono no aware* – the Japanese notion of acceptance. As a song in praise of Kannon, goddess of mercy, swells on the soundtrack, she chooses her path and bows to the temple she passes. We are left with the temple, as an alternative perhaps to fallible, transient humanity, as the scene fades.

The Life of Oharu is part of the genre known as *jidai geki* – historical films – as opposed to *gendai geki*, which are films about modern life. Mizoguchi made both, as the mood – or, since he was politically expedient, the country's mood – took him. He used the past, especially the Meiji era, to evaluate the present, and the distance – a historical equivalent of the long-shot – probably suited him, but he was perfectly adept at viewing his world in close-up. His last film, *Akasen Chitai* (*Street of Shame*, 1959), was a contemporary story about prostitutes. Still, his timing here was interesting. Japan was defeated in 1945 (a circumstance, Sato suggests, that has led to stronger Japanese women, because their men lost all confidence in their masculinity due to the vanquishing of their country). The post-war American occupation ended in 1952, the year *The Life of Oharu* opened. Under the Americans, anything 'feudal' had been banned, which effectively covered *jidai geki* (although Mizoguchi had managed to make *Utamaro o Meguru Gonin No* (*Five Women Around Utamaro*, 1946), mainly by claiming that Utamaro's profession of printmaker effectively made him a very early democrat). Oharu's fate is a vicious indictment of the feudal system, albeit one filmed with Mizoguchi's trademark concern for aesthetics – a preoccupation that was frequently attacked as overly traditional and reminiscent of the *kamishibai*, the old paper-slide theatre, or of *kabuki*. However, its attack on social hypocrisy, men's weakness and women's powerlessness, ageism and moral blindness were just as relevant in 1952. It was the year that Japanese women finally gained civic equality, which meant their rights – including that of choosing their own husband – were very much in the public consciousness. Katsunosuke, who dies crying 'I hope the day will come when all will be free to love regardless of status' (a speech, incidentally, that Mizoguchi contributed to Yoda's screenplay, and one that was deemed shocking in 1952), was very contemporary. The past claimed its place and the present could not be ignored. Mizoguchi used a modern medium – the cinema – but his shots have the grace and fluidity of *kabuki* movements. He frequently chose old stories, setting them in the distant past, yet always contriving to tell a relevant tale in a modern way. *The Life of Oharu* was a perfect example of this uneasy, but electrifying, mix.

This layering of modern preoccupations with ancient ones was partly Mizoguchi's announcement that humanity changes very little and an inescapable element of the medium. Richie pointed out that while Western cinema is the descendant of photography, with all the attendant emphasis on realism, Japanese cinema is the child of theatre; it is an art of presentation, rather than representation. But this means it is also a more complex blend of old and new, traditional and modern, which may explain the contradictions of a director whose attachment to realism did not prevent him making his greatest films about an era which, no matter how faithful the props and costumes, was impossible to mirror in the way that the twentieth century can be mirrored. Mizoguchi trained as a painter but chose cinema as his creative tool, using the medium to explore precisely those tensions between tradition and technology that the camera itself embodies. For this ongoing exploration, a period setting was useful. 'I still have a great attachment to the past', he once said wistfully, 'while having very little hope for the future.'

If I have discussed this tension between past and present at length, it is because it seems to me to incorporate so much of the fascination of Mizoguchi's work and especially of *The Life of Oharu*, which was a stylised look at a set of very contemporary problems. This prompts a return to the crimes that set in motion Oharu's story. In addition to the two visible crimes of love and disobedience, there is a further, invisible crime. Oharu cares nothing for money, as she repeatedly demonstrates. She falls in love with a poor man, rejects a seemingly rich one (the forger) and continually ignores the lessons of those, starting with her father, who tell her that she is no more than an object for sale ('You've been bought, like a fish on the chopping board', the Shimabaru brothelkeeper shouts at her). In rejecting money, she rejects modernity itself, reducing herself to the level of an animal (a 'goblin cat'), whose existence amounts to foraging for survival – and for whom survival justifies any action.

Yet, after the fall comes the rise, to serenity. Oharu's is a spiritual journey. All through the film she has been pulled towards Buddha, whether literally, as at the film's start, when the temple drums draw her in, or falling for the man-god Katsunosuke, or attempting to join a convent. Worldly forces, invariably in male form, have obstructed her, but she has overcome, and *mono no aware* is the end of a journey that began with the rejection of society's most powerful regulator: currency. Idealism has led to suffering and through it, to the ultimate ideal of spiritual peace. In keeping with a prevalent Japanese attitude to women, Oharu is no longer pitiable but a worthy object of admiration.

Mizoguchi may have been highly suspicious of modern mores, but *mono no aware* of this kind was not a virtue he ever attained ('We must wring life's neck', he said, 'suck all its blood, take everything possible from it'). But, just as his films reward the concentration they demand, his combative style won him faithful friends. He worked with the same people over and over, and years after his death (from leukaemia) in 1956, discussing him (for an interview in *Cahiers du Cinema*) could still reduce Yoda to tears. Kurosawa, whose success with *Rashomon* may have helped his highly competitive compatriot wring such wonders from *The Life of Oharu* (Yoda calls the latter film a 'bet' to match the younger director's international victory), probably summed up Mizoguchi's wonderful, infuriating contradictions most elegantly. His, says Kurosawa, was 'an exceptional nature, haunted by his own image. He was driven, unswerving in his search to create his ideal work ... In the death of Mizoguchi, cinema lost its truest creator.'

Nina Caplan

GOJIRA GODZILLA

INOSHIRO HONDA, JAPAN, 1954

Made almost a decade after Hiroshima and Nagasaki were devastated by the first nuclear attacks in history, Inoshiro Honda's *Gojira* (*Godzilla*, 1954) is a metaphor for the nuclear age, a popular monster movie hiding a cleverly crafted critique of modern science and its precarious relationship with post-war Japan. It is a narrative driven by the cause and effect of technology, namely advances in scientific and nuclear weaponry. The story primarily situates itself within the metropolis of Tokyo, a bustling modern city that is besieged by a monster of gargantuan proportions. The film is also set on Odo Island, an area off the coast of Japan, not far from a site used for nuclear testing, and where military mines still litter the water. In the film the detonation of a nuclear bomb forces the Jurassic-age reptile, named Godzilla by the inhabitants of Odo Island, from its hibernation. Enraged by the nuclear blast and driven from the area surrounding the island, Godzilla beats his destructive path towards Tokyo, destroying everything in his wake. With the annihilation of Tokyo imminent it seems that Godzilla cannot be stopped, but a secret scientific prototype, the 'Oxygen Destroyer' seems to be the city's only hope. However its effectiveness in killing the creature is questioned as its use would also destroy all other life-forms within Tokyo Bay.

Godzilla was released in Japan in November 1954, at a time when science-fiction films were commonly used as the modus operandi for enhancing or disseminating political, social and economic opinions. In a global post-war environment, opinions needed to be hidden so as not to upset the delicate status quo that had been achieved at the end of World War Two. Global opinion favoured the Japanese, who were seen as victims of American aggression, yet for the Japanese to be openly critical of the bombings was still unacceptable – thus alternative avenues of voicing the collective Japanese psyche was needed and film was considered to be the perfect medium. In order for *Godzilla* to appeal to as wide an audience as possible, Inoshuro Honda sought out the best special effects artist in Japan, who would share his vision for the film. Eiji Tsuburaya was employed as special effects co-ordinator, and particularly for his experimentation with special photographic techniques and their transformative use in the Japanese motion picture industry. Tsuburaya additionally had extensive experience in creating realistic-looking propaganda films for the Japanese during World War Two, using and filming miniature naval ships for 're-enactments' of naval battles; indeed these propaganda films looked so authentic that they were often mistaken for genuine footage. In creating and filming Godzilla, Tsuburaya broke with the special effects traditions of the time (primarily that of clay and puppet animation) and adopted a more hands-on approach. Believing that both puppetry and clay animation were restrictive, Tsuburaya had an actor don a rubber reptilian suit which allowed for more fluid and lifelike movements; the actor was able to ad-lib in real time or react according to whatever motions the script or director determined. Thus the creature was able to perform movements more naturalistically. The fact that Godzilla looked remarkably lifelike further added to its appeal to a 1950s audience, who were just beginning their foray into the science fiction genre. Tsuburaya's use of special effects in *Godzilla* afforded him the coveted Japanese Film Technique Award, additionally lending some degree of professional credibility to the giant-monster film.

The marriage of innovative special effects and exciting narrative content ensured *Godzilla's* instant popularity and ultimately contributed to the creation of numerous spin-off's and remakes – most notably the joint American-Japanese release of *Godzilla: King of the Monsters* (1956). This film (also popularly referred to simply as *Godzilla*), is the second of two films made by Honda featuring the gigantic reptile rampaging through Tokyo. *Godzilla: King of the Monsters* was released one year after the original *Godzilla's* debut in the United States. At the time *Godzilla* had only been seen by a small audience in Los Angeles and a smaller one in West Germany. The enthusiastic response by American audiences resulted in Joseph E. Levine of Transworld Pictures purchasing the American rights to the film. He enlisted director Terry Morse to oversee proceedings and added an American reporter called Steve Martin (played by Raymond Burr) as the lead role in order to help the domestic American audience identify more closely with the characters. It was thought that the post-war American audiences may find *Godzilla* too anti-American, due to the storyline focusing on nuclear science and references to the holocaust of Hiroshima and Nagasaki that had occurred just a few years before. Levine was only too aware that the conception of *Godzilla* was based in reality, and that in essence it was a politically driven film – it encapsulated the psyche of the Japanese, drawing unfavourable comparisons between the United States and Japan. While the film was an interesting marriage of science fiction that drew on contemporary themes and actual experiences of the time, it could also be potentially damaging if it was released in its original version to American audiences whose morale was at an all-time low.

There are a number of scenes in *Godzilla* that were taken from real-life events and these almost inadvertently shaped the plot of the film. The opening scenes feature a fishing trawler called the Eiko-Maru being destroyed by the ocean, or more precisely by a bubbling mass of water and fire that engulfs the entire ship and its crew before a proper distress signal is able to be deployed. The mysterious sinking of the ship is investigated as pressure increases to find a logical explanation by the loved ones of those who died. Uncertainty fills the air and the shipping company as well as the navy are unable to provide an adequate explanation. These simple scenes are symbolic for two reasons; one being related to science and the other to war. In April 1954, it was reported in the Japanese press that a group of Japanese fishermen had unknowingly sailed into an American 'hydrogen bomb' testing area close to Japanese waters. Their presence in the area subsequently made world-wide history, as they were considered to be the first civilians to be 'accidentally' exposed to radiation as a result of nuclear research. The research conducted at Bikini Atoll located in the Marshall Islands saw radiation from the blast reach the unfortunate fishermen who were 160 kilometres away, eventually killing all on board through radiation poisoning within two decades of their exposure. The bomb, labelled 'Bravo' by the American military, was 1,300 times more lethal than that dropped on Hiroshima. It is no coincidence then that Godzilla, a metaphor for nuclear destruction, is first spotted in the sea by Japanese fishermen whose ships were reportedly destroyed by 'a terrible sea of fire'.

The opening scene also alludes to the naval battles lost by the Japanese navy during the war and the reluctance in releasing information about the war effort to the Japanese people. At the time of World War Two the Japanese government placed blanket restrictions on reporting losses to the public, wishing to maintain the illusion of victory at all costs. Censorship of information was considered necessary in upholding the morale of the Japanese military and citizens, who at the time of the bombs on Hiroshima and Nagasaki had been unaware of the losses suffered by the Japanese military. The fact that the relatives in *Godzilla* are given the most scant information reflects this idea, as do the news conferences throughout the film in which the people are fed information only as the government see fit. The forced intervention and the eventual incapacitation of the military by Godzilla further mirrors the last days of the war. The allusion to censorship by the Japanese government against the people is also illustrated in another important scene, this time featuring the prominent palaeontologist Professor Yamane (played by Shimura Takashi) giving a report on the scientific origins of Godzilla. Professor Yamane believed that Godzilla's reawakening could be linked to nuclear testing in the area near Odo Island, presenting evidence of radioactive sand found in a Jurassic-age trilobolite shell as proof of Godzilla's link to the Jurassic age. Having presented his hypothesis that Godzilla's awakening was the direct result of radioactive testing to a panel consisting of important government and military officials, Professor Yamane is urged not to make his finding public – the uncontrollable spread of mass hysteria given as justification for the request. This creates a division among panel members as some believe that the public must be told of this information in order to better prepare them should Godzilla attack Tokyo. The scene in effect shows how Honda is effectively questioning whether the military and government deliberately withheld vital information about American plans to bomb Japan.

Honda's immediate experience of the war, in particular his witnessing of the bombing of Tokyo and his visit to Hiroshima in the period following the nuclear attack, shapes his presentation of the destruction caused by Godzilla. His first-hand experience is projected onto the screen through carefully designed images. Close-up and middle-range shots of Godzilla feature heavily and he is most often viewed trampling buildings and causing destruction to amenities that are considered vital for the ongoing success of contemporary society; the rampage causes the destruction of electrical towers and cables, road ways, bridges, shopping malls, markets and cars – signs of modernity and an allegory of the nuclear bomb wiping out all signs of life in two of the most populous cities in Japan. This act of destruction is juxtaposed against images of the military shooting at the huge reptile; their massive show of force incapable of stopping the advance of Godzilla. Images of naval battleships circling the waters outside of Tokyo in an act of defiance against the creature is noteworthy, as is the persistence of tanks and various military ranks firing upon Godzilla as he wades through downtown Tokyo. Honda shows that for all its military might Japan ultimately fails in its duty to protect the citizens of Tokyo from destruction. The re-creation of an environment similar to that experienced in Japan during World War Two was to directly mirror Honda's own fears and thoughts on war; he had been a sergeant in the Imperial Japanese Army and had suffered at the hands of the Chinese as a prisoner of war in China – thus he knew from first-hand experience the tragedy of war.

Furthermore, Honda's visual representation of the Japanese response to the war and the destruction of their cities is heightened by shooting his film in black and white, the starkness of which increases audience tension, as does his use of a classical soundtrack to signal the ominous approach of Godzilla. Honda wished to evoke excitement, fear and apprehension among his audience and therefore employed strong classical renditions throughout the film – especially prominent when Godzilla attacks. The film's composer, Akira Ifukube had written marches for the Imperial Army and Navy and was ideally suited for creating the film's soundtrack. The appearance of Godzilla coincides with the thunderous footsteps and a piercing roar akin to the high-velocity wind that often accompanied the dropping of the atom bomb. In *Godzilla*, the sound of the creature's footsteps are magnified and its enormous weight shakes the ground before it – the same effect as a powerful bomb.

In a scene that takes place on Odo Island, the audience first hears the sound of the footsteps then witnesses a gigantic foot crushing houses underfoot. Honda is preconditioning the audience to relate the sound of the footsteps with imminent destruction, hence minimising the need to show close-ups of the creature destroying Tokyo later in the film. The use of sound also reinforces the idea that Godzilla is himself like a bomb. Further comparisons can be gleaned, which link the monster with the atom bomb. The scene that features the first destructive on-land appearance of Godzilla coincides with a massive storm (one feature of nuclear fallout is radioactive rain that destroys all living organisms that it touches) which lashes across Odo Island and its inhabitants, increasing in strength as Godzilla tramples over houses and vegetation.

Considering that *Godzilla* is obviously anti-war, it was not surprising that the American remake of the film sought to allay growing concerns over nuclear testing and in particular American involvement in nuclear research and development. To overcome the perceived hurdle of American unease *Godzilla: King of the Monsters* became a narrative of the reporter Martin's experience and is told from his point of view. The twenty minutes of additional scenes starring Martin were shot in America and featured the reporter speaking to various characters within the film at pivotal points. Extras were called in to provide the head-shots that were used to help place Martin within the scenes without actually having to re-shoot the entire film, and without the principal Japanese actors having to participate. The Americanisation of *Godzilla* occurred with remarkable ease; the addition of bilingual security officer Tomo Iwanaga (played by Frank Iwanaga) negated the need for subtitles or a complete re-dubbing of certain scenes – the role simply was to provide Martin with a summary of what the original characters are saying, although at times it is obvious that the English rendition of 'facts' are inconsistent with what is actually occurring within the film. A particularly amusing scene involves Iwanaga translating the speech that Professor Yamane is giving to officials. It is clear in *Godzilla: King of the Monsters* that those around him are saying 'Godzilla' yet Iwangawa tells Martin that he is speaking about Odo Island and the need to interview the inhabitants. Thus a noticeable discrepancy sometimes exists between the dialogue of a Japanese character and the English translation. Arguably, the subtitling or dubbing of foreign films allows for some compensation in the degree of literal translation and thus makes no real difference to the overall presentation of the film other than to make it unintentionally comical at times.

All differences aside, the film, complete with added footage, and a somewhat loose interpretation of the original *Godzilla* was re-released in North America as *Godzilla: King of the Monsters* in 1956. Thematically the American release of the film is different to that of the original *Godzilla*. Numerous scenes were moved or completely deleted, noticeably those that referred to Nagasaki and the destruction caused by the nuclear bomb dropped at the orders of the US President. An example of this occurs when a Japanese couple are discussing the fact that they survived Nagasaki only to be faced with the terror of Godzilla crushing Tokyo. This scene was duly omitted from *Godzilla: King of the Monsters*, as it left no doubt as to where the metaphor of Godzilla originated from, likening his destruction to that of one of the bombs dropped on Hiroshima or Nagasaki. Censorship was no less prevalent in the US at the time. Moreover, the Cold War years made censorship an even more pertinent issue, especially when dealing with the regulation of film and television content. General remarks concerning the future of the world and the destructive path that scientific discovery can sometimes take is also omitted. The end result is that *Godzilla: King of the Monsters* is seemingly more optimistic while *Godzilla,* though firmly entrenched within the science-fiction genre, errs on the side of caution in examining the continuation of nuclear research and other military-related inventions.

Godzilla's greatest threat, the 'Oxygen Destroyer' is an invention that holds philosophical, moral and destructive values. In both films the Oxygen Destroyer features as a possible solution to the threat that Godzilla poses over Tokyo and ultimately over greater Japan. However the emphasis placed by each film is different, the result being that *Godzilla: King of the Monsters* is more empathetic towards military or scientific use of weaponry despite being confronted with a massive loss of life. *Godzilla,* on the other hand demonstrates more empathy towards both the scientist and the intended victims, philosophising over the role of humanity, or lack thereof, within scientific discovery. The Oxygen Destroyer was invented by Dr Daisuke Serizawa (Hirata Akihiko) in complete secrecy in his home laboratory, located in the cellar of his house, which reflects the seriousness with which the scientist regards the secrecy of his project. Dr Serizawa formulates a scientifically engineered powder that, when added to copious amounts of electricity, takes all of the oxygen out of water to render it uninhabitable for marine life. The secrecy of the project hinges on the fact that it was in the developmental stages of experimentation and thus no known antidote exists that would reverse the effects of the powder. Furthermore, Dr Serizawa has only tested it within the confines of a fish tank, and as such he cannot be sure of the effectiveness of the powder on a large target, or within a large body of water. The Oxygen Destroyer could certainly kill Godzilla, but in the process it would also kill every single life-form within Tokyo Bay.

In *Godzilla*, as it becomes clear that the Oxygen Destroyer would be the only means to defeat the monster, Dr Serizawa laments his discovery of the terrible invention and claims that its destruction would be similar to an atomic bomb and that it could possibly be used to destroy all humanity. This scene is arguably an attempted representation of the conflicting views of those who created the world's first nuclear bomb. Honda attempted to rationalise the actions and decisions made by the American military by providing a face to those who remained faceless. Using the film as a means by which to represent nuclear war Honda effectively questions whether the inventors of the atomic bomb knew of the devastating future that its conception held for thousands of Japanese people. Using Dr Serizawa, Honda also questions whether the inventors were in a similar position to those in the film. Were they distressed by the intended use of their experiment? Or did they realise, like Dr Serizawa, that their experiment held disastrous consequences for the human race and that they were powerless to stop it? Honda is able to question where the limits of scientific ethics and morals lie, through Dr Serizawa who himself is a respected scientist in the community. Dr Serizawa confronts complex ethical and moral considerations that result in his decision to become a victim of his own experiment.

As Honda drew from contemporary accounts of history, real similarities existed between Dr Serizawa's research and American nuclear research of the time. American atomic research labelled 'The Manhattan Project', which resulted in the construction of two nuclear bombs, was not publicised outside of military circles. Like Dr Serizawa's research, its intended effect to stop World War Two depended upon its grading as classified information. Furthermore like the fated Oxygen Destroyer, atomic bombs had not been tested on human targets before their detonation and thus its effects were surprising, horrific and scientifically documented for future improvements. Without actually testing on live targets first, there was really no way of knowing its true effect. Comparatively, Dr Serizawa had only tested the Oxygen Destroyer within a limited control group, nor did he actually know if it would work outside of his laboratory. The only definite way to determine its effectiveness was to test it on Godzilla directly. The film *Godzilla* was somewhat more subdued in its analysis of the dilemma that Dr Serizawa encountered with the release of his research. In comparison, *Godzilla* places more importance on the character of Dr Serizawa and his discovery of the Oxygen Destroyer, indeed, science and technology feature heavily in the Japanese version of the film. The role of science within a science-fiction film is, after all, a mandatory feature. However, Honda manages to approach it both as spectacle and as a vehicle for philosophical and moral conceptualisation. This is in direct opposition to the American 're-creation' of the film, which places more emphasis on the superficialities of a generic monster movie.

This scene featuring Dr Serizawa, often considered to be of crucial importance in relation to setting up the film as an allegory of nuclear war, was replaced by a less confronting and somewhat idealistic scene in *Godzilla: King of the Monsters*. Instead of Dr Serizawa directly questioning the validity of the Oxygen Destroyer, *Godzilla: King of the Monsters* employed the use of the character of Naval Officer Hideto Ogata (Akira Takarada) to provide a persuasive point of view that favoured the use of the device. Ogata ominously summarises that Dr Serizawa must weigh his fear of what hypothetically could occur (destruction of marine and plant life) with the reality of what *is* occurring (the destruction of Tokyo). In essence, it could be argued that the character of Ogata was used as an instrument to pacify the fears of the doctor as well as the audience. He effectively argues for the use of a weapon of mass destruction as a way of combating the destruction of the monster. The destruction of marine life in Tokyo Bay is not considered pertinent in this scenario. Changing of this scene results in a distinct change of narrative for *Godzilla: King of the Monsters*. The character of Ogata could be seen as a reflection of American attitudes towards nuclear warfare, and by extension towards the events of Hiroshima and Nagasaki. It is Ogata who views the use of the Oxygen Destroyer as inevitable, as something that must be used in order to secure the destruction of Godzilla and the safety of the Japanese people. Consequently the American remake of the film uses Godzilla as a catalyst for warfare while *Godzilla* places emphasis on the invention and the prototype of the Oxygen Destroyer as an impetus for war. As a result, *Godzilla: King of the Monsters* is much less critical and political in its intent and less obvious in its referencing of nuclear war.

Honda Inoshiro's *Godzilla* made an important contribution to both Japanese cinema and the science-fiction genre. It spawned many sequels and provided the influence for numerous of giant-monster films. However Honda's most important contribution is the moral and ethical stance reflected within the film, providing a reflection of a collective psyche damaged by the dawn of the nuclear age. The use of a Jurassic creature as a metaphor for the future, or as an allegory of nuclear warfare, would seem comical, seemingly at home in the realm of science-fiction – were it not based on a disturbing reality.

Samara Lea Allsop

SARANGBANG SONNIM-KWA OMONI
THE GUEST AND MY MOTHER

SHIN SANG-OK, KOREA, 1961

Sarangbang Sonnim-Kwa Omoni (*The Guest and My Mother*, 1961) is one of the most critically acclaimed and best loved films of the 'Golden Age' of Korean cinema, a period which is most easily placed as the decade of the 1960s, but which was initiated with the commercial success of the fourth filmed version of *Chun-hyang Jeon* (*The Story of Chunhyang*, 1955), the most beloved tale in Korean history. Beginning in the Yi Dynasty, the Confucian tale of a married woman who struggles to remain 'faithful' to her higher-class husband while being harassed (even tortured) by the new county governor has been passed down through generations and has been the subject of at least 17 Korean feature films, including the most recent, directed by Im Kwon-taek in 2000. Unfortunately, none of the first four versions have survived. Broadly speaking, the 'Golden Age' ended in the peak year of Korean film production, 1969 (229 features). Only one film survives from the first year of film production after the Korean War (1954, eight films), but from then on, the number of extant titles increased in proportion to the rapid increase in production, from 15 films made in 1955, to 111 in 1959. Approximately 14 per cent of the films made from 1955 to 1960, which Lee Young-il calls the 'revival period', have survived. The vast majority of these films were melodramas, and the second big popular success of the era, *Jayu Buin* (*A Free Woman*, Han Hyeong-mo, 1956), is amongst the survivors. *A Free Woman* is uninteresting stylistically, except for the use of crosscutting with a musical bridge to connect women caught up in corrupt webs of 'Westernisation'. Indeed, the film seems extremely reactionary today in its representation of women as willing victims of Western consumerism, while men are the arbiters of trustworthiness and traditional (hence good) morality. Nevertheless, *A Free Woman* is quite sexually explicit (relative to other Asian films of the period), showing kisses, backs being stroked while dancing, and a couple dropping down onto a bed.

The evidence points to the 1960s as being the first significant decade of sound film production in Korea, and the industry's 'classical' period. Korea's Motion Picture Law, which took effect in 20 January 1962 mandated that film companies must produce at least 15 films per year and that all films should be commercial by design. Production shifted from an artisanal practice to a studio system, and the number of production companies was immediately reduced from 71 to 16. A number of new genres began to appear – 'criminal mind dramas', a range of 'war action' films, 'spy' and 'youth oriented' films – while melodramas tended to be situated more in working- (rather than middle-)class milieus and comedies were aimed at a wider audience (and perhaps a coarser sensibility.) But it took a while for the law to fully enact a shift away from realism in art film practice, where directors were encouraged through the 'government's reward system for quality films' to rely more on literary sources, in the second half of the decade. It is possible to deduce, though, that a few leading directors continued to flourish as 'auteurs' throughout the decade. In the Korean writings on the first fifty years of Korean cinema that have been translated into English, there is little discussion of 'film style', and yet the work of three directors – Shin Sang-ok, Yu Hyun-mok and Kim Soo-yong – is very strong, stylistically, and for each oeuvre different visual parameters stand out. Kim Ki-young also falls into this category, although he is more usefully regarded as the most creative Korean director of the 1970s (an era that generally lacked cinematic creativity). He was also the first film director to be honoured with a major retrospective by the Pusan International Film Festival (PIFF) in its second edition, in 1997. In turn, from 1999 to 2002, each of these directors was honoured with a major retrospective by the Pusan International Film festival, so that now there is a much better understanding of the artistry of the Korean 'Golden Age'. One could argue that these three directors are indebted to Japanese cinema in stylistic terms, and they would, no doubt, have viewed Japanese films in their youth (under the Japanese occupation), but the period is no more influenced by Japanese aesthetics than by European or American. Thematically, all three filmmakers had a tendency to be pessimistic and to be adept at Korean cinema's specialty in representing 'the national instinct to recover from adverse conditions, and its cinematic speciality of expressing real human emotion deeply and strongly'. The tendency of all to follow the latter tenet could be regarded as a proclivity for melodrama, but it might be more useful to regard it as a distinctly Korean contemporaneous approach (rather than Japanese) of being more emotionally direct.

A self-proclaimed 'realist', Yu Hyun-Mok, is considered to be the key director of the period by many Koreans – he has won 11 Grand Bell Awards, Korea's highest (annual) honour. His work is more obviously intellectual than others, and his recognised masterpiece, *Obaltan* (*Aimless Bullet*, 1961) undoubtedly shocked audiences of the time with its harsh condemnation of Korea's post-war recovery creating marginalised victims – people who seemed to have no place in the new society. Kim Soo-yong's films of the 1960s, especially *Gaet Ma-Ul* (*The Sea*

Village, 1965), the first really successful Korean 'literary' film and *Sanbul* (*Fire in the Mountain*, 1967) make wonderful use of natural landscapes (and in the former, seascapes). On the evidence of these two films, it would seem that Kim might have been the first Korean director to work extensively in close relation to the traditions of Asian landscape painting. They were shot in widescreen black-and-white, and make full use of this format with long-shot and extreme-long-shot views, often accented by a panning camera. Perhaps, even more emotionally direct, Shin Sang-ok was clearly the most prominent Korean filmmaker of 'revival' and 'classicism' in the 1950s and 1960s. He was extremely adept at employing the close-up, not just on faces, but also on legs, feet and hands. In a word, Shin's style was 'sensuous' and he was able to combine camera movement and editing to engage the audience in the physical lives of his characters. His command of colour was supreme and his placing of brightly coloured, costumed characters in a natural landscape was uncannily similar to King Hu's, and in his *sageuk* films (historical dramas) such as *Kum* (*The Dream*, his second version of this story, 1967) and *Naesi* (*Eunuch*, 1968) his work with colour in traditional Korean dress, clearly pre-dates that of Im Kwon-Taek's. Remarkably, in *Yijoyoin Chanaeska* (*Women of the Chosun Dynasty*, 1969), Shin switched from colour to black-and-white footage at the bleakest moment of the first story (of three). A young woman is betrothed to a sick boy (he is much younger than her) who dies, but she still has to marry him! In *Kum*, he fashioned a relentlessly gripping work of oneirism, which manages to be serenely beautiful at times and jarringly physical at others: an errant monk imagines that he elopes with the governor's wife and experiences all of the sensations of the physical world in a 'dream', enabling him to reject this world and become truly Buddhist.

Shin Sang-ok was born in 1926 in Chung-jin, which is now part of North Korea. He attended art school in Tokyo for three years during World War Two, and began his film career working as an art director on *Jayu Manse* (*Hurrah! For Freedom*, aka *Victory of Freedom*) in 1945. In interviews with Kwon Yong-min, conducted in 2000, Shin claimed that the director of this film, Choi In-kyu was the person most responsible for improving film 'production values in Korea'. He learned film technique from Choi, and in 1952, with financial help from his father; he set up his own film production company and made his debut as a film director with *Ak Ya* (*Evil Night*). Shin then made a documentary, entitled *Korea* in 1954, and the first of two adaptations of the literary classic, *Kum*, in 1955. Unfortunately, all three films are now lost. Shin's next film, *Jolmun Gudul* (*Youth*, 1955) began an amazing actor/director partnership and association with his wife, Choi Eun-hee that would last off and on for over thirty years. Their third film together, *Jiokhwa* (*A Flower in Hell*, 1958) was an enormous critical success, if not a commercial one, and was the (re)discovery of the 2001 PIFF. Indeed it probably plays better now than it did when it was released, with its tale of matter-of-fact, sleazy corruption caused by the American military presence. Choi Eun-hee plays Sonya, the *yanggongju* ('flower') in the brothel-town 'hell' outside the American army base. Brilliantly, the camera never goes inside the compound, which is seen just as walls and barbed wire, and the American soldiers (clearly played by actual GIs) are just 'there', not as villains, but players in the game – they have the money. All the Korean characters, men and women, are hustlers except for Sonya's scarred boyfriend's younger brother, Dong-shik, who continually tries to persuade his elder sibling to return to the countryside with him. Everything looks bleak and broken, except the appearance of the young women in their glossy dresses, hairstyles and make-up. *A Flower in Hell* is full of passion and its melodrama is tempered by gritty realism. It is surely the finest extant Korean film from the 1950s. In 'A Flower in Hell: Fascinating Inferno of Desire', Hong Sung-nam writes: '*Yanggongju*, women who specialise in selling their bodies to "yankees" for a living, have often been represented as tragic and crucified figures in Korean films and novels. Their sad histories of bitterness and corruption resonate with Korea's national tragedy and dependency upon the powerful United States.'

In 1959, Shin was extremely prolific, directing six films including *Onu Yodaesaeng-ui Gobaek* (*A College Woman's Confession*), starring his wife, which was a big success at the box office. He made three more films in 1960, the year he established the Shin Film Company, and, at the beginning of 1961, he directed his version of the popular story, *Sung Choon-Hyang*, with Choi Eun-hee in the title role. It was the first Korean cinemascope film to be shot in colour, and, not surprisingly, it rapidly became the most popular film in Korean history; attracting an audience of 420,000 people in its 74-day run. He then made *The Guest and My Mother*, which is widely regarded as being his masterpiece. It is a much more subdued work than any of the four of his films discussed above, being virtually opposite in tone to *A Flower in Hell*. Shot on black-and-white stock and in widescreen, it resembles Yasujiro Ozu's films in its studied, gentle compositions of interior living spaces and the surrounding, natural landscape. And yet, characteristically for Shin, the story was told subjectively, through the consciousness of a young girl who wants her mother (a widow) to marry again.

The widow (Choi Eun-hee) and her daughter (Jeon Young-sun) live in the same house as the mother-in-law, in a small country town. One day a painter, Han (Kim Jin-kyu), a friend of the deceased husband, arrives from Seoul. He is boarded as a *sonnim* (guest) in a detached living room, and gradually he and the daughter become friends. One day on their return from a walk, one of the daughter's schoolmates asks her if Han is her father, following which she asks the guest if he would like *to be* her father. In her attempt to bring the two adults together, the little girl brings flowers home to her mother from kindergarten and pretends they are from the lodger. Receiving the flowers gives the mother the strength to once more play the piano, something she has been unable to do since her husband's death. The two gradually fall in love. The paternal grandmother is clearly against any future union, and is even suspicious that he has caused the housemaid's pregnancy. In reality the maid has been having an affair with a local pedlar, who sells birds and eggs door-to-door, and this parallel story is resolved by the gregarious, noisy, lower-class couple getting married. No such 'happy ending' follows the main couple though. Han sends the widow a love letter, and her mother-in-law eventually relents and suggests that perhaps she *should* re-marry, even relinquishing her rights to the granddaughter. But, the *sonnim* leaves after his sister visits, telling him that their mother is dying, but not before the widow has returned his note, asking him to 'please not stoke the fire'. Their relationship, developing slowly from sympathy and affection to mutual love, is shown very delicately and purely visually by suggestive looks and gestures – there is almost no dialogue between them. Not dissimilar to John Ford's *The Searchers* (1958), a woman's love is represented by her caressing a man's clothes. In fact, here she actually wears Han's trilby hat, looking at herself in the mirror. The most overt display of emotion is during a scene after her rejection of him, where he returns home, drunk. She brings him a bowl of water, and they hug.

Throughout *The Guest and My Mother*, Shin (with his cinematographer, Choi Soo-yung) carefully frames every composition, often using the full width of the widescreen image, even on interiors – for example with Choi Eun-hee on the right of the frame and her mirrored reflection on the left. Shin claimed that his art education greatly helped his understanding of framing and that *The Guest and My Mother* is a perfect example of this. The film also exemplifies the art and craft of editing which the director believes he really came to appreciate through reconstructing the documentary, *Korea*. Perhaps the greatest example of the combination of shot composition, camera movement and editing to subtly convey the feeling of love, is the film's last: on the dirt road to the train station, as Han leaves to walk off-frame right, the camera, in a slight low-angle, pans left to observe the mother and daughter at the left edge of the frame, with a single tree on the right. A cut closer, retaining the low-angle view, reveals them in medium-close-up, looking off-screen right and another cut shows Han boarding the train on the right, while turning to look back to the left. At this point there is a great distance between the couple, but through glance, framing and editing they are cinematically united for the last time. The film ends on another beautifully composed shot of mother and daughter, and the camera tilts down to the ground.

In keeping with the high emotionality of all of Shin's work, the end of *The Guest and My Mother* is very much a 'tear jerker', but perhaps the most interesting aspect of the film is how the story is told from the daughter's perspective. The narration is not restricted entirely to the consciousness of her character – time is spent with the guest and her mother, out of her sight. But the film begins with her voice-over and a series of detailed shots of her drawings: of her mother, her deceased father, her grandma and herself. This delightful introduction puts the film's audience very much on her side, so that, when she makes it clear that she does not care too much for her paternal grandmother, it is very easy to empathise with her against the old-fashioned, Confucian ethics of the family. We see her often with Han, and in one gorgeous shot the camera pans across the small town in the background to find the two of them seated on the side of a hill, while he paints. This shot includes in its view, a single tree which, when viewed again at the end of the film, reminds us of the closeness of the daughter to the painter. The youthful playfulness of the opening is repeated when the daughter lies about the flowers, and when she plays another trick on the adults by hiding in the attic, while everyone worries about her absence. The film certainly needs these moments of comedy (achieved through the daughter's subjectivity) to lighten its otherwise serious mood.

The Guest and My Mother was adapted from the famous Korean novella written by Chu Yusop. This story supports the Confucian ideals of acquiescence and submission for a woman, even a widow, who traditionally could not remarry. In the film, the widow always wears the traditional Korean costume and hairstyle of a married woman, and does revert to this traditional role at the end. However, as Kwak Hyun-ja notes in an essay on Choi Eun-hee entitled 'A Woman Between Tradition and Modernity', her character here does display attributes of a 'modern woman', in playing the piano, 'carrying an umbrella to block the sunlight', and sending 'her daughter to kindergarten'. Indeed it is interesting to note that she is depicted as being a Christian: she goes to church (another 'modern' characteristic), presses two of the flowers given her into her bible and, in a very brief shot, mother and daughter pray to a wall-mounted icon of Christ on the cross. As traditional as Christian rituals might seem to Western observers, they could indicate modernity to Koreans. Further, Kwak writes that 'Contrary to the original story where the *sonnim* departs without any promise of coming back, in the film he promises to return soon, of course addressing his comment not to the heroine but to her daughter, who treats him as her real father'.

The Guest and My Mother was a commercial success, but perhaps even more importantly it was a *critical* success. It was awarded the bulk of the first Grand Bell Film Awards, hosted by the Korean Ministry of Culture and Information in 1962, although another film directed by Shin, *Yeonsangun* (1962), won the top prize. Additionally *The Guest and My Mother* won the Grand Prix of the 9th Asian Film Festival, which was held for the first time in Seoul, and the film was shown at the Venice Film Festival in 1963, in the 'information' section. Shin went on to dominate the Grand Bell and Asian Film Festival awards during the remainder of the decade. His pioneering prize-winning was surprising in part because of his struggles with inadequate film technology. It is hard to believe the director's claim that *Daewongun* (*King's Father*) made in 1968 was his first complete synchronised sound film, although his complaint that there 'was only one Arriflex [sync-sound] camera in Korea' in the 1950s seems likely. Of *The Guest and My Mother*, Shin claims that he suffered from having to rely on Chopin's piano music, when the score composed for the film proved to be inadequate. It was certainly fortuitous that the central character of the widow was a pianist, and although her ability to play European art music ('classical music') may be questioned, in retrospect we may see this coincidence as a forerunner to the unfortunate dominance of Western-style piano music scores in contemporary East Asian films.

The long delay in Shin Sang-ok's work being recognised at a major retrospective – which did not take place until 2001 – may well be due of the scandalous 'kidnappings' he and his wife endured at the hands of the unfriendly neighbour, North Korea in 1978, after which they were virtually given *carte blanche* access to make films between 1983 and 1986. But for his command of the medium of cinema and the strength of his individual, sensuous (and sometimes sensual) style, his films from the late 1950s and 1960s constitute, arguably, the finest body of work in Korean film history. In any event, with the films of the three Korean film directors who produced their best work in the 1960s, we find the development of the art film during an industrial transition from artisanal realism to commercial studio entertainment. Further, the special conditions of the Korean film experience at this time – the tenacious desire to create artistically while locally-made films began to enjoy unprecedented popularity (597 film theatres in Korea in 1968 with almost 183 million moviegoers) – helped to foster a unique 'classical' period of Korean film style, of which *The Guest and My Mother* is exemplary.

Peter Harry Ris

NOTE

Part of this essay appeared as 'Neglected "Classical" Periods: Hong Kong and Korean Cinemas of the 1960s', in *Asian Cinema*, 12, 1 (Spring/Summer 2001), 49–66.

REFERENCES

Cho, Y., M. Huh, Y. Lee and D. Pak (eds) (2002) *Kim Soo-Yong: An Aesthete Bridging Tradition and Modernism*. Pusan: Seventh Pusan International Film Festival.

Kwak Hyun-ja (2001) 'A Woman Between Tradition and Modernity' in S. Han and J. Yang (eds) *Shin Sang-ok: Prince of Korean Cinema, Leading the Desire of the Masses*. Pusan, Korea: Sixth Pusan International Film Festival.

OBALTAN AIMLESS BULLET

YU HYUN-MOK, KOREA, 1961

In July 1998, the *Chosun Ilbo* newspaper conducted a survey of 31 Korean film professors, critics and film magazine editors to determine the best 50 Korean films of all time. A similar survey was held in April 2003 by local magazine *Film 2.0*, in which 74 film scholars and critics weighed in with their choices. In both lists, *Obaltan* (*Aimless Bullet*, 1961) came out on top. Directed by Yu Hyun-mok, this brooding, anguished portrayal of a nation struggling to survive in the aftermath of the Korean War was not only an accomplished work by a talented young director, but also an electrifying political statement whose content resulted in its being banned.

Today, *Obaltan* (literally meaning 'misfired bullet') is open to many different readings and reactions. The film's on-location shooting, dubbed soundtrack, black-and-white imagery and emphasis on the lower classes, strongly recalls Italian Neorealist filmmaking, which Yu cited as an influence. Creative use of sound and unusual framing provide a modernist touch and add to the work's aesthetic force. Its setting in post-war Seoul made use of numerous locations that provide a document of the struggle to rebuild a city after a war. Finally, the unflinchingly bleak narrative and the tragedy suffered by its characters still represent one of Korean cinema's most strident entreaties of the lost and dispossessed in the aftermath of war.

Obaltan's position at the top of these lists illustrates its importance in Korean film history. Internationally, it is not quite so well known. It was the first Korean film to be preserved at the Museum of Modern Art in New York, in 1996, and it screened in retrospectives of Yu's work at Aix-en-Provence in France in 1999 and at the Pusan International Film Festival later the same year. Unfortunately, the only surviving copy of the film is a worn print featuring handwritten subtitles in English, which screened at the 7th San Francisco International Film Festival in 1963. Although a great deal of effort has been put into finding a cleaner print, the poor conditions for film preservation which existed before the Korean Film Archive was established in 1974 means it is unlikely any further prints are likely to be found.

It is perhaps no accident that some of the most highly regarded works of Korean cinema – including *Obaltan* and Kim Ki-young's *Hanyo* (*The Housemaid*, 1960) – were shot in the years 1960–61; a brief window between two highly autocratic governments. The period began on 19 April 1960, when a group of 100,000 students and young people gathered in front of the presidential palace to protest the election-rigging and authoritarian practices of then President Rhee Syngman. Palace guards fired into the crowd, killing 115 people and wounding close to a thousand, setting off further protests that would end in Rhee's resignation and exile, ten days later, to Hawaii.

Korea's first-ever democratic government then took power, headed by Prime Minister Chang Myon, under which a new constitution was established and a free press emerged. In the film industry, a civilian Film Ethics Committee was established on 5 August to oversee censorship under the slogan, 'Freedom of Speech and Expression'. The successful overthrow of the previous government also had a strong psychological effect, instilling a new sense of confidence and initiative in Korea's younger generation.

However this flowering of democracy was accompanied by a sharp economic downturn, as well as chaotic debate in the political realm and a perceptible shift to the left. The instability that resulted served as a pretext for a military coup on 16 May 1961 led by Colonel Park Chung Hee. Park installed himself as president and would rule throughout the 1960s and 1970s. In the realm of cinema, the civilian Film Ethics Committee was abolished and a restrictive Motion Picture Law was established that would place severe restrictions on filmmaking. Although Korea's 'Golden Age' of cinema would continue until the end of the decade, heavy censorship and intrusive government measures would increasingly limit the activities of Korea's filmmakers.

Obaltan began shooting in 1960, during the last months of the Rhee Syngman government. The film faced a difficult shoot due to a lack of financing, with many actors or crew members working for minimal or no wages. When the April Revolution took place, Yu found himself with considerably more artistic freedom than before, and he began to work in more explicit social themes. The film took over a year to shoot, premiering in theatres shortly before the 16 May coup.

Yu Hyun-mok was born in 1925 in Hwanghae Province (now part of North Korea). He was the fifth of nine children, six of whom died at a young age, due to disease or war. After failing a physical for his conscription into the Japanese army, Yu took a job at the revenue office in his hometown and wrote plays in his free time. Following Korea's liberation from Japan in 1945, he moved permanently to Seoul and entered Dongguk University as a Korean language major. After hearing a lecture on screenplay writing, he took an interest in cinema, spending time on the set of *Jayu Manse* (*Hurrah! For Freedom*, aka *Victory of Freedom*, Choe In-gyu,

1946) as an observer and later assisting on Shin Sang-ok's debut feature *Ak Ya* (*Evil Night*, 1952). He made his debut, *Gyocharo* (*The Crossroad*) in 1956, and would direct six more films, including the critically praised *Ilheobeolin Cheongchun* (*Lost Youth*, 1957), before starting work on *Obaltan* in 1960.

Yu has been referred to by many Korean film critics – most notably film historian Lee Young-il (1931–2001) – as 'the father of Korean realism' and a companion book published for the retrospective of Yu's work at the 1999 Pusan International Film Festival is titled *Yu Hyun-mok: The Pathfinder of Korean Realism*. However, a look inside the book raises doubts about this claim. Film professor Yi Hyoin notes that much past criticism has been based on a vague application of the term 'realism', and that even *Obaltan* – considered the most 'realist' of Yu's works – adopts narrative and stylistic elements that fit more easily into modernist or expressionist conventions.

As in many of Yu's films, *Obaltan* eschews a central hero in favour of a group of charaters. Much of the film's focus is on a large family, consisting of accountant Chul-ho, his war veteran brother Young-ho, younger sister Myung-sook, mother, wife and two children. Chul-ho is a dutiful worker and husband who refuses lunch in order to work an extra hour, hands over all of his pay-check to his wife each month and who suffers from intense toothache throughout the film, refusing to spend the money to get it treated. Despite his full-time job as an accountant, his meagre salary does not provide him with enough money to buy proper shoes for his children. His son has dropped out of school, trying to earn money by delivering newspapers. Actor Kim Jin-gyu, who also starred in *The Housemaid* and *Sarangbang Sonnim-Kwa Omoni* (*The Guest and My Mother*, Shin Sang-ok, 1961), portrayed Chul-ho as a weary, passive man who works with fanatical devotion only because he sees no other option for himself.

Young-ho is younger, good-looking, and has escaped the Korean War with only scars on his stomach (unlike his friend Gyeong-shik who walks with crutches). Although he has tried exhaustively to find work, he remains unemployed and spends much of his time hanging out with his wartime buddies. Ruled by his passionate nature, he takes a radically different approach to life than his brother, refusing to accept his lower position and willing to compromise his morals if necessary, in order to get ahead. Young-ho was played by Choi Mu-ryong, a popular star who made some of the biggest headlines of the decade for his extramarital affair with actress Kim Ji-mi, for which he was briefly jailed. Choi (the father of contemporary star Choi Min-soo, who has appeared in *Gyeolhon Iyagi* (*Marriage Story*, Kim Ui-seok, 1992) and *Libera Me* (Yang Yun-ho, 2001)) acted in over five hundred films throughout his career.

08

OBALTAN

THE CINEMA OF JAPAN AND KOREA   85

The brothers represent two different responses to the challenge of surviving in post-war society. Seoul in the late 1950s was slowly trying to recover from the destruction of both its economy *and* infrastructure. During the Korean War, the city had changed hands four times as advancing armies shelled its buildings into little more than rubble. Poverty reigned in the subsequent years, and for most citizens neither hard work nor risky enterprise could deliver them of their fate.

One of the few ways of making money at that time was to have connections with the US military presence, or with the Korean government, which disbursed the large amount of US aid flowing into the country. In this sense the sister Myung-sook, who ultimately prostitutes herself for US soldiers stationed in Seoul, represents a third path. Although by the end of the film she has achieved a small degree of material success (it is ultimately she who finances Chul-ho's visit to the dentist), she suffers in other ways.

Yu depicts his characters with a great deal of empathy for the bleak situation they face. 'At that time the streets were filled with the unemployed. They felt despair, without any hope or belief in the future', he said in an interview at the 1999 Pusan festival. The limited choices faced by the characters in the film are most eloquently expressed by a recurring sense of confinement. Physically, psychologically and in the possibilities available to them, the film's characters are confined and hampered from achieving their goals.

Obaltan opens with a credit sequence featuring Rodin's 'The Thinker' set in front of an iron grillwork, with a translucent window and series of flashing lights behind. The rather heavy-handed symbolism implies a human being trapped in a confined space, where thinking and intellectual struggles are constrained by outside forces. We then cut to a scene involving Young-ho's friend and war comrade Gyeong-shik, a former captain who now walks with crutches. After leaving a bar in which they drank more than they can pay for and break a window, Gyeong-shik and his war buddies admit to missing the war. The poverty and uncertainty of the present are such that the danger they once faced seems more inviting, and they sing a war song to comfort themselves ('Chun-woo-ga' or 'Comrades' Song', which also appears to different effect in two films from 2001: *Sorum*, directed by Jong-chan Yun and *Goyangileul Butaghae* (*Take Care of My Cat*, directed by Jae-eun Jeong)). 'We were brave men then', notes Gyeong-shik, implying in some sense that they have become lesser, emasculated figures since the war. Indeed, in the following scene Gyeong-shik is sought out by his former sweetheart Myung-sook, and he refuses to restart their relationship due to his disability and lack of a job. 'For a long time I wished for one of us to die, so that at least we might have a beautiful memory', says Gyeong-shik. 'But now I am useless, like a spent shell left over from the war.'

We then see our first view of Chul-ho and Young-ho, outside of their home. The family lives together in a dilapidated house at the top of a steep hill (interior scenes were shot on a set designed by Yu). The inside of the home is a scene of utter hopelessness; Chul-ho's mother, who became insane as a result of shell-shock during the war, lies helplessly in the centre of the house, only to cry out from time to time, 'Let's get out of here!' Her calls are repeated throughout all of the scenes shot within the home, and although the family ignores her completely, she gives a verbal embodiment of all the characters' desire to escape. Just as the crazed woman cannot leave behind her imagined aggressors, so the rest of the film's heroes are confined in with their predicament.

At home, Chul-ho's impetuous daughter Hye-ok steals rice while her tired mother, pregnant with a new child, looks on, too weary to protest. Hye-ok asks her uncle Young-ho to buy her new shoes, and when he tells her he will do so the next day, she calls him a liar. Meanwhile the son, Min-ho, has stopped going to school in order to sell newspapers and earn a bit of money. Young-ho scolds him for this, but is not able to stop him.

We next move to a teahouse, and the first glimpse of Miri, the one character who has found economic success by becoming an actress. After speaking briefly with Myung-sook, who asks her to find a job, she runs into Young-ho outside the teahouse. She is in love with him, yet in an echo of the situation between Gyeong-shik and Myung-sook, he refuses to commit to her unless he can find a job. Later, Miri will take matters into her own hands and line up an acting job for him. Young-ho shows an interest in the role, however when he arrives on set and learns that the role is of a wounded veteran who, like himself, has large scars across his stomach, he flies into a rage at the thought of having his wounds exploited – shouting, 'These wounds are not for sale!' he gives up the role, although later regrets his actions.

At the same time, Young-ho runs into a beautiful nurse named Sul-hee, who treated his war wounds. He walks her home, accepting an invitation to go to her room, at the top of a high building. On the way, they pass a young poet from the same building who gazes up at them with angry, jealous eyes. On a later day Young-ho comes to visit her late at night, at which point the poet knocks on her door, sees them together, and runs away. Sul-hee explains that the poet loves her, and comes to visit every night. He says he wants to compose only ten poems ('because there is only enough inspiration in the world for ten poems' – another form of confinement), and will then kill himself. Young-ho and Sul-hee spend the night together, but the following day when he comes again to visit, he learns that the poet threw her off the ledge and then followed her.

Meanwhile, Myung-sook does not return home one night, and the following morning Chul-ho receives a call at the office from the police. Myung-sook has been arrested working as a prostitute near the American military base in Seoul. Shocked, Chul-ho collects her. Yu illustrates the shame both feel in a striking sequence, of the two walking home, neither saying a word to the other but the physical space between them (Myung-sook in the foreground, Chul-ho in the background) empasising the emotional and psychological rupture caused by her actions. On another day, when he is taking the bus, Chul-ho overhears two passengers talking about a prostitute in a soldier's jeep next to the bus: 'A pretty good business – she doesn't need to invest anything ... Later she'll probably get married. Just looking at her, you can't tell if she's a college student or an office girl.' Their talk adds to his despair and he moves to another section of the bus.

Gyeong-shik, after being scolded by Young-ho for abandoning Myung-sook, is on his way home when he bumps into her near the US military base. She runs off, pursued by a US soldier, and Gyeong-shik realises the decision he has forced upon her by refusing to marry her. He disappears the next day, presumably unable to face his guilt, suggesting to his landlord that he may be only a short way from his own death.

Obaltan's climactic sequence comes when Young-ho, despairing of having no opportunities in life, takes the risky decision to rob a bank. After determining the time of day at which the bank is most vulnerable, and promising Miri and his family that he is on the brink of good fortune, he enlists the aid of a fellow veteran to drive a jeep (without telling him what they are to do). As Young-ho disappears inside the bank, a period of calm descends over the screen. Without any clue to what is happening with the robbery, the viewer watches as Miri arrives, having followed the jeep, and a church procession passes. Finally the sound of gunshots are heard, causing Young-ho's friend to drive off in fright, and a long chase sequence follows with Young-ho, carrying a sack full of money, pursued by the police and Miri. The chase leads him through various neighbourhoods of Seoul which portray some of the difficulties faced by its citizens: he passes a labour strike, the cavernous underground of a covered road, a woman who has hanged herself with a still-living baby strapped to her back (a scene that was cut by censors for the domestic release), and then an empty factory. Finally Miri, worried that he will be shot, catches up with him and he hurls down the money and his gun, surrendering to the police. Young-ho's dreams of wealth and success are over, and his exploits make headlines on the newspapers sold by his young nephew.

Chul-ho receives another phone call from the police, this time to learn that his brother is in jail. At the same time his wife goes into labour and dies giving birth to their child. Unable to decide whether to go to the hospital or the jail, Chul-ho wanders the streets of Seoul in excruciating pain from his decayed teeth, finally going to the dentist to get them removed. Listless from lost blood and overcome with despair at his situation, he gets into a taxi and tells the driver just to go, without giving him a destination – echoing the words of his insane mother.

Adrien Gombeaud of *Positif* magazine noted that due to the Korean War, 'post-war cinema' arrived in Korea nearly a decade after continental Europe. As such, films like *Obaltan* may have struck international audiences as being somewhat regressive and overly dependent on the traditions started by Italian Neorealist filmmakers in the late 1940s and early 1950s. Nonetheless a closer look implies that many of the similarities tend to reside on the surface, and that *Obaltan* represents an individualistic and thoroughly modern work for its time.

One striking aspect of the film is its unconventional narrative. In contrast to the dominant mode of storytelling in most Hollywood and international cinema, there is no one strong central hero in *Obaltan*. More importantly, the psychological motives and goals of the characters do not function as the film's major causal agents. Given the limited choices available to them, characters tend to react to, rather than bring change to their surroundings – for example, despite the diametrically opposite approaches to life taken by the brothers Chul-ho and Young-ho, both end in ruin, implying that the choices we make in life will ultimately come to nothing in the face of more powerful social conditions.

Obaltan also employs stylistic innovation in its use of sound and camera angles. Using post-dubbing for the film's soundtrack, Yu inserts sound effects that are disconnected from the action on screen; trains and airplanes are heard but not seen, at times overpowering the scene at hand, babies' cries can be heard off screen, presented without any explanation. In the same way, tilted camera angles shot from below or above a character can emphasise a certain mood – Shots of Chul-ho in the midst of his despair are often shot from below, emphasising his solitary nature and making him stand out against the landscape. Such stylistic effects give the film a more modern feel and highlight the bleak situation faced by its protagonists.

Obaltan was greeted with a warm response by critics and intellectuals upon its release in early 1961. A review in *Yeonae Seupocheu Sinmun* (Entertainment Sports Newspaper) from 14 April 1961 read:

> Yu Hyun-mok is a director who each year directs one of the three most important films of the year. However of the seven films he has directed before *Obaltan*, only his most famous work *Lost Youth* succeeds in showing Korea's social situation as it really is, and that being an adaptation of a Japanese film, it is not a work that one can take great pride in ... At long last, a film depicting 'our problems' has arrived before us.

Although the review went on to criticise the film's narrative as being chaotic and unorthodox, it praised the director's intention and called for more socially conscious filmmaking. Alas, a month after the review was written, a military government took power and would eventually ban all screenings of *Obaltan*, claiming it to be a socially disruptive work. It would take two years before the film was granted permission to be re-released in theatres, but much more time would pass before such criticism of society would ever be produced by Korean cinema again.

Darcy Paquet

KOROSHI NO RAKUIN BRANDED TO KILL

SEIJUN SUZUKI, JAPAN, 1967

Deafening gunshots over the Nikkatsu Corporation logo seguing into a melancholy jazz score herald the beginning of Seijun Suzuki's seminal hitman opus, *Koroshi No Rakuin* (*Branded to Kill*, 1967), a film that would irrevocably redefine and subvert the *yakuza* (gangster) film, whilst simultaneously prompting Suzuki's exile from the filmmaking fraternity for a decade.

Following on from the perceived esoteric excesses of 1966's explosively lurid *Tokyo Nagaremono* (*Tokyo Drifter*), Suzuki was warned by Nikkatsu president Hori Kyasuku to tone down his work and create something more palatable to a mainstream, commercial movie audience. Whilst *Branded to Kill* was arguably a a more accomplished film than *Tokyo Drifter*, Suzuki's cinematic style nevertheless caused further annoyance to the studio and its president.

Japanese genre cinema has always had its detractors, who complain about everything from elliptical and obtuse storytelling, to ponderous pacing, pretentious imagery, impenetrable plot contrivances and illogical shifts in tone. However, Suzuki seems to have been singled out by Hori for these supposed crimes against linear narrative conventions, resulting in his firing. But were Suzuki's cinematic transgressions so serious as to merit this unceremonious termination, or has history vindicated him with critical opinion that has come to regard *Branded to Kill* as something of a landmark in Japanese film? There was undoubtedly something absurd in a filmmaker as unpretentious, self-deprecating and modest as Suzuki being identified as the scapegoat for Nikkatsu's financial travails.

Never as highly regarded or internationally recognised as contemporaries such as Kon Ichikawa or Shohei Imamura, Suzuki's reputation seems to have suffered due to his choice of subject matter. Incredibly prolific in the years prior to *Branded to Kill* (at one point he was making six films a year), Suzuki happily tackled everything from *yakuza* movies and comedies to *kayo eiga* (pop song movies), *mukido sieshun eiga* (alienated teen movies) and *mukokuseki* (westerns). It is all too easy to dismiss filmmakers by placing undue emphasis on the genres they work within, rather than the way they transcend genre with their treatment of the material itself. In this respect, Suzuki is a true auteur in that his films are unmistakably 'his', infused with his own personal sensibilities and methods of storytelling, creating films that often have a theatrical, slightly artificial feel to them.

Shot in glorious 'Nikkatsuscope' (in stark contrast to the blindingly bright colours that pop off the screen in *Tokyo Drifter*), the crisp look and slick production design are fundamental to the appeal of *Branded to Kill*. The films that Suzuki made during his time at Nikkatsu were known as 'program pictures', equivalent in many ways to American 'B-movies'. The fact that *Branded to Kill* was shot on black-and-white film was purely a budgetary consideration, and not one that Suzuki had any control over. Similarly, Suzuki claims that the vast majority of shots were improvised during shooting due to logistical, time and budgetary limitations. It would seem, therefore, that much of Suzuki's greatly admired and genuinely unique style was a result of foruitous accidents.

The beauty of Suzuki's films in general, and *Branded to Kill* in particular, is the sheer playfulness he indulges in; toying with conventions for no other reason than to entertain his audience, despite the fact that for years fans and academics alike attempted to attribute significance to moments that were nothing more than playful experiments and undermining preconceptions of what genre cinema is 'supposed' to be; to create memorable, and above all, entertaining moments of pure cinema. Suzuki always vehemently maintained that his films contain no meaning, and his sole aim was to entertain. However, the films of Seijun Suzuki are not intended to be seen as either satire or parody, although they have often been perceived in such a way; his more off-key and extreme moments are merely introduced in order to keep things interesting for both Suzuki *and* his audience.

As the opening titles appear, three miniscule flashing white dots slowly traverse the screen, before a thundering noise lets us know that a plane carrying our protagonist is landing at Haneda Airport. The hamster-cheeked Shishido Jo plays Hanada Goro, otherwise known as Number 3, the third best hitman in the business. It is clear from the beginning that Hanada fits the classic archetype of the laconic loner. Decked out in an immaculate black suit, not a hair out of place, and his ever-present wraparound black shades concealing his eyes – Hanada is a man of few words. This iconic image culled from American *film noir* and pulp fiction was released in the same year as French filmmaker Jean-Pierre Melville's celebrated and stylised take on the noir thriller, *Le Samuraï*. And through the years, the film has continued its influence, from from Chow Yun-Fat in John Woo's *Ying Huang Boon Sik* (*A Better Tomorrow*, 1986) to numerous gun-toting anti-heroes in the films of Quentin Tarantino. Such a strong signifier successfully acts as a visual shorthand, alerting the audience to the kind of man Hanada is. Such economical use of visual grammar is a hallmark of Suzuki's work, where his 'show, don't tell' direction efficiently imparts information to the audience. However, Suzuki himself would contend that there was *no* visual grammar employed in his work.

With his use of Western iconography, Suzuki's works are littered with references to and influences of Western popular culture. In 1959 the John Cassavetes television series, *Staccato*, about the eponymous hipster detective, aired on American television in a similarly snappy black-and-white style, replete with jazz on the soundtrack and a restlessly roving camera. Directors like Nicholas Ray, with films such as *In a Lonely Place* (1950) and *Johnny Guitar* (1954) and Robert Aldrich with *Kiss Me Deadly* (1955) were also manipulating traditional portrayals of masculinity in film, and exploring how those characters can be ripped apart and put back together again within genre cinema. The amalgamation of Japanese and American conventions and influences, and the way they are chewed up and spat out in Suzuki's film, is part of its enduring allure. It is heartening to know that Suzuki's contribution to cinema has, likewise, been digested and reformed in numerous iterations by subsequent generations of filmmakers, from its play with generic conventions through to its idiosyncratic visual style.

As the journey at the opening of *Branded to Kill* ends, Suzuki unleashes the first of his trademark flashes of inventive surrealism. Asked by a bartender what they would like to order, Hanada's wife Mami (Ogawa Mariko) requests a double scotch for herself and some boiled rice for her husband. After being assigned his latest job by the Syndicate, Hanada stands in the kitchen of the bar, leaning over a steaming pot of rice, noticeably aroused by the smell. Prior to this, a former hitman for the Syndicate, Kasuga, imparts a neat piece of foreshadowing: 'Don't drink, don't touch women. Drink and women kill a killer.' But being turned on by the odour of freshly steamed rice does not appear to qualify as a debilitating impediment for a top assassin.

From this point on, *Branded to Kill* hurtles deliriously through a series of warped action set-pieces and softcore sex scenes, before the *femme fatale* of the story Misako (Annu Mari) approaches Hanada with a job that sends the movie spinning off in another direction, as a botched hit results in the need for Hanada to be rubbed out by the mysterious Number One (Nambara Koji). Number One is an almost-supernaturally gifted assassin who has never been seen by anyone who has lived to tell of his existence, but will Hanada run scared, or does he have more than a fair shot at stealing the Number One crown for himself?

The plot itself is secondary to the way Suzuki weaves his threads together, and when scrutinised too closely, it is clear that much of the story makes little sense. For example, at one point Hanada is hired by the Organisation to carry out four assassinations, yet he only executes three of them; the fourth is never referred to again, even in an expository scene later on, when the background to the series of killings is half-heartedly explained. The screenplay refuses to clearly resolve various plot strands, and Suzuki's unorthodox editing cuts in and out of scenes with little regard for the flow of the story. It is worth noting that the screenplay for *Branded to Kill* was credited to 'Guru Hachiro', an alias used by a group of filmmakers (including Suzuki) who wrote numerous action movies together.

The true delights of *Branded to Kill* lie in the incidental details and Suzuki's delirious direction. The story is often difficult to follow and takes some time to make any sense, buried as it is amongst all the 'strangeness', as well as Suzuki's unerring sense of *iki*, the Japanese aesthetic of sophistication, eroticism and style that permeates much of the film.

Suzuki's jagged and disjointed editing is exhilarating and frustrating in equal measure. In their minimalist home where pop art design assaults the eye in the most unashamedly blatant way, Hanada and his wife engage in all manner of aggressive sex. In the bathroom Suzuki employs a strange technique where it looks like water from a showerhead is falling only directly in front of the camera, regardless of where in the room the couple are having sex. In another scene, the sounds of sexual activity are prominent on the soundtrack, but the camera remains focused on an empty bed, whilst the action continues to take place noisily off-screen. Hanada and his wife seem to have sex everywhere in their home, *apart* from in the bed. Interestingly, whenever Hanada is alone with a pot of steaming rice, he is gentle and tender with it, but when he is seen making love with the insatiable Mami (or forcing himself upon the aloof and icy Misako), he is rough and assertive.

Ironically, whenever Hanada interrupts their interminable sex sessions in pursuit of a bowl of rice, Mami berates him. 'You're kinky!' she screeches at him, as she carries on wandering around naked or hurling herself at men. At another point, Mami says to Hanada: 'We're beasts.' Later on in the film, however, when Hanada has realised that Mami has betrayed him to the Syndicate, and just before he kills her, his parting words are: 'We're beasts? I'm not!' Hanada's newly revealed humanity is only just starting to rise to the surface, but at this point he is some way from complete regeneration.

Suzuki's penchant for superfluous over-the-top moments of intense surrealism and bizarre imagery is something of a double-edged sword in the case of *Branded to Kill*. Whilst such moments fill the screen with indelible images that remain in the memory longer than more conventionally-filmed scenes, they also result in jarring jolts that remove the audience from the story. On balance, however, it is precisely these moments that have made *Branded to Kill* a film that is 'rediscovered' on a regular basis. How many films have featured a doctor casually plucking an eye out of a patient's socket, before giving it a thorough rinse in the sink; the hitman in flames running screaming towards his killer; the hair of a dead woman floating in a toilet; or the assassin deliberately urinating down his leg into a perfectly-shined shoe so he does not have to take his eyes off his target? Admittedly, in the years since Suzuki's film was first released, filmmakers such as Takashi Miike have employed similar shock tactics. However, few directors made it appear so effortless as Suzuki managed to do at the peak of his abilities, perhaps playing these little celluloid pranks to satisfy his creative frustrations.

It would be unfair though to dismiss all of Suzuki's visual trickery as meaningless. Birds and butterflies, often lifeless, appear throughout the film to signify Hanada's obsessive desire for Misako. Misako has a dead bird impaled on a nail hanging from the rearview mirror of her car on the night she first finds Hanada in the rain. Her home is littered with dried leaves, birds and butterflies. And, of course, it is a butterfly that causes the sequence of events that leads to Hanada's reversal of fortune and the loss of his defining status as Number 3.

There is a pleasing streak of black humour that runs through the film and Suzuki uses certain scenes to point out how ludicrous, stupid and messy death can be. Death is treated as something vaguely comical, without the usual gravitas found in *film noir*, such as scenes where an assassin falls down dead, but uses his final seconds of life to take off his jacket and cover his face before collapsing with inappropriate dignity. Or the scene where a man in an executive armchair is shot and the force of the bullet causes the leather chair to rotate on its wheels, as the victim's blank gaze whirls around the room.

Hanada's hits are remarkably complex set-pieces, showcasing his competence as a top assassin, whilst simultaneously displaying Suzuki's directorial finesse. One scene in particular, where Hanada uses an elaborate mechanical billboard that appears to be advertising a brand of cigarette lighters is ingeneously constructed. The billboard shows a huge cardboard flip-top lighter that flips open at timed intervals. Hanada's intended victim is standing on a train plat-form waiting for a train. When the top of the cardboard lighter flicks open, the tip of Hanada's rifle pokes out of the tiny hole between the two halves of the lighter, and we see through the rifle sight that Hanada manages to shoot his target between the carriages of a moving train.

Working in black-and-white accentuated the use of lighting the film and also afforded Suzuki the opportunity to indulge in quirky and unusual optical effects. At one point, as Hanada wanders around in a state of confusion, primitive-looking birds, raindrops and but-terflies are superimposed over the image, whilst the soundtrack features a cacophony of bird sounds and the patter of rainfall. Suzuki also employs numerous shots full of backlit characters, or scenes shrouded in darkness with only the face of the character in the centre of the frame lit. Misako is frequently shown with her face lit from beneath, giving her a menacing appearance. And in the tradition of *film noir*, shafts of light cut through the menacing darkness of rooms, hallways and stairwells. This look may not enhance the storytelling, but it conjures up an evocative moodiness. As the film progresses, there are a handful of scenes lit with natural lighting, but it is the studio-bound shots that catch the eye.

Just as important to the composition of Suzuki's films is the sound design. There is little or no ambient or background noise and in a film with such sparse dialogue, the isolated noises accentuated on the soundtrack are all the more noticeable, from the rainstorm towards the beginning of the film, to the sound of Mami scratching a pane of glass with her fingernails in a jealous frenzy, the noises are penetrating and forceful. And there are sections of the film that are absolutely silent, or filled solely with the moody lament that opens the film.

As his theatrical stylings attest, Suzuki's work is influenced in no small measure by *kabuki* theatre and its traditions. Literally translated as 'the art of singing and dancing', Suzuki used kabuki as his model when structuring his movies. As Katherine Monk has stated, 'There are three points: the love scene, the murder scene and the battle scene. Translated into film, those are the three basic ingredients of entertainment.' Strangely, Suzuki has no theatrical experience himself, but nevertheless employs the *kabuki* model successfully in his work.

Suzuki also delights in exploring the middle ground between conflicting styles, from prodding at the tensions inherent in the concepts of *mu* (nothingness) and *keren* (artifice), or from the pulp roots of the subject matter, wavering somewhere in-between the squalid cynicism of Mickey Spillane and the romantic idealism of Raymond Chandler. Hanada possesses all the moral fibre of the heroic Chandler protagonist, tainted by the perversity of Spillane's twisted anti-heroes.

Although *Branded to Kill* is firmly located in a fictitious underworld of killers and criminals, both Hanada and Number One remain loyal to classic *samurai* codes of honour, in particular that of *bushido* (the code of the warrior) and *giri* (the code of obligation, loyalty and duty). Both men are considered to be consummate professionals, carrying out their orders efficiently and without question, wielding their pistols like swords, in a world where cunning is just as important, if not more so, than the bullets at their disposal. And Hanada exists in a world where the perfectly planned assassination and the pleasures of the flesh are everything, but outside of action and eroticism, nothing else matters.

Hanada slowly transforms over the span of the film from cold and calculating professional, to an emotional wreck; as we know clearly from the opening minutes of the film, 'Drink and women kill a killer.' Having finally fallen for the chilly charms of Misako, Hanada is devastated to come home to discover a reel of film playing on the wall of his apartment, showing Misako's capture and torture at the hands of the Syndicate. Throughout her vicious ordeal, Misako refuses to cry, her inscrutable Mona Lisa smile twisted in pain without yielding. The killer stroke comes when she mimes the words 'I love you' to Hanada in the midst of her suffering. In turmoil, Hanada hits the bottle. His familiar black suit gradually gives way to the anonymous dress code of the average guy; a nobody.

The eventual conflict between the two warriors is fraught with tension, and continues unalleviated for the final third of the film until the dénouement. Suzuki's action sequences transform into the slow and sustained psychological torture of Hanada by Number One, who shows off his deep sense of honour, expertise and cruelty, as he tries to unbalance his rival, never allowing him to sleep and watching him round the clock from a concealed position in an adjacent tower block. As Number One tells Hanada: 'A killer must not be human. He must be tough and cold.' However, it is a combination of Hanada's vulnerability and humanity, which does not surface until he is made to suffer, that makes the audience care for him, but it is his steely resolve and ability to do what he does best with precision and concentration that allows him to have a chance of succeeding. It takes a return to his professional armour, sharp as ever in his smart black threads, and a repudiation of his hard boozing ways to return to form. The classic redemption of the tragic hero is just around the corner.

The final confrontation between Hanada and Number One takes place at a deserted boxing ring, a visually arresting metaphor for their chosen arena of battle, and with all the suitable visual cues that suit the *faux noir* feel that the film aimed for, with its eye-catching use of sharp horizontals and verticals, and harsh use of polar opposite blacks and whites, light and dark. And the battle itself has a (quite literally) killer twist.

For many years the ending of *Branded to Kill* was deemed ambiguous. As the film draws to a close with Hanada's muffled cry of 'I am a Champion!' he finally succumbs to his injuries and topples over the edge of the boxing ring. The question over whether Hanada had died was finally answered in Suzuki's belated sequel to *Branded to Kill*, *Pistol Opera* (2001). Although it had eventually been revealed that Hanada had survived to sniff rice another day, Shishido was unfortunately not hired to reprise the role; the part going instead to Hira Mikijiro.

Over the years both Seijun Suzuki and *Branded to Kill* have garnered notable admirers as diverse as Wong Kar-Wai and Jim Jarmusch. Jarmusch in particular has paid homage to *Branded to Kill* with his film *Ghost Dog: The Way of the Samurai* (1999), which references many elements of Suzuki's film, from the assassination carried out via the plumbing beneath a washbasin to his use of bird imagery throughout the film. Jarmusch even went so far as to show Suzuki the film, who declared it a little too slow for his tastes; Jarmusch's pace is typically measured and deliberate, unlike the breakneck speed with which Suzuki rushes from scene to scene.

After his dismissal from Nikkatsu, Suzuki finally managed to successfully sue his former employers after three and a half long years of legal wrangling. However, just like Hanada at the end of *Branded to Kill,* it was a pyrrhic victory in that he was prevented, due to blacklisting at the hands of a cartel of major production companies, from directing another movie until 1977. By committing cinematic *seppuku* (ritual suicide) on his career with *Branded to Kill,* Suzuki never again captured the inspired insolence and mischievous liveliness of his most notorious and beloved film.

Anthony Antoniou

NAGISA OSHIMA, JAPAN, 1976

Nagisa Oshima's *Ai No Corrida* (*In the Realm of the Senses*, 1976) can be viewed as an important contribution to contemporary Japanese cinema, and indeed international art cinema, in that it confronted sexual taboos head-on and placed the viewer in the precarious position of voyeur. Set on the eve of war with China, the film is based upon the real story of Sada Abe. On 21 May 1936, Sada Abe was found wandering the streets of Tokyo with a knife, a rope and her lover's castrated penis in a carefully folded bag. She claimed that the owner of the penis, her dead lover Kichizo Ishida, would have wanted her to possess it so that she was able to pleasure herself with him even in the event of his death. She killed her lover three days prior to her arrest, using a meat cleaver to cut off his penis and scrotum, leaving a message on his thigh, written using his own blood, declaring that they were now bound together. After a controversial trial in Japan where Sada and Kichizo's sexual practices were aired in public, Sada was sentenced to six years in prison but was later released under a general amnesty that coincided with the twenty-sixth anniversary of Emperor Jimmu's ascension to the throne. Sada had committed the ultimate act of possession which had stemmed from a deadly two-month relationship centred around the subjugation and domination of both participants.

Filmed and released in the mid-1970s *In the Realm of the Senses* was not the first Japanese film to attempt to portray such a sensitive and controversial story. Noboru Tanaka's *Jitsuroku: Abe Sada* (*A Woman called Abe Sada*, 1975) was released the year before Oshima's film, yet failed to establish an international presence and has been all but forgotten. With a strictly domestic audience in mind it had conformed to the strict censor guidelines, consequently focusing less on the sexual relationship between Sada and her lover. More recently, Nobuhiko Obayashi's *Sada* (1998) created a resurgence of interest in the story and contributed to the rising domestic and international interest in Oshima's film. Yet it was more of a homage to contemporary Japanese art films and techniques than a new take on the events that took place nearly seventy years ago. Unlike these and other more tame cinematic depictions of the illicit relationship between Sada Abe and her lover, *In the Realm of the Senses* directly challenged the strict traditional Japanese social paradigm where hardcore pornography was illegal and sexual taboos were rife, presenting the audience with a shocking, but truthful, insight into a human sexual relationship.

Censorship has always been an issue concerning Japanese film and the meeting of traditional and modern Japan have not always sat well together. As a result of Oshima's frankness (full frontal nudity and the lucid close-ups of both actors' genitalia) the film endured countless censorship hurdles. The depiction of genitalia was expressly forbidden under strict censorship laws in Japan and was also considered in the late 1970s and early 1980s to be too controversial to show audiences around the world. It was subsequently banned from the New York Film Festival of 1976 where it was supposed to make its North American debut. Australian film festivals in both Sydney and Melbourne required that it be released in a censored version before it could be shown to audiences, with the uncut version being made available on DVD as recently as the late 1990s. Additionally, the film was confiscated at the Berlinale Film Festival as suspected pornography but was released in its original form after 18 months. These set backs were obviously of no surprise to Oshima, who had decided that in order to maintain full creative control over the picture he required an international, rather than a domestic, investor. Anatole Dauman, a French producer and financier, produced the film, offering Oshima the creative license he had been dreaming of. Post-production in France allowed Oshima greater control over his film; had he stayed in Japan he would have been forced to conform to strict censorship laws and regulations thereby damaging the film's content and tone. Thus the history of *In the Realm of the Senses* is as controversial and as colourful as its story, but by no means does this detract from the artistic conventions and ideas that Oshima successfully infused within it.

Contextually *In the Realm of the Senses* is an exploration into the five human senses and their interaction within a given situation. Oshima succeeds in illustrating the importance of each of the senses in a relationship where words or conventional communication are often less meaningful than touch, taste, sight, smell and hearing. However, the over indulgence of each of the five senses ultimately leads to the destruction of life and all that contributes to its meaning. Kichizo (Tatsuya Fuji) and Sada (Eiko Matsuda) are victims of their own morality and the human need for intimacy marks their downfall. The episodic nature of the film only serves to highlight the emphasis on each of the different senses, although often they have been hidden within images of sexual debauchery. In portraying Sada and Kichizo's relationship episodically Oshima is able to emphasise the two lovers' growing obsession with each other and their increased need to dominate each other's primary senses.

The opening credits, complete with the French title *L'Empire des Sans* (which was required for the French and European release), is a construction of images that provides the first all-important insight into the themes of the film. Traditional Japanese music plays in the background while the predominant image on the scene is rice paper, the kind used as a wall divider in the antechamber of a traditional Japanese middle-class house. The paper has thick black bars running across it and the curious reflection on the paper reveals itself to be trees blowing in the wind, or possibly water running down a stream. As rice paper is a non-reflective surface, the reflection on it instantly creates a paradox for the viewer, who is forced to look for subtextual meaning; to delve deeper into the image. The marriage of the reflection and rice paper coupled with the thick bars points to caged beauty, or rather a captive sexuality that, when reflected back to itself, becomes destructive. Rich with examples of multilayered visuals, the strength of the film lies in the fact that one is able to appreciate the complex textual meanings hidden within the images as well as appreciating the stylistic features of the entire work as a whole.

Sight is usually considered to be the most important of the human senses and can be argued to be a predominant theme within *In the Realm of the Senses*. Oshima's achievement is his successful engagement of his audience in the unfolding relationship between Sada and Kichizo, while at the same time alienating these characters from their own filmic world. The viewer becomes entangled in the story and engrossed by the images presented to them on the screen as the characters become more introspective and preoccupied with themselves – increasingly requiring no external interaction. This theme of distraction and isolation is carried through with the inclusion of the Japanese iconic figure of the *geisha*, traditionally viewed as being expert in entertaining, having been schooled in traditional arts such as Shamisen playing, dancing, conversation and the tea ceremony. As well as being socially adept, the *geisha* were relatively independent and able to manoeuvre within the patriarchal world in which they performed. Their role demanded that they portray an image of refined seclusion, as it was detrimental to her patronage to be less than available. Furthermore the *geisha* existed only when she was required, her life being a distraction for those who pay for her skills. Similarly, Sada cannot exist without Kichizo. Her insatiable sexual appetite and knowledge becomes worthless if she cannot share it with him and, like the *geisha*, her life outside of the relationship becomes a distraction. Her very existence becomes threatened when she is separated from him and she fails to function within her own environment. In addition, Sada experiences hallucinations about Kichizo running naked (with her Kimono flowing off his back) through the fields as she is leaving to acquire money from her *Dana* (Master).

As their relationship progresses, Sada begins to mistrust one of her senses – that of sight. She becomes suspicious of Kichizo and stalks him from the shadows, to ensure that he is not returning to, or sleeping with, his wife. This is a key emotional moment for the character of Sada as she is transformed from the lover who will have sex anywhere and in front of anyone, to the jealous and dangerous mistress who fantasises about stabbing the wife so she can obtain the husband. Similarly Kichizo begins his metamorphosis from a lover to a possession and hence the beginning of the end of his life.

One could argue that the constant appearance of traditionally attired *geisha* is the antithesis of Sada and Kichizo. Both appear in direct contrast to the *geishas'* projection of visual beauty; their stylised movements and appearance illustrates just how far removed from traditional Japanese society Sada and Kichizo are. The character and appearance of Sada is crude compared to the refined nature and looks of the *geisha*. In fact Sada mimics the *geisha* during a bout of lovemaking where she strides Kichizo while playing the Shamisen and singing a song that she once heard Kichizo singing (he in turn had picked it up from the *geisha*). Sada effectively transforms *geisha* and their traditions into a spectacle. Oshima has used the *geisha* both as an illustration of the modernising of traditional Japanese values, these in part embodied by Sada and Kichizo, as well as a basis on which the viewer draws deeper meaning concerning wider Japanese cultural values and notions.

Oshima's vision draws influence from traditional Japanese arts such as the *ukiyo-e* whose literal meaning is 'pictures of the floating world' and refers to Japanese woodblock prints of *geisha*, brothels and other sexually referential images. Characters are often framed by the environments around them; similar to the way an artist uses composition in a painting to provide a focal point for its intended audience. Oshima also employs the 'Rule of Thirds' technique, which is used by photographers to break an image into thirds (horizontally and vertically), thereby allowing him to create a tiered image. Sada and Kichizo's farcical marriage ceremony is a case in point, as it displays similarities to a *ukiyo-e* print while utilising the idea of 'Rule of Thirds'. Sada and Kichizo remain as the focal point in the middle of the screen dressed in traditional wedding attire; they are kneeling next to each other as tradition dictates while before them lies their wedding feast. This feast serves as the second tiered image within the frame – the 'guests' at the wedding, who themselves initially serve as passive onlookers form the final tiered image. This image of traditional Japan and its conservative values is completely transformed when the entire wedding brigade participate in an orgy as a celebration of the mock wedding.

A voyeuristic theme runs though the film and it is not only the audience that partakes in the ritual of watching Sada and Kichizo's affair. Their sexual experiences usually involve passive characters watching, with the exception of the wedding *geisha* and the old teahouse owner. These characters watch through windows, screens or simply sit in the same room as the two lovers and can be argued to represent the audience, as passive participants in this sordid affair. Each scene is really a window into the fleeting and deadly relationship of Sada and Kichizo.

Oshima uses costumes as a way of expressing emotion and, abstractly, to represent the human sexual organs. A kimono is one of the most recognisable symbols of Japan yet it turns out to be the harbinger of death for Kichizo. Sada's kimonos are made up of either soft pastels of green, red or pink or of more solid colours – which could be seen to represent the colour of the female sexual organs and arousal – while Kichizo dresses in strong masculine colours. At his weakest moments, when Sada is in Tokyo with her other lover, he dresses in her summer kimono and thus assumes a fragility that is as submissive as it is 'female'. By wearing Sada's kimono he assumes the role of the woman; his position changed from a strong masculine identity to a feminine one and it is in this guise that he refuses to eat, languishing around the teahouse waiting for Sada's return. The kimono is also important in that Sada uses a part of it to unwittingly strangle Kichizo – her sexual games and prowess, which are strikingly modern and open in their approach, resulting in the strangulation of Kichizo by kimono tie. Hence Kichizo's death is caused by a traditional Japanese icon wielded by a woman whose attitude was more modern woman than traditional Japanese.

In the Realm of the Senses is a highly stylised film. Every object, every movement and every interaction between characters within the film has been carefully crafted. Subtextual meanings have been hidden within images so that the discerning film viewer, is able to extract them and glean a higher meaning from the visuals. The human sense of taste, coupled with touch within the film, is equally important. Together they provide a platform from which Sada and Kichizo are able to initiate, maintain and then destroy their relationship. Each tries to manipulate the senses for their own personal sexual, physical or emotional satisfaction. Sada is the first to recognise the importance of taste in her relationship with Kichizo and uses it to manipulate and dominate him. Her place of employment, owned by Kichizo and his wife, is a teahouse that also provides prostitutes for its male customers. Sada herself was employed, both as a prostitute and a cleaning woman. She touched men and saw to their needs while she also cleaned after them. Kichizo loved to dine with *geisha* which was a historically expensive 'hobby' in Japanese history, and one that his middle-class status affords him additional luxuries not available to the majority of Japanese (such as Sada). He also likes to be waited on, a task that Sada delights in completing. Thus it was not difficult for Sada to realise that, for Kichizo, life revolved around taste; indeed his very livelihood depends upon food. While on the other hand Kichizo realises that Sada is equally dependent upon him, for lodgings, employment and sexual satisfaction. Their mutual knowledge of each others' dependency is used both in favour of and against the relationship – in their own way they are as destructive as each other.

Food is needed to maintain life and Sada is quick to equate Kichizo with this fact, often using her body as the medium by which he gains it. We again return to the argument that Sada views Kichizo as *essential* to her life. She views sex as important as food is to the survival of the human body and indeed Oshima has succeeded in his presentation of Sada, not just as a nymphomaniac but as one who cannot live without sex. An important scene occurs between the two characters when Sada attempts to manipulate Kichizo's association of food by coating it with her pheromones – obtained by rubbing it on her genitalia. It is not the first time that the association of food, pheromones and life has appeared within the film. The first is when Kichizo licks his finger after fondling Sada. At that moment she has her period and his licking of her menstrual blood alludes to the fact that he has little respect for her. In Japan, as in other Buddhist countries, it is considered to be a mark of disrespect for both the woman and the unborn 'being' that is being shed. Consequently, by using the mushroom as a way to lure Kichizo into another session of sex Sada is attempting to reassert her status as a 'respectable' woman (stereotyped as a homemaker and thus cook). She coats food with her body secretions, thereby implying that sex and food are one and the same in her relationship with Kichizo. Kichizo, for his part, recognises the attempt at being manipulated but continues with the charade, eating the mushrooms that Sada offers him. The impression appears to be that he is completely under Sada's spell. However, he then cleverly resumes his traditional patriarchal role and becomes the dominant partner without Sada realising it. He achieves this by placing an egg between Sada's legs and telling her the only way she will get it out is to do as hens do, and to lay the egg.

The insertion of the egg into Sada can also be viewed as a symbol of fertility, the egg is intended to highlight the biological reasons for human mating. Kichizo transforms the egg into an object of humiliation – implying that this is the closest Sada will ever come to creating life with him. It must be remembered that Kichizo is married and this is *simply* an affair. He finds it amusing that Sada must act like an animal and give 'birth' to an egg. The insertion of the egg also reaffirms Sada's belief that food and sex are intertwined and her strong oral fixation continues throughout the film. Her first instinct after dropping the egg from her womb is to clutch on to Kichizo and say, 'See what I'd do?'; she has humiliated herself at his mere request and becomes the submissive woman while he, smiling at his power over her, refuses to have sex with her. His withholding of sex only serves to humiliate Sada further and arguably lays the foundation for her descent into dangerous jealousy. In humiliating Sada, Kichizo teaches her a valuable lesson: that sex can be used as leverage or as a way of obtaining what she wanted. It is from this moment that Sada begins to physically threaten Kichizo using a knife, telling him that she would castrate him and even holding it up to his throat. It is also an important indicator of just how far each has subjugated themselves to the other.

The lack of any substantial dialogue between the two characters does not imply that the sense of hearing has been neglected; rather it highlights how intimate sounds can be just as important in a relationship, and dangerous. Kichizo's lying to Sada about sleeping with his wife only causes her to be suspicious, yet the intensity of his breathing during the last bout of love-making causes Sada to strangle him out of sheer sexual pleasure. A breath can be sensual, while a laugh can cause as much hurt as joy.

The complete domination of the senses occurs precisely at the point where Sada strangles and ultimately disfigures Kichizo. Their final sex scene shows Sada on top of Kichizo twisting the kimono tie around his neck tighter. She has completely dominated his sense of touch by restricting his movements. His sense of smell and taste is impaired as he is being strangled, albeit as part of a sexual game, while his sense of hearing is slowly diminishing as he looses consciousness. Sada's ultimate act of domination is the castration of his penis, a symbol of both the love she had for him as well as the power it held over her.

Arguably *In the Realm of the Senses* is pornographic; yet it is portraying no more than a relationship between two people, and as such is honest in its representation. Oshima directly challenged the dichotomy of Japanese society that allowed such sexual representations as *ukiyo-e* and *geisha* to flourish but objected to celluloid representations of the same things. It may have been the intensity and open display of sexual gratification by both Sada and Kichizo that shocked audiences. As the film is presented from neither of the characters viewpoints it is the audience that must identify with one or the other and that, at times, proves uncomfortable. Nevertheless *In the Realm of the Senses* certainly contributed to the rising interest in Japanese cinema that continues into the twenty-first century and Oshima remains a distinctive figure within that country's cinematic landscape.

Samara Lea Allsop

SALINNABILEUL GGOTNEUN YEOJA KILLER BUTTERFLY

KIM KI-YOUNG, KOREA, 1978

The link between realism and modernity has long been assumed. Both mark a shift away from the divine to a secular humanism. Here, human observation and rational analysis are understood as the measures of truth, and problems are assumed amenable to logical and linear resolution in a progress that suggests perfectibility. Leading scholars have dubbed Hollywood studio-era moviemaking as 'classical' realist cinema manifesting these characteristics and constructing this culture. As Kim So-young has pointed out, in South Korea, major film historians and critics have also emphasised realism as an ideal to aim for.

The late Kim Ki-young, director of *Salinnabileul Ggotneun Yeoja* (*Killer Butterfly*, 1978), has been lauded as one of the three fathers of Korean realism, along with Shin Sang-ok and Yu Hyon-mok. This critical framework casts his career as an early burst of neo-realist brilliance in the lost films of the late 1950s culminating in the 1961 classic, *Hanyo* (*The Housemaid*), an expressionist watershed followed by a long and slow decline into muddled genre cinema. The late Lee Young-il, South Korea's pre-eminent film historian, notes bluntly that, 'since 1965, he has not made great works that compare to his early works' and dismisses his 1970s films as 'enervated' in comparison with the 'strong realism' of his earlier work. Unless I have missed a startling botanical discovery, *Killer Butterfly*'s title alone announces that it is not a realist film.

However, I want to challenge the longstanding neglect of Kim Ki-young's later works. This is in line with recent reassessments of Kim's oeuvre, which argue that his films trace a struggle to develop a cinematic mode appropriate to the experience of South Korean modernity. As well as participating in this reassessment, I also aim to insert the discussion of Kim's later works into two other debates. First, the very assumption that realism is the dominant mode of modernity has itself come into question in other contexts. For example, critics have argued recently that the pre-eminent mode of Hollywood studio-era cinema is not realism at all, but melodrama. However, melodrama, although exaggerated, is not completely outside the parameters of plausible mimesis that ground realism. *Killer Butterfly*, on the other hand, is both a pre-eminently modern film and outside those realist parameters; the dominant mode of this fragmented film is the fantastic. In other words, melodrama may expose the ideological underpinnings of realism's claim to truth from within, but the use of the fantastic mode suggests an altogether different aesthetic and culture of modernity.

What is this different aesthetic and culture of modernity? This takes us on to a second debate, linking the turn to the fantastic in Kim's later works to the specific experience of modernisation in the era of the Park Chung-Hee regime that lasted from 1961 to 1980, and drawing on Kim So-young's crucial insight into the importance of the fantastic for understanding the connection between colonial and post-colonial violence and Korean modernity. In light of this analysis, the apparent chaos and disorder that characterises *Killer Butterfly* emerges not as a sign of failure but as an apt characterisation of South Korean modernity as an experience more delirious than rational. Furthermore, Kim's work and the Korean experience of modernity it expresses challenge us to think again about our assumptions concerning modernity and realism in the cinema. Commentators have started to speak of 'alternative modernities' in their efforts to acknowledge different social and economic modern structures constructed in different parts of the world. Works such as *Killer Butterfly* indicate that we need to extend this model to think about alternative cultures of modernity that render its violence and irrationality.

The shift away from realism in Kim's films is fundamental to Lee Young-il's account of South Korean film history. He discusses the trilogy of Yu Hyon-mok, Kim Ki-young and Shin Sang-ok and their use of realism to regenerate South Korean cinema in the late 1950s in his *The History of Korean Cinema*. After the defeat of Japanese colonialism and the restriction of communism to the northern half of the Korean peninsula, this was a time when there were high hopes in South Korea for the production of democracy and economic development. So, it is not surprising that a critical realist mode might have existed in this period. Lee also notes Kim's shift from realism in the late 1950s to a more expressionistic style in the 1960s and in his article for the book released at the retrospective of Kim's work at the Pusan International Film Festival in 1997. However, this shift away from realism is not only produced across Kim's films, but also within *Killer Butterfly*. Like so many of Kim's films, *Killer Butterfly* is a generic hybrid, and the generic shifts inscribed within the film trace a movement away from realism and towards the fantastic. This suggests that a reassessment of the modernist ideology of realism is not only inscribed across Kim's oeuvre but also internal to *Killer Butterfly*.

The protagonist of *Killer Butterfly* is a young student called Kim Yeong-geol. The film opens with Yeong-geol out on a butterfly hunt with friends. The soft-focus scene and cheerful music are hardly typical of the nitty-gritty urban neo-realism loved by critics and which we are told characterised the lost films of the late 1950s. However, regardless of the romanticism, the genre it invokes still falls within the broad parameters of plausible mimesis. This genre is the youth film, an optimistic cycle of South Korean cinema emphasising aspirations for romantic love, upward economic mobility and the appurtenances of Western-style modernity. In other words, in *Killer Butterfly*, the mark of realism no longer attaches to a critical discourse emblematic of the democratic spirit of modernisation, but instead to a genre that emphasises materialist plenty alone as the hallmark of modernity.

However, *Killer Butterfly* only dwells in the bucolic romping of the student film for long enough to reveal dangers lurking in the undergrowth. A young woman wearing a butterfly pendant spikes Yeong-geol's drink in an effort to make him die with her. Yeong-geol survives and wears the butterfly pendant from now on. At this point, the film has taken one step further away from realism, moving into the mystery of the suspense and murder genre, as Yeong-geol wonders why the woman tried to kill him. However, although this genre complicates the innocent pleasures of the student film, it is also not completely beyond the realms of plausible mimesis.

Yeong-geol finds he has lost the will to live, and becomes a recluse. He attempts suicide, but an old bookseller breaks in and interrupts him. He tells Yeong-geol that the will to live can be stimulated by the desire to kill someone else. After enough interruptions, Yeong-geol's desire is to kill the bookseller. However, he finds that stabbing and burying him alive are not enough to finish him off. Eventually he has to burn the old man. But when he tries to turn himself in to the police, they claim the ashes he has brought as evidence are not human, and release him.

With the nearly immortal bookseller and his ashes that are not human, *Killer Butterfly* has entered the territory of the fantastic, and in particular the horror film. This is confirmed in the next sequence, when Yeong-geol and a friend go on an archaeological expedition to retrieve a skeleton from a cave. Raindrops bring the skeleton back to life as a young woman from the *Shilla* dynasty of two thousand years go. She is looking for a man so that she can reproduce, but also announces that she needs to eat human liver within ten days or she will die again. Yeong-geol goes to look for a liver, but is unable to locate one.

Instead, he returns with a rice-cake machine, intending to use it to earn some money for himself. As the untended machine pops rice cakes across the room like frizbees, Yeong-geol and the *Shilla* woman make love. Afterwards, she cannot bring herself to kill him and eat his liver, so after ten days she dies. With this sequence, an unstable mixture of absurdism and erotic film are added to the horror genre, and this mix is maintained through the remainder of the film.

11

SALINNABILEUL GGOTNEUN YEOJA

Yeong-geol takes the woman's skeleton to Professor Lee and becomes his assistant, moving into his Western-style home. The house is dark, and shot with a wide-angle lens and from high and low angles to create a gothic house typical of the horror film, a setting common to many of Kim's films. Yet the absurd elements continue. For example, over a breakfast of notably Western foods, a bottle of Aunt Jemima's pancake syrup looms lifelike on the counter, adding an unlikely footnote to the career of this already bizarre icon.

Yeong-geol notices that the Professor's daughter has a butterfly pendant just like his. She tells him that her dead friend returned in a dream, demanding that she poison Yeong-geol so that he would join her in death. A skull arrives for Professor Lee, and later a whole head. Yeong-geol becomes curious and begins to investigate the source of the head. Out drinking one night, a friend spikes his alcohol. A parcel arrives with Yeong-geol's head. But Yeong-geol's head speaks its will to live. Professor Lee attacks Yeong-geol's head, but the head wins. The dead Professor Lee turns into an enormous butterfly and ascends, his daughter clinging to his tail. Yeong-geol and his friend awake from a drunken stupor and go out into the streets of Seoul.

This conclusion produces a standard trick used in fantastic genres, whereby the elements of the film considered implausible within the ideology of secular modernity are excused as a dream. Earlier on, when Yeong-geol goes to the police with the bookseller's 'ashes', the inspector suggests he must still be delirious from the poison the woman had given him earlier. However, these excuses beggar disbelief. Despite the 'it was all a dream'-style ending, *Killer Butterfly* remains a representation of South Korean modernity as a living delirium. Why might this be?

The characteristics of *Killer Butterfly* can be related to those of the South Korean experience of modernity itself, but how? This question cannot be answered by any direct allegorical interpretation. It is highly doubtful whether the butterfly motif itself, or the archaeological trip, or the Professor's bizarre experiments can be said to refer to some particular historical or contemporary events. However, there are other ways in which the connection can be understood. First, the sudden incongruous genre switches in *Killer Butterfly* parallel the sudden and disorienting shifts in modes of modernity experienced on the Korean peninsula. Second, the shift away from the glossy materialist realism of the student film and towards the fantastic parallels the bizarre career of modernisation in South Korea after the Korean War. Third, as in so many of Kim Ki-young's films, Western and specifically American goods appear as a fetish, suggesting they cover a fundamental lack at the heart of Korean modernity. Fourth, the archaeological theme of the film relates to ethnic nationalism – the attempt to trace an ancient bloodline as a way of assuaging the anxiety produced by the new and flimsy nature of the South Korean nation-state always haunted by its northern counterpart. Each of these points necessitates further elaboration.

First, for most of the world, modernity arrived as a foreign phenomenon; Korea was no exception. But the Korean experience of this imported and imposed form featured more than one competing model of modernity. This led to a series of sudden and disorienting disjunctures and shifts not only between pre-modern and modern culture, but also within the Korean experience of modernity. These zigzags are in some sense echoed in the unstable generic shifts of *Killer Butterfly*. It was clear during the late *Chosun* dynasty years at the end of what is now retrospectively known as the nineteenth century in Korea that modernity came from the West. But in the early part of the twentieth century those bearings were challenged by Japan's colonisation of Korea and establishment of a regional empire of its own. Even though the modern continued to be traceable back in the last instance to the 'West', it arrived from the east, via Tokyo, between 1910 and 1945. After Liberation in 1945, two (and possibly three) new competing centres of modernity presented themselves for emulation. First, there was liberal capitalism represented by the United States. On the other side of the Cold War divide were the socialist models of modernity, represented by two powers that saw eye to eye in the early 1950s – the People's Republic of China and the Soviet Union – but were at loggerheads by the end of that decade.

Turning to the second point, after the Korean peninsula itself was split into two republics corresponding to competing socialist and capitalist modernities, the South Korean 'Republic of Korea' was itself buffeted by sudden regime changes and shifts. Most recently, it has been transformed from one of the most repressive right-wing dictatorships in the world to one of the most liberal multi-party democracies in the region. *Killer Butterfly* was made in 1978, in the middle of the dictatorship. While it is now possible (at a stretch) to construe South Korea's history as demonstrating the common ideological assumption that more capitalist development means more democracy and freedom, the opposite must have seemed the case in 1978. This helps to explain the turn to the fantastic mode in *Killer Butterfly*.

In the late 1950s, in the wake of the Korean War, the Republic of Korea was impoverished and beset by social problems. Kim Ki-young's first films have not survived, but Lee Young-il compares them to Italian neo-realist works in their on-location realism and social critique. The deployment of the realist mode in these and other films from this period suggests a progressive and developmentalist imagination, where implicit in the representation of a series of social problems in a manner recognisably similar to what an audience member might imagine encountering in daily life is the possibility that they might be addressed by material development and government policy. In 1960, the *Syngman Rhee* regime was replaced by a democracy after a series of student demonstrations culminating in the 'April Revolution'. It must have seemed that the progressive imagination of the future was accurate.

However, this was short-lived. In 1961 a military coup took place and Park Chung-Hee came to power. Park's regime confounded the progressive imagination. On the one hand, it ushered in an era of unparalleled material development and economic growth. In 1961, per capita GNP was at $68, but by 1979 it had reached $1,662. On the other hand, this process of development did not banish the tyranny that modernist ideology assumes characterises 'feudalism'. Instead, the greater the amount of material growth and development, the stricter and more brutal Park's dictatorship became; it was notorious for its paranoid Cold War vision of international relations and violent suppression of any political dissidence. In these circumstances, the possibility of any direct representation of social critique was impossible. Furthermore, the trope of haunting and its associated fantastic mode becomes an appropriate means for expressing the appearance in the present of that which has supposedly been consigned forever to the scrap heap of the past by the decisive break that characterises the founding of the modern era.

An Jin-soo has related the emergence of expressionism and horror film conventions in Kim Ki-young's watershed work, *The Housemaid*, to the anxieties of a failing economy and fleeting democracy. By the time of *Killer Butterfly*, in 1978, both the Park dictatorship and the disturbing equation of political repression with economic development must have seemed so entrenched that they were fixed. In these terms, it is entirely suitable that the first ghostly apparition in the text should be the old bookseller. He appears to haunt and torment Yeong-geol not with a text of ancient superstition but with Adolf Hitler's *Triumph of the Will* (1934). The title of that book simultaneously grasps the forced modernity projects of the Park regime and the ideologically repressed underside of modernity. The significance of the more ancient connections of other supernatural events will be discussed below, but here it is worth noting that both the reincarnated *Shilla* skeleton with her craving for human liver and Professor Lee's ghastly graveyard thefts of human heads are carried out in the name of supposedly enlightened and progressive scientific experiment. Here again, the deployment of the supernatural tropes of the fantastic mode enable the film to emphasise the uncanny quality of Park Chung-Hee's dictatorial modernity as it brought people back into touch with the very things it was supposed to abolish.

Third, in the face of these deeply troubling experiences that undermine the supposedly solid ground of modern rationality, Western culture emerges in *Killer Butterfly* as a fetish that characters hang on in a desperate effort to cover up the contradictions produced by the experience of South Korean modernity. This pattern occurs throughout Kim Ki-young's surviving works. A fundamental paradox animating his films is that it is precisely the quest for these modern fetishes that produces the fantastic eruptions that both undermine modernity and motivate further desperate desire for it. For example, An Jin-soo points out that the two-story Western-style house the wife desires in *The Housemaid* is the very cause of the family's downfall, because it is too much for her to manage and so they have to hire the maid.

The Western-style house also looms large – literally – in *Killer Butterfly*. Before Yeong-geol meets Professor Lee and becomes his assistant, the screen is filled with a shot of Lee's very substantial Western-style home, which contrasts strongly with the shack Yeong-geol has been living in. This associates Lee with his house, and for the rest of the film almost all the scenes featuring Professor Lee and his daughter are set in this impressive home. However, the home itself is not the only Western thing associated with the Lees. Indeed, their extreme attachment to Western culture is emphasised at the first dinner Yeong-geol attends in the house. When candles are lit at the request of Professor Lee's daughter, Yeong-geol remarks that this is very traditional. She corrects him immediately stating that, as the subtitles put it, it is 'occidental'. The Lees eat with Western cutlery; Professor Lee smokes a Sherlock Holmes-style Western pipe; the Lee family home is full of stained glass; breakfast consists of heaps of bread and butter, which Yeong-geol consumes ferociously; Professor Lee's daughter is trained in Western-style realist painting; and there is a reproduction of the Mona Lisa on the wall. At the same time as the Lees pursue everything Western as though it is the panacea for all ills, as in his other films, Kim shoots the Western-style house as a claustrophobic gothic mansion. The staircase is open, enabling him to film through it so that the image is cut across with horizontal bars. Other woodwork and stained glass enables similar barring and confining effects. The dark woodwork and candlelight create an eerie effect and invoke the conventions of the ghost film.

Fourth, at the same time as Professor Lee pursues the West as emblematic of modernity, in his scientific endeavours he pursues the Korean past. This element of the film draws attention to the nationalistic aspect of South Korean modernity under Park Chung-Hee. Professor Lee seeks out *Shilla* Dynasty skeletons and tries to use the skulls he collects to prove links between modern-day Koreans and Mongol ancestors going back to the days of Genghis Khan, if not earlier. The nation-state is itself an invention of modernity, and, as Homi Bhabha points out, it is narrated into being through moves such as Professor Lee's. Furthermore, as Benedict Anderson has pointed out, the narrative of the modern nation typically constructs a glorious past and intervening trauma, with the modern narrative of progress itself constructed as a climb back to former glories in modern form. Professor Lee's supposedly scientific activities echo those carried out by archaeologists in South Korea. They work to anchor the very recently invented state of South Korea in a bloodline that leads back to the glories of *Shilla* and the Mongol Empire. However, in Kim Ki-young's rendering of these activities this bloodline is also bloodstained. Rather than a tidy genealogical diagram of a national family tree organised as a progress of generations, the present is haunted by a past that literally seeks to consume it and the desecration of corpses in the pursuit of so-called knowledge.

This is a disordering of progress – the ideological timeline of modernity – by what its own logic configures as eruptions from the past. It makes the fantastic mode in the fragmented and demented later works of Kim Ki-young particularly suitable manifestations of the delirious experience of forced modernity under the Park Chung-hee regime. This delirious experience is also a postcolonial experience of modernity as a violent imposition that projects its own brutalities back into a past that it claims to have moved beyond. As such, it is both specifically South Korean but also has wider significance. Furthermore, the postcolonial fantastic corresponds to the vast majority of the world population's experience of modernity, for whom it arrived as just such a violent imposition. Therefore, we may need to consider it as well as realism and melodrama as one of the dominant cinematic modes of modernity.

Chris Berry

REFERENCES

An, J. (1999) '*The Housemaid* and Troubled Masculinity in the 1960s', in C. Berry and S. Kim (co-ordinators) *The House of Kim Ki-young*. Seoul: Korean National University of Arts, http://www.knua.ac.kr/cinema/KKY/Window/AJS.htm.

Berry, C. (1999) 'Genrebender: Kim Ki-young Mixes It Up', in C. Berry and S. Kim (co-ordinators) *The House of Kim Ki-young*. Seoul: Korean National University of Arts, http://www.knua.ac.kr/cinema/KKY/Stairway/CB2.htm.

HIMATSURI FIRE FESTIVAL

12

MITSUO YANAGIMACHI, JAPAN, 1984

Himatsuri (*Fire Festival*, 1984), justly considered as the finest of the films directed by Mitsuo Yanagimachi, is a fresco of unusual proportions, portraying the same peculiar world his cinema has always been preoccupied with. Made in 1984, it also marked an important turning point in Yanagimachi's career as it contributed to his world-renowned and opened up his work to international appreciation. Today it stands as a strong reference point for the new generation of Japanese film directors.

Before shooting *Fire Festival*, Yanagimachi had already experienced unexpected success with *Barak Emporou* (*God Speed! You Black Emperor*, 1976), *19 Sai No Chizu* (*A 19-Year-Old's Plan*, 1979) and *Saraba Itoshiki Daichi* (*A Farewell to the Land*, 1982), three low-budget movies produced by his own independent company, Production Gunro. Starting with these films, Yanagimachi showed himself to be particularly preoccupied with the innermost aspects of Japan, of those parts of the country injured by modernisation even though still filled with traditions. However, rather than telling of a mythological but now-lost past, he preferred a straight and bare portrait of the Earth, which from his own perspective is responsible, from ancient times, for all degradation and grief. This is not due to a kind of ineluctable fate, but, according to Yanagimachi, to human beings themselves – even if strictly related to their environment – whose physiological fears of progress and of change manifest themselves in the form of violence and crime.

It is natural that Yanagimachi should be interested in the work of a writer such as Kenji Nakagami – co-author of the screenplay of *Fire Festival* – whose short novel he had already adapted for *A 19-Year-Old's Plan*. Nakagami was born in the Kumano area, where *Fire Festival* is set. He had devoted most of his works to the mysterious aspects of his land, giving emphasis to the physiological and blood relation among the people who lived in the small villages of the region. With Yanagimachi, his approach to the human condition was especially directed toward the less well-to-do individuals who lived far from the big cities and their trappings. However, neither the director nor the writer had any intention to investigate the political cause of their condition, nor to raise their dignity. Rather, they preferred to demonstrate the emptiness of their existence, showing how each character runs a short distance in the human cyclic existence, leaving behind nothing but a mark – often a negative one – before disappearing, only to be replaced with a new and near identical mankind. As Yanagimachi has often declared in interviews, at the centre of each story, and especially in *Fire Festival*, is a kind of 'Spirit of Earth', a witness of the never-ending return of human existence. It acts as a measure of capacity of human history, where each individual character's reality gradually disappears – an idea shared by the co-author Nakagami.

At its most basic *Fire Festival* tells the story of a man who exterminates his own family and himself. Inspiration for the story was a short article that he had read in the newspaper some five years earlier. What had especially struck Yanagimachi about the actual incident was that the murder was apparently motiveless. Wondering what could have given free rein to the man's madness, he came to the conclusion that the reason could be nothing other than a peculiar relationship that Man had established with Nature, from ancient times unchanged and imbibed with animistic elements. In other words, preferring an interpretation in terms of religion to a psychological analysis of the event, Yanagimachi believed that the man had, by degrees, assimilated all the animistic emblems which the inhabitants of the area had always worshipped; the gods that, according to Shintoism, dwell in the stones, the trees, the waterfall and in all aspects of Nature. Since these values were in his opinion gradually diminishing as a result of modernisation and the cultural homogenisation of Japan, the murderer represented (to Yanagimachi) a rare and heroic example of how these ideals could be preserved in the memory. Further, the director and the writer had chosen a man born as an outcast (a *burakumin*, Japan's pariah caste, as Nakagami himself was), 'impure' enough freely to overcome the morality of his society and thus capable of such blasphemous acts as killing animals.

Initially Yanagimachi and Nakagami had chosen as a title *Mori To Umi No Shukusai* (*The Festival of the Forest and of the Sea*), but later thought this may not have been truly representative of the story. *Otomatsuri* (*Light Festival*, from the name of a typical festival which takes place in the area celebrating the Goddess Amaterasu) was then considered before they finally opted for *Himatsuri* (*Fire Festival*) after it was decided to insert a scene of such a festival into the narrative. The background chosen for this film is itself deeply meaningful. It is set in a small sea-village surrounded by mountains. This contrast between sea and mountains (distinctive of the whole Japanese archipelago whose mythological history relates that the islands, mostly mountainous, emerged from the sea) is a means of underscoring a continuum and, at the same time, a first line of demarcation between two worlds traditionally in conflict with each other.

Here the urbane reality of the village has been offset by the largely uncontaminated aspect of the mountains, where a marine park is being constructed to bring to the inhabitants economic stability and a modicum of modernisation. Both Yanagimachi and his cameraman, Tamura Masaki, pay particular attention to the environmental setting. It is clear that the realistic and partly documentary-like imprint derived from the first works of the director (and obviously from the long experience of Tamura on the subject), particularly when nature is framed not only by long-shots as a huge and impressive entity endowed with life, but also observed through the characters' eyes, thus revealing her hidden and usually unnoticed appearance. Thanks to this peculiarly voyeuristic way of filming, in many of the scenes Nature acts as a true character, demonstrating her influence over Man. To capture this sensation, Yanagimachi had for a long time walked across these places, trying to understand in detail which kind of camera techniques, which spots and atmosphere could best fit the representation of what he had, by instinct, felt from that earth. This is an undeniably unusual method of working but one that Yanagimachi says he has inherited from his most loved film director, Kenji Mizoguchi, thanks to whom he could foresee, in advance of filming, the final effect it would arouse in the audience.

The leading character, Tatsuo (Kitaoji Kinya, at this time specialising in action movies), is a woodcutter who spends most of his time working in the dense nature of the mountains. In actuality, the murderer on which the character was based worked as a stone-breaker, yet Yanagimachi and Nakagami decided to change his profession to that of a woodcutter so as to immediately represent the gods with whom he was going to establish a symbiosis. Moreover, according to the director, cutting trees would become a symbol of the castration of Tatsuo himself, from which he would be able in turn to transform himself into a god. To this image is linked the choice of his name, Tatsuo, since in Japanese 'tatsu' is a verb also meaning 'having an erection'. Tatsuo works with a small group of colleagues, including his young 'disciple' Ryota, who is destined to succeed him, symbolically at least, after his death. Tatsuo lives in a house in the village with his two children, his mother and his wife – all of whom fully comply with his beliefs and values, and who will all be sacrificed because of them.

Several characters in the course of the film contribute to quickening Tatsuo's awakening. There is Kimiko (Taichi Kiwako), whose name phonetically recalls that of Himiko, a mythical princess and shamanic figure in Japan. Kimoko comes from nearby Shingu by means of a small boat and, like Himiko, she carries with her an umbrella. She is a childhood sweetheart of Tatsuo's and now works as a bar-tender and as a prostitute. When she reaches the village, Tatsuo's awakening begins and, upon her departure, he will be ready for the final sacrifice. Here represented as human, the 'goddess' Kimiko has the power to communicate with Nature. When she makes love with Tatsuo, with an old man or with the young Ryota in the middle of the mountains or immersed in the sacred waters, Nature always spies on her; the film projects her presence through the sudden movements of trees and plants.

The 'Goddess of Nature' (in Japanese called *Shizen shin*) is also passionate. Her iconography is based on the changes of her seasonal cycle and on a constant pattern of depiction. She is then taken as motionless and timeless within the bounds of a kind of framework, so as to perceive her invisible strength and inner turmoil. She often appears as impressive while vertically shot from the ground towards the sky (a difference from the lateral dollies used for filming 'human' characters). She may also become a maternal entity, as in the case of the frequent scenes of ablution in her waters by Tatsuo, Kimiko or Ryota.

Tatsuo appears different from the other men. He does not allow human laws to rule over the natural order of things, whose power he is aware of. Nonetheless, his attitude towards the goddess is both profane and of deep love. For example, he does not hesitate to bathe in the sacred waters, even if he knows it is forbidden as taboo except on solemn occasions. But when his friend Ryota breaks a branch off a sacred tree to construct a trap, Tatsuo forces him to prostrate himself before the goddess by showing her his sex. Moreover, Tatsuo has learnt how to communicate with Nature. He has a confirmation of this privilege in the scene when the furious goddess provokes a violent storm in the forest that makes all the woodcutters, apart from Tatsuo, run away. He then embraces the sacred tree (a paraphrase of a long and passionate sexual embracing) so that the rain gradually stops, and again he drinks the water of the river to abate the wind. This is one of the fundamental scenes of *Fire Festival*, which possesses a refined beauty. For a while, the general realism of the movie is broken off and we perceive the fantastic nature and the oneirism of their relationship. From now on, Tatsuo completely devotes himself to Nature through a spiritual exercise consisting of both love and death instincts.

In *Fire Festival*, a few animals (always present in Yanagimachi's films) play the role of a kind of watershed between the irrationality distinctive of mythology and the blind reason peculiar to mankind. Tatsuo owns some dogs and he loves and takes care of them with an affection he never shows to other human beings. The dogs' instinct represents one more manifestation of Nature and is also a symbol of the sacrificial offerings common to any religion. Tatsuo sets the dogs on a wild boar, encouraging the animals' blood lust, rather than attempting to stifle it. In a scene similar to the one of the storm in the forest, Tatsuo spends some time with his dogs on a beach, embracing them with unusual tenderness and rolling together with them in the sand;

a play that is at once funny and sensual (in fact, Yanagimachi expressly asked the actor Kitaoji to simulate sexual intercourse with the dogs). Also Kimiko, before leaving, lets the dogs out of their cages and lingers to caress them, which in a way anticipates the final murder by Tatsuo who is now freeing his instinct. Finally, in the very last scene after Tatsuo's death, his dogs look as if they are praying whilst remaining motionless and staring at Nature.

As in a religious ceremony, other animals in *Fire Festival* become sacrificial victims as Tatsuo transforms into a god. The more he changes, the worse a fish murrain (caused by oil spilled in the water) becomes – the fishermen suspect Tatsuo wants to hinder the building of the marine park. In this sense, the fish, no longer edible, represent what happens to nature whenever man tries to rule over it. In different scenes, Tatsuo and Ryota kill some monkeys, sacred animals according to Shintoism because of their anthropomorphic aspects, and Tatsuo covers his arms with the blood of a bird caught by Ryota, as a form of ritual ablution.

As we have seen, many different contrasts constitute the thematic background of this film – between tradition and modernity, sacred and profane, what is pure and what has been polluted, man and nature, and finally, between criminal instinct and the form of reasoning employed by humans. A further theme subtended to the story is the urge of human beings to travel, as Yanagimachi has said in interview: 'I am interested in those individuals who, however much they try, will not succeed in entering society at all, who never are successful, never manage to enforce their own radical position. If we consider it according to Buddhism, to these people there is nothing more to do than move around along society's boundaries and never enter, forced to travel continuously, hoping to find an opening to infiltrate through. Maybe I am one of them, even if I'm not so interested in entering, actually.'

In *Fire Festival*, in addition to Tatsuo's symbolic and initiatory travel from life to death and to his own deity, this theme is suggested in more scenes. For example Kimiko often moves, unable to settle in a single place. In the sole flashback of the movie, when we see both Tatsuo and Kimiko in 1959, still in their teens but ready to 'travel' towards their adult lives, there takes place the opening ceremony of the railway line which will also run through the village. The train itself further represents a passage towards modernisation.

The never-ending moving of those who are forced to travel is also represented by a peddler's little van which goes through the village playing a jingle through shabby loudspeakers. It reaches the village at the beginning of the story and then leaves after the murder, playing its music quietly, like a requiem. A further symbol of the travel theme is represented by a tunnel that is often crossed by the characters. According to Yanagimachi, it indicates 'the vagina at the moment of birth, and is also a cinematographically perfect space. It is dark, with a light in the end. If you wonder how men are born, then the answer is in the tunnel's image.'

Fire Festival hence displays a dense system of symbols and rites to enforce deification. They include the umbrella brought by Kimiko and the one used as a sunshade by a knife manufacturer in the village. To Yanagimachi, the umbrella is not only a symbol of the deity, but also a means of circumscribing a small space and a little world – this is why he over-emphatically shoots some sequences through the umbrellas. Another recurring symbol is represented by all the traps arranged by Tatsuo and Ryota in the forest. They are a means of capturing not only animals, but also the Goddess of Nature (the trap set for her is a fruit composition resembling the male sex) and men – indeed, a trap containing money, which to Yanagimachi represents the ordinary people's god of today, almost cuts off an old man's arm.

As for the rites, in addition to the one when Tatsuo calms down the storm in the forest, there is a scene in which three young people come to the village riding their bikes before suddenly dancing in front of the amused villagers, symbolising the uninterrupted duration of mankind and its culture. Later, the rite of the Fire Festival begins, which has taken place at Wakayama since ancient times. Only men participate in the rite, each bringing a torch that has to be lit from a sacred fire in the temple. For Yanagimachi, the fire from the past has always been considered a violent means of salvation and purification, which then becomes a strong symbol of the passage to adulthood. However, as in the case of other religious beliefs, it tends gradually to disappear and become a meaningless practice, the inevitable result of modernisation. This is the reason why, during the festival, Tatsuo assails a man who has tried to light his torch from a different fire, a 'false fire'.

The final rite, of course, occurs when Tatsuo murders his family before taking his own life. We reach this scene after having gradually followed Tatsuo's catharsis, when we have already learnt to recognise his inner strength and have realised that he actually loves life. Therefore, the multiple murders give neither a sensation of anguish or terror. By his death, Tatsuo plans a better future and wants to take his beloved family with him. His children, while he smilingly hunts them, think it is nothing but a game and therefore die without fear. After the massacre (of which we hear only the rifle shots without seeing them) the camera explores each body in silence. The spectator can do nothing but identify with the camera's eye (which is at the same time Nature's eye), moving over the bodies in search of Tatsuo's corpse.

As he had previously done with the killed bird, Tatsuo covers his body with the children's blood, which is, according to Yanagimachi, the visible symbol of their existence. The director, who had taken inspiration from the writer Yukio Mishima for the character of Tatsuo and his *seppuku*-like suicide, demonstrates that the concept of evil is a human invention. As I have previously stated in a study of the director, 'I don't want to judge a man who kills a fellow-man. It is not this that scares me, but it is the intervention of the society that terrifies me, since the changes are irreversible. Murder and suicide are ways of escaping from the implacable flowing of modernisation and are attempts to refrain from social impositions.'

Tatsuo's murder and suicide occur in broad daylight. Light is not only a proof of paradise, but in Japan is also considered frightening because, dazzling, it hides from view something thus not fully comprehensible. The use of lighting in *Fire Festival* was fundamental to Yanagimachi who says he was inspired by the effect Jean Renoir achieved in *Le Déjeuner sur l'Herbe* (*Picnic on the Grass*, 1959). He therefore for the first time used HMI lamps, at that period rare in Japan, and avoided shooting on sunny days, preferring cloudy ones so that, thanks to the lamps, the colours of the bodies would become particularly sharp and unreal. For example, in the scene when Tatsuo and his friends bathe in the river, the lighting is gradually intensified, offering a sharp contrast between the water and the men's bodies, exalting the epidermal surface.

In addition to the lighting and to the fundamental soundtrack by Takemitsu Toru, very significant in *Fire Festival* is the abundance and range of camera work, new to Yanagimachi's cinema. Tamura Masaki utilises both the crane and the handycam to penetrate with the gaze every viable ravine of nature, also giving the sensation of a multiplication of the visual angles. Last, with considerable use of medium and long shots, the film keeps the audience always at a distance and like a documentary it never tries to be didactic in describing the situations.

Fire Festival has the power to draw us into a never-ending mystery. In spite of the richness of themes, sometimes difficult to interpret for people who do not know Japanese culture in detail, and thanks to its fascination, its being stateless with the universal messages it carries, and to its strong and dense fiction, it won the Silver Leopard at Locarno Film Festival and international fame for its director.

Maria Roberta Novielli

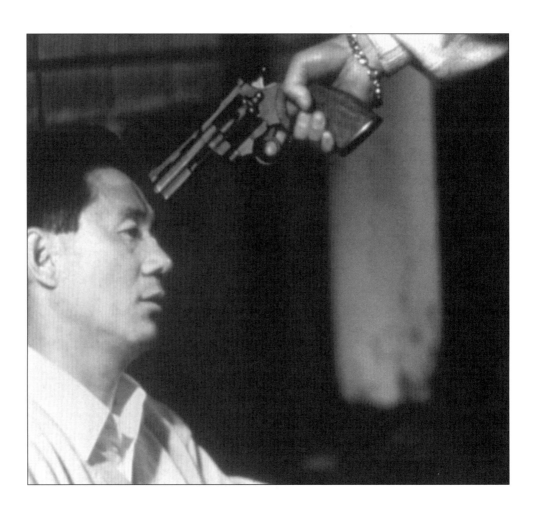

SONO OTOKO, KYOBO NI TSUKI VIOLENT COP

TAKESHI KITANO, JAPAN, 1989

Before one can assess *Sono Otoko, Kyobo ni Tsuki*, (*Violent Cop*, 1989 [US release, 1998]) it is vital to consider the phenomena of its director, star and uncredited writer, 'Beat' Takeshi Kitano. Kitano, a one-time strip-club host who went on to become a veritable one-man Japanese entertainment industry, made his mark in Japan as one-half of the 'manzai-style' comedy team, 'Two Beats' (the other 'Beat' being Kaneko Kiyoshi, who appears in a small role in Kitano's *Kikujiro no natsu* (*Kikujiro*, 1999)), before establishing himself as a television comedian/host and then movie actor. His work rate is manic, appearing on as many as eight television shows a week. He is undisputedly the most identifiable popular culture icon in Japan.

After conquering the entertainment arena, Kitano expanded his field to include writing (magazine articles, serious books, poems, scripts) and painting (his paintings are featured in *Hana-bi* (*Fireworks*, 1997)). His breakthrough film in North America came with his acting role of Sgt. Gengo Hara in Nagisa Oshima's *Merry Christmas, Mr. Lawrence* (1983), who delivers the memorable final line of the film: 'Merry Christmas, Mister Lawrence.' Takeshi Kitano was at first only slated to act in *Violent Cop*, but the (reported) illness of original director Kinji Fukasaku, who had helmed numerous *yakuza* films during the genre's heyday of the 1960s and 1970s, thrust Kitano into the role of director. Exactly why Fukasaku relinquished the director's chair is not known but it is a moment of serendipity as significant as Riccardo Freda 'playing ill' to allow cinematographer Mario Bava to complete the directing of *I Vampiri* (1956);

Violent Cop was followed by *3-4x Jugatsu* (*Boiling Point*, 1990), *Ano Natsu, Ichiban Shizukana Umi* (*A Scene at the Sea*, 1992), *Sonatine* (1993), *Minna Yatteruka* (*Getting Any?*, 1995), *Kidzu Ritan* (*Kids Return*, 1996), *Hana-bi* (*Fireworks*, 1997), *Kikujiro no Natsu* (*Kikujiro*, 1999), *Brother* – his first English-language film in 2000, *Dolls* (2002) and *Zatoichi* (2004). Throughout these films he took on the roles of actor, director, writer and editor. Between *Sonatine* and *Getting Any?* Kitano was involved in a near-fatal motorcycle accident which left his face with partial paralysis, scars, and a noticeable tic. Such a disastrous accident could have destroyed any actor's career. Not the case with Kitano, who was able to productively exploit the accident to the benefit of his taciturn persona, to the point where it has helped his onscreen 'tough guy' image.

According to figures taken from Brian Mertens' 'Japan's Entertainment Exports to Asia are on a Roll' from Asian Business of October 1996, 1958's cinema attendance in Japan peaked at an impressive 1.1 billion spread across more than 7,000 movie theatres. By 1994 the figures plummeted to 123 million ticket sales in only 1,700 cinema theatres. In addition, 60 per cent of films screened in Japan are foreign. In counterpoint, the numbers merely reflect the changing media and entertainment landscape, where film must vie for consumer dollars with a myriad of competing mediums and spectacles (pachinko, which is a Japanese version of slot and pinball machine parlours, the expanding home video industry, cable satellite, terrestrial television, manga, internet, computer games, and so forth). Additionally it is estimated that the Japanese spend an average of seven hours a day watching television, the highest level in the world.

Japan, the first Asian country to make Western inroads with the international success of Akira Kurosawa's *Rashomon* (the Golden Lion Award at the 1951 Venice Film Festival), had largely taken a back seat on the international scene since the rise in the mid-1980s of such national cinemas as Iran, China, Taiwan, Hong Kong and South Korea. But Japan has rebounded strongly thanks in great part to Kitano's multiple prize-winning *Fireworks*. Since its release, Japan has made significant inroads on the competitive international scene with such young (and not so young) directors as Takashi Miike, Hirokazu Kore-eda, Sogo Ishii, Kiyoshi Kurosawa, Hideo Nakata, Shinji Somai, Seijun Suzuki and Nagisa Oshima. Takeshi Kitano, who has thrived largely because of his media diversification, has played a key role in Japan's international rebirth – although perversely his films have performed poorly in domestic markets.

Because of his relatively advanced age (he was born in 1947), Kitano is an anomaly among the pack of new Japanese directors. Whilst directors in the Japanese studio system once had to work their way up to director, younger directors are now finding quicker, alternative roads to directing – principally through television, commercials and music videos, and in some cases through the 'Roman Porno' film industry. Kitano also worked his way to films through television, yet his cinematic directorial debut came at the age of 41. This stands in comparison to other directors who made their debut films around the same time at a much younger age: Shinya Tsukamoto (1988 at age 28), Junji Sakamoto (1989 at age 31), Hashiguchi Ryosuke (1989 at age 27), Rokuro Mochizuki (1985 at age 28), Shinju Iwai (1992 at age 29), Kiyoshi Kurosawa (1983 at age 28) and Takashi Miike (1995 at age 35). Of his contemporaries, only Takashi Ishii debuted at an older age – 42 in 1988.

This generational difference may explain Kitano's filmic sensibility, patterned on an aesthetic of repetition and minimalism, which seems far removed from the younger generation's fever-pitched, consumerist and technophile mindset. It may also explain the strident conservatism that surfaces in his films, showing as early as *Violent Cop*. Most pronounced is the right-wing vigilante attitude of Kitano's character, Azuma (and in nearly every US review *Violent Cop* was compared to *Dirty Harry*). Secondly, there is his distrust of youth and respect for the elderly, or more directly, the way he maintains the hierarchy of seniority: the older the person, the more fitting they are of respect, usually at the expense of the young, who are continually slapped, pushed and ridiculed in his films. There is also a link made between homosexuality and criminal pathology. The most obvious examples are the vicious gay hitman Kiyohiro in *Violent Cop* and the bisexual *yakuza* leader Uehara in *Boiling Point*). Some of this conservatism may in fact stem from Kitano's background in comedy, a tradition where taboo areas such as race, sex and gender are acceptable targets. Conversely Kitano demonstrates a fondness for children, the weak and the ill, such as his sister Akari in *Violent Cop*, his terminally ill wife Miyuki and the suicidal, wheelchair bound detective Horibe in *Fireworks*.

Although *Violent Cop* is more plot-driven than his later films, there is a sense that Kitano, learning as he went along, whittled away plot as the filming/editing progressed, in favour of mood and theme. *Violent Cop* also has a less complex narrative structure, opting out of the unexplained flashbacks/flash-forwards and elliptical traces that structure most of Kitano's subsequent works (the same could be said of *Boiling Point*, both of which Kitano did not edit alone).

In *Violent Cop*, Kitano's character, Azuma, is a single, 'old school' police detective who spends all his time and energy chasing crooks and caring for his mentally ill sister. While trying to solve the murder of a drug dealer he and his rookie partner Kikuchi become embroiled in a drug ring that exposes Azuma's police detective friend Iwaki as a *yakuza* accomplice. Azuma's investigation leads to the *yakuza* murder of two police officers, Emoto and Iwaki, and to an inevitable confrontation with the *yakuza* ringleader Nito and his loyal henchman Kiyohiro. The film contains all the crime/gangster film clichés: the weathered cop who teams up with the rookie, the new police chief who wants to put a stop to Azuma's effective yet dubious methods, the pathetic drug pushers, the corrupt police officers, the slick *yakuza* leaders and their psychotic henchmen. Yet *Violent Cop* energizes these clichés through its unique style and sensibility. Whilst a debut film, there is a sense of icy control in every shot which, in a world of imminent aggression and violence, produces an unnerving stoicism slowly building to a hellishly bleak finale. But, unlike the recent trend in Japanese action and gangster films to push the 'over-the-top' aesthetic, Kitano maintains the film's formal control right to the end.

Violent Cop projects its internal calm through a use of static camera and long- and extreme-long-shots that engender an aesthetic of mild distanciation; a stylistic trait which has become a Kitano hallmark. A case in point is the opening scene, where a group of bicycle-riding teens taunt, push and kick an aged homeless man in a suburban street. One of the boys is given a stern lesson when Azuma quietly talks his way into the boy's home, disarms the his mother with his calm assurance ('Leave us alone, don't worry'), enters his room and then proceeds to reduce the boy to tears with slaps and a well-placed head-butt. This seminal Kitano moment is book-ended by two static extreme-long-shots framed from high up and behind a tree looking down at the suburban home. The distance and bird's-eye view of the camera adds to the apparently serene setting which belies Azuma's violence.

The scene is important not only in establishing the film's visual style but its social import and meaning. It instantly establishes Azuma's personality; a quiet, cool disciplinarian not averse to taking the law into his own hands when he sees fit. He willingly abides by the law but when that law fails him, he resorts to a more rigorous personal code that has more in common with the *bushido* – the *samurai* code of the warrior – than any contemporary set of rules. Indeed, in a Japan where *yakuza* leaders wear Armani suits, police officers collude with drug pushers and *yakuzas*, and teenagers beat up defenceless old men, to Azuma, modern laws *do* often seem to be failing.

For any resident of urban Japan the opening scene of the violent teens is a direct allusion to the social problem of the *bosozoku* ('speed tribes') – teenage bike gangs that first appeared in Japan in the mid-1960s and reached their peak in the mid-1970s, when there were an estimated 30,000 to 40,000 gangs across Japan. According to Japan's National Police Agency figures taken in 1999, the *bosozoku* were responsible for more than 80 per cent of serious juvenile crimes, and approximately 40 per cent have links to the *yakuza*. Hence with this opening scene of marauding teens, Kitano foreshadows not only the *yakuza* world we are soon to enter, but perhaps makes a nihilistic social comment on Japan's youth. A quote from Takeshi Kitano, taken from Mark Schilling's *Contemporary Japanese Film*, seems to confirm this and serves as a blueprint for this opening scene:

When we look at Japan today and wonder why we have all these problems between parents and children, with drug use – well, we just have to look at America and see what kind of country it's become, where their form of democracy has taken them. Parents have become scared of their own kids. It used to be that adults would scold kids who were running around and making trouble on the train, but now no one does that. When I was a kid I used get scolded by adults all the time, but that doesn't happen anymore. We've lost the ability to distinguish between rights and duties. Now the emphasis is totally on rights – no one talks about duties any more and we're going in a very strange direction as a result.

The bleak vision presented in *Violent Cop* of a modern Japan driven by consumerism, conformism, internal corruption and random violence would become a thematic constant in Kitano's later films.

One of the overriding themes of Kitano's directorial debut is the blurring of the worlds of law and crime, cop and criminal. Kitano quickly establishes himself as a formidable director by using visual and cinematic means to highlight the confused boundaries. In a sequence which recalls Fritz Lang's classic *M* (1930), he crosscuts between Azuma and Kikuchi looking for Kiyohiro, and Kiyohiro looking for an informant; blurring the distinction between criminals and the police. This is further accentuated by the fact that the *yakuza* run their business out of a large, barren modern office that is always bathed in white light and which contains only two desks, one for the *yakuza* leader Nito, the other for his emotionless secretary. Likewise, the new police chief is always seen seated behind his desk in a similarly under-furnished and over-lit office.

The invisible 'changing of the guard' from honest (law) to corrupt (criminal) cop plays out in the way Kitano revisits a shot from the film's second scene in the final scene. In the early shot the camera is placed at one end of a pedestrian overpass while Azuma enters the frame from below and walks toward the camera (a telephoto lens compresses the space, making the walk seem interminable). In the later shot Kitano reproduces the camera set-up, only now we see his rookie partner Kikuchi walking toward the camera. The first impression is that Kikuchi has become the new 'violent cop'. Yet in the proceeding shot Kikuchi enters the *yakuza* office and accepts an envelope from the new *yakuza* leader becoming, instead, the 'new Iwaki'.

One of the most powerful signifiers of this blurring between police and criminal is in the layered doublings between Azuma and the henchman Kiyohiro. Both Azuma and Kiyohiro are loyal foot soldiers unappreciated by their respective bosses. In several parallel scenes, Azuma and Kiyohiro are called into their boss's office and reprimanded. In the final instance both are relieved of their duties, making them servants without a master, in essence modern-day *ronin* (unemployed *samurai*). Although they are on opposite sides of the law, Azuma and Kiyohiro both share the *samurai* qualities of loyalty, self-sacrifice, self-control and fearlessness. Once a warrior, the *samurai* must remain a warrior until death; this is why Azuma and Kiyohiro seem all too aware of their destiny to confront each other.

By the film's adrenalin-fuelled finale, Azuma and Kiyohiro are reduced to fearless, suicidal killing machines. Director Kitano builds up to the violent ending by slowly stripping the film of its surface sociality (dialogue, secondary characters, social interaction) and in the process sinking the audience deeper into the depraved world of hired killers and angels of death. Azuma, who in relation to later Kitano characters is positively loquacious, barely speaks a word in the last third of the film. Kiyohiro kidnaps Azuma's sick sister and has his three minions viciously rape and drug her. Meanwhile Azuma calmly enters Nito's office and kills him, while his second-in-command and secretary passively watch on. When Kiyohiro receives news of his ex-bosses demise he prepares himself for the showdown with Azuma. Kiyohiro gives the three 'punks' given the task of holding Akari hostage a choice: either they stay and face Azuma or die by his hand, coldly stating, 'in either case you are dead'. With the house cleaning complete, a wounded Kiyohiro takes a suitcase full of weapons and waits in the car park for the inevitable showdown. Azuma arrives and slowly walks toward Kiyohiro, unperturbed by the barrage of bullets Kiyohiro is firing. Some of the bullets appear to hit Azuma, yet he remains standing. Azuma stops a few feet in front of Kiyohiro, who is lying against the wall in a reverse of the earlier back-alley scene where Kiyohiro stood in front of a fallen Azuma. At point blank range, the two warriors exchange their final bullets, with Azuma claiming the final fatal blow directly into Kiyohiro's face (one of the few instances in *any* national cinema of an explicit, on-screen facial bullet hit.) In a bitterly ironic and tragic moment, a mentally shattered Akari appears from the dark and begins to crawl over Kiyohiro's corpse, sifting through his pockets in search of drugs, failing even to acknowledge the presence of her brother Azuma. As if to respect the privacy of the moment, the scene cuts to an extreme and partially obstructed long shot. The expected mercy killing of Akari comes when a single gunshot is heard off-screen. Azuma begins to walk toward the exit, but is shockingly felled by an anonymous bullet to the back of his head. The interior car park lights are turned on and the shot cuts to the source of the gunfire: Nito's once second-in-command and newly-minted *yakuza* leader. Looking over the bloodbath, he utters the telling phrase, 'Everybody is crazy', and turns the lights back out. The shot cuts to our final view of Azuma, lying still on the garage floor, cast in a sharp triangular light. The intense, relentless drive of the two combatants, and their near superhuman ability to absorb bullets, was undoubtedly an influence on the 'over the top' endings of Takashi Miike's 'Dead or Alive' films and other recent super-charged gangster films.

The cumulative violent encounters between these two warriors suggests more than a hint of homoeroticism. In the scene where Azuma and Kikuchi arrest Kiyohiro at his apartment, they discover a young man in Kiyohiro's bed. When Azuma sees the attractive man he comments, 'Nice taste'. As a point of contrast, Azuma is unmarried and shows no interest in woman. At the police station, Azuma tries to beat a confession out of Kiyohiro and forces the barrel of his gun into Kiyohiro's mouth – later Kiyohiro stabs at Azuma's abdomen but Azuma manages to grasp the blade of the knife. During the same altercation Kiyohiro finds a wounded Azuma sitting against a back-alley wall and pushes his foot against Azuma's stomach wound. He then takes a gun to Azuma's head, but is thwarted when Azuma picks up the fallen knife and jabs Kiyohiro in the leg. These jabs and thrusts of phallic weapons 'climax' in the orgiastic exchange of bullets in the closing scenes. Kitano even employs the equivalent of pornography's patented 'cum shot' with the final bullet to Kiyohiro's face.

To fully understand the impact of *Violent Cop* on the gangster genre, and in particular its brusque, laconic treatment of violence, one must remember that the film was made five years before *Pulp Fiction* (Quentin Tarantino, 1994). Much was made of the way Tarantino deployed violence in an offhand manner, pointing to the scene in a car where a gun accidentally kills Marvin, the unsuspecting back-seat passenger. The template for this type of 'off the cuff' violence may certainly have been influenced by Kitano's approach to violence, as evidenced in a wonderfully choreographed scene where an innocent bystander is killed by a stray bullet from Azuma's gun. The moment occurs during the scene noted earlier where Kiyohiro confronts Azuma on a city street and stabs him in the abdomen. Azuma lessens the impact by gripping the blade with his bare hand. While struggling with the knife Azuma pulls a gun, but Kiyohiro deflects his arm, causing the bullet to veer left killing a young woman standing behind them. The unfortunate victim crumbles to the street while her stunned friend lets out a horrified scream. In Kitano's miniature set pieces, the angel of death comes quick and suddenly. Often the audience does not even have time to register who has died. Kitano's approach to violence is in many ways an antidote to the slow-motion approach favoured by Sam Peckinpah, John Woo and their imitators; quick and to the point rather than slowed down and expanded; brutal and ugly rather than balletic and poetic. Although he does choreograph some violence in slow-motion, it is hard to accuse Kitano of glorifying his violence.

Violent Cop is by no means Kitano's masterpiece, yet it remains a most self-assured debut, featuring certain stylistic devices that resurfaced in a more refined form in many of his later films. After his sister Akari's release from the hospital, Azuma takes her to an amusement park.

The short scene ends with Azuma and Akari momentarily stopping to have a seaside talk. This setting, which only occurs a few times here, foreshadows what will become an important Kitano trademark: scenes set on the beach and/or by the seaside. Such scenes appear in almost all his subsequent films. As depicted by Kitano, beaches are a place where *yakuza* and other assorted criminals play games, act the fool and can, momentarily, return to the cares of childhood. Other elements in *Violent Cop* that continue through his oeuvre include Kitano's habit of slapping people, often to comic effect, and the use of piano-driven, meditative music which sometimes runs as an emotional counterpoint to scenes of violence. The appearance of his mentally ill sister also introduces a common Kitano plot element: the pairing of a strong, silent character (usually played by Kitano) with a physically or emotionally weak character. For example, the quiet, shy boy and hapless 'bikers' in *Kikujiro*; the terminally ill wife and wheelchair-bound detective in *Fireworks*, and the sad loser from *Boiling Point*. These characters often serve as comic foils, but also 'soften' the film's hardened world. The world may be filled with violence and cruelty, but it also features weakness and vulnerability.

Violent Cop may seem a world apart from the meditative *Fireworks* or *Dolls*, but Kitano remains consistent in the emotional pendulum he achieves from one film to the next, shifting from the violent, hard-boiled male world of the *yakuza* to the contemplative world of 'quieter' characters and even to worlds where the two poles appear in harmony. What unites the two emotional poles is Kitano's distinct poetic style. To varying degrees, the *yakuza* is featured in all but two of Kitano's films: *A Scene at the Sea*, a quaint, contemplative film about a young deaf man's infatuation with surfing; and *Getting Any?*, Kitano's first and thus far only outright comedy. Even *Dolls*, an esoteric and minimalist *bunraku* doll theatre fable of undying love, features an aging *yakuza* as an important secondary character. Yet *Violent Cop* remains Kitano's *purest yakuza* film, and therefore casts an enormous shadow over all his subsequent films.

Donato Totaro

REFERENCE

Schilling, M. (1999) *Contemporary Japanese Film*. New York & Tokyo: Weatherhill.

TETSUO THE IRON MAN / TETSUO 2 TETSUO 2: BODY HAMMER 14

SHINYA TSUKAMOTO, JAPAN, 1988 & 1992

When Charlie Chaplin released *Modern Times* in 1936, the film's signature image of the humanist Tramp literally lost in the cogs of oppressive industrialism was already something of a cultural and aesthetic banality. Fritz Lang's *Metropolis* (1926) and René Clair's *A Nous la Liberté* (1931) had preceded Chaplin's criticism of the fascistic underbelly of industrial capitalism, and Aldous Huxley's novel *Brave New World* (1931) had prophetically satirised the corporate state with its story of eugenic hatcheries mass-producing identical children programmed to turn the capital engines of machine labour. Meanwhile, Futurist ballets such as Prokofiev's *Le Pas D'acier* (1926) and Alexander Mosolov's once-sensational *Iron Foundry* (1928) had even glorified the futuristic symbiosis of man and machine, in accordance with then-fashionable Constructivist ideologies. So when we turn to Shinya Tsukamoto's *Tetsuo* (*The Iron Man*, 1988) and *Tetsuo 2* (*Tetsuo 2: Body Hammer*, 1992), it is little advance on the high modernist sentiments of the 1920s to say that Tsukamoto's cyberpunk descents into errant evolution, technological mutation and man-machine hybridity present an intricately fetishised critique of industrial dehumanisation.

That cult film demography has unceremoniously lumped together the *Tetsuo* dyad with similarly techno-erotic Japanese science fictions such as Shozin Fukui's *964 Pinocchio* (1992) and *Rubber's Lover* (1997) only muddies Tsukamoto's themes further, making them difficult to analyse and articulate beyond stock clichés of technophobia and mad-science-run-amok. But, remarkably, the *Tetsuo* films are not merely the visually striking exercises in nihilism their cult popularity suggests, and unlike the largely decorative sadomasochistic futurism of Fukui's films, or Kei Fujiwara's maddeningly solipsistic *Organ* (1996), Tsukamoto's work invites rather than resists close interpretation.

Nevertheless, Tsukamoto's *Tetsuo* films have secured such a rarefied place both in Japanese science fiction and in international cult cinema that we must begin by disentangling them from modernistic clichés and the convenient categorisations of the cultish. Though *Tetsuo* is, even more than *Modern Times*, a narrative of literal dehumanisation, Tsukamoto dehumanises not the anonymous, lower-class factory worker represented by Chaplin's Tramp, but the equally anonymous, middle-class, post-industrial businessman who regularly figures as Tsukamoto's protagonist. Though the influences of David Lynch's *Eraserhead* (1976) and David Cronenberg's *Videodrome* (1982) must be acknowledged, Lynch's influence is superficial and purely stylistic, and the kinship with Cronenberg is obvious without being terribly revealing. While *Videodrome*'s Kafkaesque metamorphoses and fears of contamination are thematically akin to Tsukamoto, Cronenberg's film is ultimately a culturally specific satire of the mass media, far removed from Tsukamoto's abstract expressionism. Likewise, if *Tetsuo*'s anarchic punk wastelands are nominally presaged by Sogo Ishii's *Kuruizaki Sanda Rodo* (*Crazy Thunder Road*, 1980), the similarities end there. While Ishii's post-apocalyptic bikers are a stylised burlesque of the politics of youthful rebellion – the favourite theme of 1960s Japanese new-wavers – *Tetsuo* has no clear point of cinematic departure.

Tsukamoto's avant-gardism also refutes the traditions of generic science fiction, which, as exemplified by landmarks such as Fritz Lang's *Woman in the Moon* (1929) or William Cameron Menzies' *Things to Come* (1936), presented probabilistic fantasies based on pseudo-scientific explicability. But with minimal dialogue and no linguistic or 'scientific' explanations for their frequently unintelligible action, the *Tetsuo* films owe more to the discontinuously edited Surrealism of the 1920s, the non-narrative abstractions of Stan Brakhage and the stop-motion grotesqueries of Jan Švankmajer than they do to the atomic-age Inoshiro Honda epics to which they tangentially tip their cinematic hats. The deliberate unintelligibility of the *Tetsuo* films' narratives, however, is part of Tsukamoto's very point, for, as we shall see, his are futures where knowledge has no precious place, and which hinge on wilfulness alone.

Of all Tsukamoto's influences perhaps Cronenberg remains most trenchant, for in both of their worlds ever-escalating technology is conflated with both infectious disease and evolution; two elements inextricably locked in the Darwinian tango of natural selection. Both directors' unrestrained fetishising of the haplessly diseased 'technological man' cruelly satirises the phenomenon that Alvin Toffler, writing in 1970, called 'future shock', or an exponentially 'accelerated rate of change in society', where an alienated populace is no longer able to rationalise technologies spinning out of proportion to its understanding and control. If Japan's high-tech boom of the mid-1980s fostered and commodified the young professional's technophilia and Japanese society's neophilism, and if *anime* from the sugar-coated *Baburugama kuraishisu* (*Bubblegum Crisis*, 1987) to the more reputable *Kokaku Kidotai* (*Ghost in the Shell*, 1995) fantasised that humans could switch their cybernetically protective second skins as often and as peacefully as one slips into a new suit, Tsukamoto will have none of it, bitterly mocking Japanese pop culture's 'diseased' way of fetishising – or rationalising – accelerated future shock with his darker brand of fetishism, where the organic and inorganic are inextricable, even indistinguishable. In the *Tetsuo* films, future shock's 'sped-up' evolution is realised quite literally with Tsukamoto's trademark, breakneck stop-motion animation that regularly launches lost souls on disorienting journeys through physically sterile, eerily dystopic urban sprawl. His use of this kinesthetic technique is traceable to the early amateur short *Futsu Saizu no Kaijin* (*The Phantom of Regular Size*, 1986), basically an 8mm storyboard for *Tetsuo*, and the medium-length *Denchu Kozo no Boken* (*The Adventure of Denchu Kozo*, 1987), whose blatant slapstick seems an adolescent phase soon exchanged for the drier, deadpan humour of his features.

On the one hand, Toffler's future shock is the inevitable modernist outcome of a post-war Japan too abruptly thrust from militaristic imperialism into Americanised egalitarian democracy. Still, it may seem that Tsukamoto's films also fall into the post-modern rubric, where 'hybridity' of all sorts – here, *Tetsuo*'s cyborg hybrid of the organic and inorganic – announces the destruction of obsolete categories and their anachronistic value judgments. Post-modern critic Donna Haraway, in her *Simians, Cyborgs and Women: The Reinvention of Nature*, appreciates the cyborg as a crypto-socialist, utopian myth 'about transgressed boundaries [and] potent fusions', whose quasi-sexual 'coupling' of man and machine signifies a futuristically liberated technological reproduction that elides the whimsical tyrannies of biological fertility and the heterosexual family unit that forms the base of capitalist economies. Indeed, the obsessive heterosexual relationship at the core of *Tetsuo* becomes a dead-end, eventually abandoned in favour of a chaotic cyborg life whose cathartic, revolutionary anarchies remain the only thing in the film resembling the futuric or 'reproductive'. But at *Tetsuo*'s end, the cyborg's unstoppable reproductions turn apocalyptic, and it becomes an ironically animalistic, raving hybrid poised to refute postmodernism's easy utopias.

Instead of regurgitating an ideologically stale 'modernism versus postmodernism' schema, it is preferable to frame the *Tetsuo* films, to the degree that they are about evolution, as satires of anthropological and evolutionary adaptation. Describing evolutionary adaptations in the modern human, some anthropologists have appropriated two psychoanalytic terms Sandor Ferenczi popularised in the 1920's: the 'alloplastic', or behaviours by which humans use their intelligences to speedily and wilfully manipulate the external environment to meet their own needs, and the 'autoplastic', or the more primitive, instinctual behaviours through which species undergo evolutions to fit the demands of the external world – such as a chameleon's automatic, and therefore unwilling, camouflage. Consider anthropologist Weston La Barre's views on the alloplastic human, whose all-adaptive, tool-making hands have rendered any further genetic evolution unnecessary:

> The human hand is the adaptation to end all adaptations: *the emancipated hand had emancipated man from any other organic evolution whatsoever.* Machines not only do man's flying, diving and superhuman seeing and hearing, but also *they do his evolving for him* … Since man's machines evolve now, not anatomical man, he has long since gone outside his own individual skin in his functional relatedness to the world.

What La Barre calls 'evolution-by-prosthesis' allows humans to evolve by proxy as they attach prosthetic or mechanical devices to their limbs: 'man's very physical ego is expanded to encompass everything within reach of his manipulating hands'. In light of this, Tsukamoto envisions pandemic prosthetic evolution as something more fearsome (or fearful) than a merely communicable Cronenbergian disease. Alloplasticity, which should benefit humankind, has been robbed of its 'wilfulness', and human hands no longer use technology to manipulate the environment, but are manipulated by the environment when technology spins out of control.

Plot synopses have never done justice to Tsukamoto's experimentalism, but we will need to consider the texts of both *Tetsuo* films, which must be considered as a complementary pair, before we continue. *Tetsuo* opens with a title reading 'regular-size monster series', a spoof of Japan's apocalyptic, nuclear-age *kaiju-eiga* (monster movie), where *Gojira* (*Godzilla*, 1954), represents the logical outcome of nuclear technologies unbound, symbolising not so much future holocausts but an endless memorial to Hiroshima and Nagasaki. In his *Science Fiction: The Complete Film Source Book*, Phil Hardy remarks that in the *kaiju-eiga* imperilled Tokyo 'bizarrely stands in for America', but this substitution is actually sensible, for modern Tokyo is the product of post-MacArthur, Americanised technology, and thus represents simultaneously American imperialism and the Japanese spirit that, in the 1980s, attempted to better American industrialism by producing higher-quality electronics. But if the genre's Tokyo-smashing monster-sprees present the architecture of modernity itself as a villain to be joyously squashed, in both *Tetsuo* films the metropolis is an invulnerable, labyrinthine stage to be (barely) navigated at high speeds, while newly fashioned cyborgs misdirect their frustrations, sexual and otherwise, at each other.

In *Tetsuo*'s opening montage, we see photographs of athletes strewn about a metal wasteland, announcing the film's themes of bodily mechanisation and a new sexuality, not of athletic training but of industrial reconditioning. Soon, a character usually dubbed the 'metal fetishist' or 'techno-fetishist' (his character is unnamed in the film) slices open his leg and willingly inserts a long metal screw, whereupon the images of athletes suddenly burn to ash, asserting, in Cronenbergian fashion, the end of the 'old flesh' and the arrival of a being ultramodern yet non-virtual and materialistic. Frightened by maggots festering in his wound, he flees in panic only to be struck by a car driven by Tsukamoto's trademark 'salaryman', clad in thick-framed glasses and business suit, who in the credit sequence had been presented at odd camera angles spastically writhing amidst an iron foundry, apparently suffering from symptoms of modernist withdrawal. This spineless, oft-mocked Japanese salaryman can be seen as the democratised, emasculated incarnation of the *samurai*, who, like his feudal forefather, is apparently masculine yet in fact servile to centralised institutions, be it the corporate state or, in the case of the *samurai*, a feminised feudal lord wholly dependent on his retainers.

After his automotive (and thus technological) run-in with the techno-fetishist, the salaryman, looking in the mirror, discovers shards of circuitry sprouting from his cheek in a scene recalling Jeff Goldblum's analogous revelation of insect hairs in Cronenberg's *The Fly* (1986). He is next accosted on a train platform by a woman, similarly undergoing a monstrously mechanical transmutation, apparently at the hands of the techno-fetishist as he observes her through an odd-looking machine. As she pursues the salaryman, this female monster pauses to admire her new body in the mirror (a satire of beauties perfected through technologies of make-up and face-lifts), and speaks in a male voice (apparently that of the controlling techno-fetishist), her electrically frazzled hairdo a travesty of *The Bride of Frankenstein* (James Whale, 1935). After she rams her metallic fist down his throat – an obviously sexual contamination – his own arm, too, becomes a festering machine; his foot is now equipped with an engine that sends him along delirious stop-motion journeys through city streets. He then fantasises that his girlfriend sodomises him with a mechanised, snaking fistula – similar to the tentacles that in *hentai anime* so often substitute for the taboo penis – as if his penetration were an extension of the humiliated salaryman/neo-*samurai* 'feminisation' at the hands of Japanese technocracy and corporatism.

Returning home, he attempts to suppress his masochistic fantasies by ravaging his girlfriend. Yet he remains sexually insecure: 'Promise you'll never leave me', he begs, at which point his penis, fulfilling the predictable demands of his mechanical morphosis, becomes a great boring drill, a ridiculous terror first witnessed in *The Phantom of Regular Size*. Certainly this uncontrollably monstrous phallus parodies cyberpunk's emphasis on adolescent masculinity (and unwittingly self-parodies the film's own popularity with testosterone-fuelled young males), but it also heralds the reappearance of a sexuality so chaotic as to repudiate the servility of the salaryman. To his girlfriend's plea of 'How the hell did this happen?' he can only respond, 'It is a punishment', a curiously theistic explanation for technological irreverence, as though technology (and by extension, knowledge and human curiosity) could now be judged original sin. Frightened and ashamed, the drill overpowers his egoistic human will, whereupon he tries to rape and kill her; when she defends herself with a frying pan, his metallic body absorbs it, as it will all other metal objects it touches, and La Barre's notion of 'evolution-by-prosthesis' is stretched to nonsensical extremes. He laughs maniacally, hoisting his drill in both clumsy triumph and visible pain, finally grinding the girlfriend in a gory orgy of spewing bodily fluids.

We return to the techofetishist, lingering in the iron foundry that seems to be his new home, his arm morphed into a torch-like cannon. As he threateningly raises his arm, the image superficially recalls James Woods' literal 'hand-gun' in *Videodrome*, but the torch-cannon also clearly parodies the perceived imperialism lurking behind the American Statue of Liberty. Finally, the fetishist challenges the salaryman to a cybernetic duel to determine who has better mastery over their new bodies, leading to hyper-masculine melée so intimate and intertwining that it foreshadows the expressly homosexual sadomasochism engaged by the two rival boxers of Tsukamoto's subsequent *Tokyo-ken* (*Tokyo Fist*, 1995). In their stop-motion melée, their bodies absorb first all the nearby accessories of the modern world – stray tools, televisions, all the electronic accessories of capitalist production – and finally each other. Unlike the sentimentalised cyborg juggernaut of Otomo Katsuhiro's *Rojin Z* (1991), which seeks to reclaim for all a long-forgotten humanity and spirituality, in *Tetsuo* there are no greener pastures to recapture, and the two combatants synthesise to conquer (or absorb) the world.

While it seems the techno-fetishist has been, in some impossibly obscure fashion, orchestrating *Tetsuo*'s chaos, the original cause of the chaos remains unnamed and free from identity. If mankind now evolves not by manipulating objects but by being environmentally manipulated by them, creativity itself lies within the object and not the hands that once manipulated them. Inverting the werewolf legend, which supposes essential animal-man has yet to come to terms with his shaved modern skin, Tsukamoto's films rationalise the ungovernable machines raging in man, machines which are supposedly alloplastic and wilful, but behave more like wild, autoplastic animals. La Barre states: 'Man's evolution is through alloplastic experiments with objects outside his own body and is concerned only with the products of his hands, brains and eyes – and not with the body itself.' Yet in *Tetsuo* it is precisely the body itself that comes under 'autoplastic' attack, and the 'emancipated hand' is *too* emancipated, becoming an illiberal, apocalyptic cannon, ironically fulfilling its dictum as the evolution to end all evolutions.

Keeping these ideas of ever-mutating autoplasticity and alloplasticity in mind, we can now begin to consider *Tetsuo 2*, which vitally introduces the idea of wilfulness into Tsukamoto's vision of cybernetic evolution. Our mock-heroic salaryman returns afresh, this time moderately affluent and equipped with a young wife and infant son, but still he, like his predecessor from the prequel, psychically flashes back to images of himself writhing in despair in a modernistic iron foundry. His suit and tie may be the new armour of post-industrial life, but the repressed industrialism on which it is founded will feverishly resurface in the shape of the iron-man's own, more physicalised armour. *Tetsuo 2* also offers a more conventional narrative, for now Tsukamoto psychoanalyses his previously abstract hero: an orphan adopted into sterile modernity, he dreams of long-lost parents and an idyllic childhood. For utopian postmodernist Donna Haraway, the unnatural reproductions of the cyborg myth make the oppressively patriarchal 'father-creator … inessential' so it is perhaps no accident that our alienated and soon-to-be cyborg hero is without parents. But this time he confronts not an individual anarchist but a fascistic collective of techno-fetishists who, by kidnapping his child, seek to render the salaryman's own patriarchy 'inessential'. Additionally, the villains' punk-fetishist makeup in *Tetsuo 2* is distinguished from the salaryman's suit, signifying economic disenfranchisement far more than the punkishness of *Tetsuo*'s techno-fetishist. Made at the height of Japan's industrial power, *Tetsuo* was a critique of rampant economic modernisation; but in *Tetsuo 2*, made during the economic decline that befell Japan in the early 1990s, the villains' counterculture guise comes to serve as the decorative marker of the underclass, just as theatrical make-up marks the disenfranchised folk classes in Tsukamoto's *Soseiji* (*Gemini*, 1999).

Emasculated after only barely rescuing his son from the skinhead thugs, the salaryman stands amidst fast-motion shots of urban life, reminiscent of *Koyaanisquati* (Godfrey Reggio, 1983), while superimposed infernal flames lick across the screen to symbolise human anger and the raging fires of the modernistic foundry that haunt his memory. Attempting to assuage his inferiority complex and imbue himself with godlike Olympian spirit, he futilely attempts to weight-train in a parallel montage that juxtaposes his soft-bodied masochism with the hard-bodied, cultish fascism of the techno-thugs who, we learn, have been technologically mutated by an organised cadre of Frankensteinian scientists. Under the scientists' control, the thugs finally kill the salaryman's son and chloroform him, penetrating his memory in experimental procedures that dredge up a stew of disturbing childhood memories and prompt a mighty phallic canon to burst from his angrily mutating chest, much like the liberty-torch of *Tetsuo*. When one of the scientists comments, 'The will to kill … that's what counts', the newly-emboldened salaryman rips himself from the chair and proceeds to slaughter his oppressors, just as the brainwashed techno-fetishists now revolt against the puppet-master scientists. When the salaryman mortally wounds the villain who murdered his child, the dying thug says, 'He was a god … the man who can make us all gods', an implicit variation on Nietzsche's familiar sentiment, 'There cannot be a God because if there were, I could not believe that I was not He', which at first seems to mistakenly remove the will from the individual to an external force (presumably, the controlling scientists), but can also be interpreted as an ironic foreshadowing of the rampaging hero's climactic absorption of humankind into his allegedly godlike whole. It would also seem that the fit, Darwinian physiques of *Tetsuo 2*'s fascistic thugs are a red herring, for though they do revolt against the scientists who forged them, their allegedly steel wills are easily conquered by the less 'fit' but more psychically wilful salaryman.

When the salaryman's wife is then kidnapped, he shoots recklessly at the getaway car with an arm transformed into a cannon, prompting the kidnapper to remark, 'He doesn't seem to care much for you' – as in *Tetsuo*, the militaristic technology rioting from his body has overpowered his emotions. In fact, his cannon has become more powerful than the cult leader's own cybernetic appendages: 'He used will-power to transform himself', he concludes. Through psychiatric flashbacks, we discover the salaryman and cult leader are long-lost brothers; soon the salaryman's family memories resurface and we learn he murdered his parents with an earlier incarnation of the arm-cannon, apparently part of his psyche all along, after beholding their primal scene. After much stop-motion-animated combat, the salaryman rusts his brother's metal body, yet his still-living head injects into the salaryman an umbilical pipe which channels through his brain a hyperactive montage of abstract images climaxing in the vision of a spinning silver ball: the whole Earth made metal. We flashback again to their childhood, where the father, an inventor, uses an esoteric machine to clumsily unite organic and inorganic matter, allowing the two boys to cleave their alloplastic wills to handheld weapons. We return to the present, where the salaryman injects multiple mechanical umbilical cords into the remaining horde of techno-fetishists, absorbing them into a new conglomeration that anarchically takes to the street. However, unlike the exclusively male *Tetsuo*-monster at the close of the first film, this time the salaryman is joined by his wife, optimistically restating affective bonds laid to waste in the prequel. In an ambiguous (and probably unnecessary) coda image, we see the salaryman, his wife and young son peacefully together again, wandering haunted industrial wastelands that imply the nightmare is about to begin anew.

Despite his valued insights into the alloplastic human, La Barre ultimately reveals an anthropologist's moral conservatism by insisting that the 'family is the factory of human sexuality'. But in the *Tetsuo* films, where the heterosexual family unit has been fractured, the factory, to punningly usurp his metaphor, now becomes the family of sexuality, as new specimens are spawned by the 'living', self-governing technologies of *Tetsuo*, or by an uneasy alloy of technological umbilici and human will in *Tetsuo 2*. The sequel's re-centring of the nuclear family also draws attention away from the sadistic male-on-male aggressions at play not only in the second half of *Tetsuo*, but throughout the masculine cyberpunk genre. In *The Terminator* (James Cameron, 1984), the godlike perfection of Schwarzenegger's body is mirrored in the futuristically unattainable perfection of the machine that hums beneath his cyborg skin. His musculature, however, is decorative rather than functional, for Schwarzeneggar's heroic action muscles are trumped by his cyborg's handheld, alloplastic utilisation of mechanical weapons (guns, cars and trucks) which redirect the sexuality suggested by his physique in more socially acceptable, less eroticised ways as he perpetrates meaty sadisms against lesser bodies. But in the *Tetsuo* films, pipeline penetrations into human flesh turn it metal, and soon we can no longer distinguish between flesh-against-flesh violence and metal-against-flesh violence, between organic interior and iron exterior – unlike the fiery climax of *Terminator*, which reassures the audience that beneath fantastic organic perfection lies a sterile metallic skeleton. But despite its subversive sexualisation of the inorganic, *Tetsuo 2*'s climactic reintroduction of the nuclear family may seem, if not an optimistic assertion of the hero's ego, an oddly conservative gesture.

Though less enigmatic than *Tetsuo* narratively, *Tetsuo 2*'s insistence on humanising its hero actually makes it more difficult to assess, as it problematically places the abstractions of the first film within a framework that begs for a more conventional analysis. Indeed, the (psycho)analytic revelations undergone by *Tetsuo 2*'s salaryman are too familiar – the young hero driven mad after witnessing parental coitus is a cliché of countless B-grade horror films. However, the sequel's new emphasis on the notion of parentage refocuses our attention on the notion of 'origins' in Tsukamoto's evolutionary plan. The *Tetsuo* films are, in a sense, reversing Darwin – instead of natural selection weeding out the unfit, the iron-men's future-shocked alloplasticity *weeds in* all of humanity and its hand-made creations. But what force is actually undertaking this (un)natural selection? It seems clear that both *Tetsuo*'s techno-fetishist and salaryman have little control over their metamorphoses (even if the fetishist voluntarily introduces metal into his body, he cannot anticipate the aberrant consequences), but we are unsure to what degree *Tetsuo 2*'s salaryman wilfully controls his transformation, and to what degree he is being controlled by it.

In *Tetsuo*, the salaryman apparently has minimal voluntary control of his prosthetic evolution: his transformations occur *automatically* and lacking wilful reason he can only rage in destructive anarchy. In *Tetsuo 2*, however, the hero's cybernetic transformations occur at strategic moments – when his wife is kidnapped for example – and are thus existential assertions of the will. Nevertheless, even as he is wilful, *Tetsuo 2*'s salaryman behaves irrationally (he continually endangers his wife's well-being).

Despite Tsukamoto's overenthusiastic suggestions of the iron-man's godliness, even at his very best, *Tetsuo 2*'s iron imperialist is no *Übermensch*. He remains self-centred, barely mastering his ego, let alone superego, and activates his imperialistic will mainly to redirect corrupting social forces in his favour. Even if he subversively encourages those technological forces to bloat to critical mass, he remains in their thrall, himself becoming a new false idol that, for all its scathing caricature of materialism and alloplastic, capitalistic consumption, fails to raze old idols or offer a viable alternative way of being. Tsukamoto is clearly not interested (even on an ironic level) in resurrecting the blissfully ignorant noble savage; it is too late to return to naïve autoplasticity, and the Humanist dichotomy of soulless science and soulful humanity has been forever erased by technologies that have themselves become alloplastic mutations, an intrinsic part of nature, not opposed to it. Of course, like all surrealists, Tsukamoto does not want to tell us how to live; the mind-bending artistic experience should itself be the catalyst to change, with Tsukamoto himself assuming the role of godlike father-creator. Still, we are trapped within a critique of techno-fetishism that is itself techno-fetishistic, as if the only way we alloplastic decadents can escape our alienation is to drive ourselves further into it. But if technology is the ultimate drive, and cinema the most ubiquitous of technologies, the *Tetsuo* films leave open the question as to whether cinema is itself an alloplastic Master techno-fetishist forcing its audience of salarymen to absorb the bulk content of its post-industrial, prosthetic image-making – or an evolutionary medium that somehow liberates an audience's wills from a future shock that paradoxically returns, again and again, to the solace of fetishising its egoistic despair.

Andrew Grossman

REFERENCES

Haraway, D. (1991) *Simians, Cyborgs and Women: The Reinvention of Nature.* New York: Routledge.
La Barre, W. (1954) *The Human Animal.* Chicago: University of Chicago Press.
Toffler, A. (1970) *Future Shock.* Pan.

SEOPYEONJE SOPYONJE

15

IM KWON-TAEK, KOREA, 1993

Conventionally, cinema has been defined by two main categories, entertainment and art, each of which are assumed to constitute the two opposite poles of cinema's spectrum. The dichotomy, however, works well only in the modern Western context. Many non-Western films, which are invariably embedded in the social, defy this simplistic categorisation. Im Kwon-taek's masterpiece *Seopyeonje* (*Sopyonje*, 1993) is such a film. The film might be classified as an art film, since it was made with a small budget, no stars, an episodic and convoluted narrative, no reliance on generic formulae, and is imbued with the all-important role of the filmmaker's personal vision. Yet the film also possesses traits of commercial mainstream cinema. It was made in Chungmuro, the South Korean equivalent of Hollywood, and enjoyed record-breaking commercial success.

Sopyonje marks a peak of Im's prolific work. Having made more than one hundred films since 1962, he is a towering, magistrate presence in Korean cinema. Born in 1936, Im had an ill-fated childhood. Persecuted for the Leftist elements in his family background, he had no opportunity to experience a decent education. He worked as a general hand in the impoverished film studios in the late 1950s and soon began his directing career as a commercially-oriented filmmaker. He eventually turned to 'serious' films in the late 1970s. Thereafter, traditional culture has been one of the two major themes which Im has tackled time and again – the other being ideological conflicts between the right and the left. In an interview, Im expressed a concern about the disappearance of traditional culture:

> My personal desire has been to capture elements of our traditional culture in my work … The fear is, of course, that those aspects of Korean culture that are not favoured by the terms of this new international and more aggressive culture may be absorbed and, in the end, disappear.

Im has dealt with Korea's traditional art and customs in a number of films ranging from *Chokpo* (*The Genealogy*, 1978) to *Chihwaseon* (2002). But it was with *Sopyonje* that he confronted traditional culture from a critical standpoint and succeeded in translating its meanings for contemporary audiences. Even Im's later films with traditional themes, such as *Chunhyang* (2000) and *Chihwaseon*, fall short of evoking the profound social implications that *Sopyonje* brings into life.

Sopyonje is acknowledged as a landmark, not only in Korea's cinema history but also within its cultural history. Above all, the film was an unprecedented success both in terms of box-office and critical reception. Released in April 1993, *Sopyonje* stirred the entire nation, becoming the biggest box-office hit in the nation's cinema-going history. Furthermore, domestic critics were in unison in applauding its artistic and commercial achievements. Its phenomenal success reinvigorated the film industry and *Sopyonje* sparked popular interest in domestic cinema, which the majority of Koreans have shied from, favouring instead the cinema of Hollywood and Hong Kong. Many even saw in the film a new hope for Korean cinema, which was, at the time of the release, at its lowest ebb, in terms of popularity, since the 1960s. The total attendance for domestic films in 1993 was a meagre 7,690,000 – 15.9 per cent of the total audience attendance for the year. The film even spawned unprecedented industrial practices: the first original soundtrack album and the first film book dedicated to a single film in Korean cinema. The former was also a commercial hit and the latter, *Sopyonje Movie Book*, edited by the director himself, documented these successes.

Additionally, *Sopyonje* revived public attention in the film's subject matter, *pansori*, the almost forgotten, traditional Korean art of dramatic singing, and created a sudden boom in the desire to learn the art. Its unparalleled popularity ignited a debate on retro-mode, which was in vogue in early 1990s Korea. Mass media covered the so-called 'Sopyonje syndrome' and offered various analyses of it. Ultimately one of the short serial stories from which the film was adapted was anthologised in a Korean textbook. *Sopyonje* was also – until the recent boom in the popularity of South Korean cinema – arguably the most internationally recognised of all Korean films; garnering a number of international film festival prizes and becoming the first Korean film ever to be included in the permanent collection of the Museum of Modern Art in New York. It has been widely seen internationally through numerous festival screenings and regarded as a quintessential film in identifying Korean identity. The film's importance is demonstrated in the only English book dedicated to Im's work, *Im Kwon-Taek: The Making of a Korean National Cinema* (2002), which dedicates three of the book's nine chapters to the film.

Sopyonje traces the vicissitude of an itinerant Korean folk-artist family from the early 1940s to the late 1960s. The storyline itself is perfectly simple: A man in his thirties, named

Dong-ho (Kim Kyu-chol), wanders the countryside, ostensibly to purchase herbal products, but actually in search of Song-hwa (Oh Jeong-hae), the stepsister with whom he grew up. It is revealed through multiple flashbacks that theirs was a bitter childhood – both were orphans adopted by and apprenticed to a *pansori* artist Yu-bong (Kim Myung-gon), who pressured them to sacrifice everything for their art. Dong-ho rebelled and ran away; Song-hwa stayed, lost her sight at the hands of Yu-bong, ultimately outliving him.

At first glance, *Sopyonje* is an artists' film, apparently dealing with a *pansori* family and as the title – meaning the 'Western school of *pansori* singing' – suggests, *pansori* plays a crucial role in the film. Director Im recalled that although he had wanted to visualise *pansori* within his medium for decades, it had not been possible until he found his leading actress, Oh Jeong-hae, who was an excellent *pansori* singer in her own right. The *pansori* singing dramatising ancient moral tales in impassioned, keening and guttural tones offer the main appeal – especially for young Koreans and foreigners who are unfamiliar with the traditional art. *Pansori* lyrics are also adroitly interwoven into the narrative to convey the singer's situations and feelings and to make a smooth transition from one scene to the next.

In some respects the father, Yu-bong, and his stepdaughter, Song-hwa, resemble the modern ideal of artist: they are indifferent to and ignorant of mundane life, devoting themselves to the perfection of their art. Unlike most artist films, however, the film does not tell of artist's achievements; rather it concerns their failure. Yu-bong and Song-hwa never receive public recognition; the stepson Dong-ho resigns his training and runs away. More importantly, their failure as artists does not stem from their lack of talent and passion but from their art's deteriorating social status. As the film masterfully demonstrates, both Yu-bong and the mature Song-hwa are legitimate *pansori* artists in their own right. Yu-bong never gives up an ardent passion for *pansori* throughout his life. When he encounters his old friends who are on *pansori* tour, he scolds them, remarking of their performance, 'Do you think that is *pansori*? Mind your singing first.' Yu-bong is so obsessed with *pansori* that despite his extreme destitution, he offers money to learn *pansori* from his friend, an opium addict. Likewise Song-hwa strives hard to reach the state of master. The climactic reunion scene shows that she has indeed mastered her art – her singing having been recorded by Ahn Kuk-seon, a *pansori* master christened as a human national treasure.

Despite their hard work and talent, Yu-bong and Song-hwa are destined to fail. They resist their art's doomed downfall with all their might to no avail, precisely because of *pansori*'s overall decline in popular reception – although, initially, their failure appears to be attributable to Yu-bong's own failings. Yu-bong, once the best trainee of a master-teacher, was banished by the master because of his affairs with the master's concubine. He squanders the opportunity to perfect *pansori* and perform on prestigious stages. As the narrative unfolds, it becomes obvious that *pansori* is no longer favoured in the rapidly changing society and that *pansori* in general is in decline. The marginalisation of the art is vividly presented by the marked contrast between an early sequence depicting Yu-bong's performance in a squire's birthday party and subsequent performance sequences by Song-hwa and Yu-bong. In the former, Yu-bong confidently and masterfully displays the artistry of *pansori*, receiving warm responses from audiences. But, years later, it is no longer valued. The performance sequence in the market epitomises *pansori*'s destiny: Song-hwa and Yu-bong sing in front of a very small audience of children, whose attention soon drifts to a cheerful brass band advertising a Westernised show. Thus the trajectories Yu-bong's family has taken go beyond the world of art and *pansori* comes to have social implications beyond the personal. In this way, what is at stake is the wider context in which the family is situated, rather than their personal successes and struggles.

The way in which *Sopyonje* involves the social dimension is both subtle and nostalgic. The film evokes past memories through Dong-ho, a character who traverses East and West, the pre-modern and the modern. Significantly, the film opens with Dong-ho visiting a dilapidated tavern on a hill. A woman in traditional clothes greets him; he is dressed in Western clothing. Dong-ho, hired by a herbal medicine firm, is a visitor from Seoul, an emblem of the urban, modern and secular world. Through the conversation between Dong-ho and the tavern owner, we learn that Dong-ho is searching for his family. This opening scene encapsulates the film's preoccupations: the encounter or confrontation between East and West, the pre-modern and the modern, past and present. Several long flashbacks ensue, revealing Dong-ho's family's past. We learn that he was trained as a *pansori* drummer and his stepsister, Song-hwa, as a singer, by their stern stepfather Yu-bong and that he ran away both because of Yu-bong's maltreatment and the family's destitution – additionally some may interpret sexual rivalry between Dong-ho and Yu-bong over Song-hwa into these scenes.

Dong-ho traces the vestiges of the family he deserted long ago to find Song-hwa. The woman at the tavern and others he meets during his search are only able to give scant recollections about the lost family. Typically their recollections begin with 'A long time ago...' suggesting that the object of his search is now gone and mostly forgotten. In this sense, it can be argued that the family he looks for no longer exists in this world as flesh and blood, but only in the form of past memories. Dong-ho discovers lost memories and guides the audience to the forgotten past, not merely of *pansori* artists but of the surroundings and processes into which they are thrown. His journey is nothing other than a return to the past through revived memories.

The past that *Sopyonje* portrays is social and historical rather than personal. Thus the reconstruction of the past through Dong-ho re-evokes bitter memories to Korean audiences. When seen in the historical context of extensive modernisation that the Korean people underwent, *Sopyonje* ceases to be a mere artist film. It narrates the discord with social reality changing in the irrevocable process of modernisation. Thereby, the film retells the modern history of Korea at its deepest level. Within this tumultuous period of contemporary Korea, the film implicitly addresses the memories of modern history – those cataclysmic, often disastrous changes such as the Japanese colonisation (1910–45), the Korean War (1950–53) and the intense industrialisation under military dictatorship (1961–79.)

In *Sopyonje*, traditional Korean values represented by *pansori* are subject to marginalisation in the historical process of modernisation and Westernisation. However, the process of modernisation is largely invisible in the film. Instead, through the description of the artists' hapless resistance to the decline of *pansori*, the film subtly suggests modernisation's destructive effects on the art. Here *pansori* serves as a thread to past memories, representing the marginalisation of traditional culture by the encroachment of modern Western culture. In fact, Yu-bong's family loses its means of living when confronted by Western culture: having made their living by performing to promote a peddler's products on the street, Yu-bong's family is eventually fired by the peddler. The employer, doubtful of *pansori*'s attraction, decides instead to hire a violinist who may provide an exotic, attractive cultural experience for the Korean audience. When Dong-ho shouts to his stepsister, 'Now we can't make our living only by *pansori* in this world!' he succinctly expresses the marginalisation of *pansori*.

Sopyonje as a text, and Korean audiences' unexpected enthusiastic response to it, cannot be fully understood without understanding its wider context. The emotional resonance the film evoked stemmed from the fact that the film forced Korean audiences to recall their own past through the characters' experiences. Thanks to shared memories of the painful processes of modernisation, the marginalisation of *pansori* represented to them the whole process of the marginalisation of the Korean/traditional/spiritual values by modernisation. There is an underlying sense for Korean audiences that the defeat represented by Yu-bong and Song-hwa is actually a defeat of 'us'. The audience possibly realises that they have paid a price for favouring the Western/material civilisation. Like the *pansori* artists, 'we' have been marginalised and victimised by Western influences, being alienated from 'our' traditional culture. 'Our' way of life and 'our' value systems have been eroded, eventually replaced by Western customs and values which modernisation necessarily introduces. Through the very process of modernisation we, Koreans, have become quasi-Westerners, 'inferior' Westerners, feeling 'ourselves' as 'the other'. Cultural critic Choi Chungmoo calls this process the 'colonisation of consciousness' of the postcolonial subject by Western discourse. As an audience community, 'we' could not help sympathising with the characters that desperately try to escape from the overarching power of modernisation. In short, Yu-bong and Song-hwa become 'our' father and sister, while *pansori* is not just 'our' art but also the metaphor for 'our' lost past.

The most remarkable aspect of *Sopyonje* is that emotional resonance (including sympathy and identification in the film) is induced not by cinematic devices such as point-of-view shot, but by historical collectivity which the filmmaker and the spectator share. The sympathy with Yu-bong and Song-hwa differs from secondary cinematic identification, a notion used by the renowned film theorist Christian Metz to designate spectators' identification with characters. The spectator cannot identify with Yu-bong or Song-hwa on the individual level, because despite their embodiment of the collective past experience, they are somehow beyond our worldly existence. What the spectator in fact identifies him or herself with are not characters but the particular socio-historical situations in which characters have existed. By recalling the situations he or she previously experienced or internalised as his/her own memory, the spectator feels as if he/she were in the same situation of the characters. For many Korean viewers, figuratively speaking, Dong-ho's search for his sister occurs on *their* behalf. Through his journey, they eventually come to recognise that it is they who in fact deserted Song-hwa and made her blind, and it is they who long for reunion with the forgotten sister. Thus this search might be the redemption of the Korea's forgotten memory. The *Sopyonje* phenomenon can be interpreted as a result of the audience's reconciliation with their past, which most Koreans were ruthlessly forced to forget and, furthermore, to negate in the rush to development. By offering memories of the past, *Sopyonje* reminds Korean audiences of the bitterness of the past and the splendour of traditional culture.

In this way, *Sopyonje* was concerned with modernisation as the constitutive social memory of Korea. It primarily constructs the past as a counter-memory by presenting the modernisation process as marginalisation of national culture, which is seldom told in the official history of Korea. Instead the official history has been enthusiastic to glorify the Korean economy's achievements by modernisation. Given that 'social memory thrives on remaking the residue of past decades into material with contemporary resonance', *Sopyonje* would be read appropriately in relation to the social memory it embodies.

Sopyonje's success in recalling the past for Korean audiences and in allowing them to face it was due not only to its compelling narrative but also its characterisation and stylisation. The configuration of three main characters constitutes a microcosm of a society in transition. Although the three are all the same in that they are attached to a disappearing traditional art and exist on the fringe of a radically modernising society, they respond differently to the changing reality. Yu-bong is a stubborn traditionalist who sticks to pre-modernity, symbolised by his traditional art. Yu-bong adamantly disavows his art's decline, insisting that *pansori* must prevail in the future over Japanese *enka* and Western popular songs – he refuses to accept the new reality modernisation brings about, because it is harmful to his art. He is a man of dignity but unwilling to change. This character is also ultimately responsible for the tragic act of blinding Song-hwa.

In opposition to the character of Yu-bong is Dong-ho, who is exceptional in that among three main characters, he alone reaches a compromise with contemporary life. Dong-ho chooses to come out of Yu-bong's world of traditional art to the mundane, modern world, not because he sees an illusion of social utopia in modernity but because pre-modernity is incapable of providing basic conditions of survival and comfort. Tired of poverty and maltreatment, he runs away from his stepfather. This same exodus was seen to occur *en masse* in Korea from the 1950s to the 1970s. In this sense Dong-ho is not just a rebellious son, but can be seen as the alter ego of *any* common Korean. Perhaps after years of striving, Dong-ho manages to successfully settle in a city, where he finds a job and raises his own family. Only then can he afford to look back upon the past. He starts a journey in search of his sister Song-hwa. His journey is also toward *pansori*, an art he used to play, and the past that he had deserted.

Meanwhile, Song-hwa is situated in a somewhat unrealistic transcendence. If Yu-bong resents the changing reality, she is totally indifferent to the outside world. Song-hwa's world is entirely centred around *pansori*. When her brother grumbles about their ill fate as itinerant singers, she retorts, 'I like singing. When I am singing I forget every suffering.' Naturally, she does not follow Dong-ho's path; Song-hwa literally and symbolically closes her eyes to reality – Yu-bong blinds her by tricking her into taking a fatal herb, either in order to keep her beside him or possibly to provide her with *han* (deep grief) in order to perfect her *pansori*. Song-hwa forgives Yu-bong's cruel act, accepts his art as hers wholeheartedly and eventually becomes the ultimate master of the art. Thus she transcends the mundane world, elevating herself to a state of sublimeness, a utopian quality which the audience likewise wish to attain both in contemporary life and, if possible, in a reassessed past. However, her transcendence is not a condition of pure bliss, since it is not the result of her desire alone but a state compelled by the loss of sight. Ironically, Yu-bong, the proponent of tradition, acts as the agent of blindness in a desperate reaction to the destructive effects of sweeping social change. The transcendence is the culmination for art, but in reality it means nothing more than a defeat.

It should be noted that Song-hwa's transcendence is deeply nostalgic as it is achieved through *pansori*, the signifier of the pre-modern past and the forgotten traditional culture. This quality is immensely desirable but at the same time is absent in reality. This offers a very reasonable answer to the questionable ending in which Dong-ho leaves his stepsister after the emotionally-charged reunion. If Song-hwa is a nostalgic image of the past and seeing Song-hwa construes seeing the idealised side of that past, Song-hwa's transcendence could be kept intact only by remaining in the past. If she comes out, led by Dong-ho's hands, to the present, modern world in which pre-modern and non-Western values are overridden by materialist logic of capitalism, how is it possible for her to maintain her transcendence? There is no room in reality for nostalgic imagery.

As previously seen in *Mandala* (1981) and *Chukje* (*Festival*, 1996), in *Sopyonje* Im Kwon-taek weaved episodes into a coherent narrative with incredible economy, going back and forth within four flashback sequences that coherently portrayed the family's past over several decades. Cinematic techniques were kept to a minimum. For instance, close-ups (on faces) and point-of-view shots, both of which are devices used for character development through psychological realism, were scarcely used. Instead, protracted static long-takes and slow-moving panning-shots were employed. This technical minimalism perfectly matched with the context or ambience rather than specific characters. With the help of cinematographer Jeong Il-seong, one of his long-time collaborators, the director visualised the artists' discord with the modernising reality through the desolateness of cinematic space. There are no modernised urban places in the film. Every place that the protagonists inhabit is peripheral and, sometimes, unattended. Particularly, the recurrent scenes of the aimless travelling of Yu-bong's family, carrying only a few small bags and a drum, their only means of living as well as their art, bring to mind the devastating diaspora which so many Koreans experienced in the process of Japanese colonisation, the Korean War and ruthless industrialisation. This is the film's characteristic way of relating its cinematic space to the social memories of modernisation.

Im controlled temporal space as consummately as he did physical space. After being fired by the medicine peddler, the family embarks on another journey without destination. They sing a famous folk song, 'Jindo Arirang', together in order to raise their spirits. The camera captures without any movement their steady approach, in which they sing at first timidly and later with recharged enthusiasm. This take, 5 minutes and 30 seconds in duration, vividly accentuates the last gasp of the family and *pansori*, both of which were soon to face disintegration. In contrast, a number of scenes featuring Yu-bong and two children – and later, with only Song-hwa – compress time. The best example is the scene in which Yu-bong sings a folk song leading the blind Song-hwa that shows, in a sequence that combines four scenes but is edited to resemble a single take, four seasons passing, which perfectly matches the lyrics of the song that refers to each season while lamenting the singer's aging and decrepitude.

Sopyonje has become an essential text in analysing the tensions and conflicts between the declining, pre-modern tradition and rapidly advancing, modern, Western culture. It engaged with the Korean people's contemporary collective experience, represented by the radical transformations made by modernisation. Considering this, it seems quite natural that *Sopyonje* cannot be pinned down using conventional categories of art and entertainment. Contrary to a great many Hollywood films, particularly Hollywood blockbusters, which carefully efface the historical social dimension in the text and openly encourage audiences to forget it, *Sopyonje* sets a model of non-Hollywood popular cinema by bringing up and consoling the nation's collective memories with incredible emotional resonance.

Han Ju Kwak

REFERENCE

Im, K. T. (1993) *Sopyonje yonghwa iyagi* [*Sopyonje Movie Book*]. Seoul: Hanul.

PERFECT BLUE

SATOSHI KON, JAPAN, 1997

Billing itself as the world's first animated feature-length psycho-suspense thriller, it is fair to say that prior to its first international screening at Montreal's Fantasia Film Festival in 1997 there had been little to pave the way for the phenomenal *Perfect Blue*. Taut, visceral and strikingly cinematic, Satoshi Kon's adaptation of Yoshikazu Takeuchi's pulp novel of the same name (his debut work, published in 1991) sent shock waves that reached out far beyond the circles of *anime* fans to the broader film community. It earned theatrical releases across Europe and the US, proving to legions of doubting cynics that by neatly side-stepping the restrictions set in place by adhering to more traditional means of depicting reality, the 'cartoon' format is more than capable of delivering challenging, thought-provoking works for adult audiences.

The bloody tale of a former all-singing, all-dancing teen idol named Mima Kirigoe, caught within the machinations of the media machine and hounded by a psychotic stalker, toys with such concepts as the fragmentation of the self – hammered home in the film's oft-repeated line 'Who are you?' – and the twisted mutual dependency that exists between star and fan-obsessive. It does so within a disorienting and disarmingly sophisticated narrative that rattles along at an impressive pace throughout its 81-minute running time.

At the film's opening, we see Mima leaving the all-girl pop group, Cham, to pursue a career in acting. 'The idol image is suffocating me', she later tells her mother over the phone. But there are hints that the decision may not have been entirely her own. 'Well, pop idols just don't make money these days', a fan muses at Mima's farewell concert, and with Cham still striving to make an impact on the singles chart, it makes more sense for the talent agency, run by the mercenary Tadokoro, not to put all its eggs in one basket. Not everyone is happy with the decision it would seem, as that evening Mima receives an anonymous fax with the word 'traitor' scrawled over it.

Meanwhile, her initial one-line appearance in the psychological TV-drama 'Double Bind' seems unpromising. But then the show's producer, Tejima, and scriptwriter, Shibuya, hit upon an idea to boost ratings by introducing a trite *Silence of the Lambs*-styled murder plot. In order to elevate her on-screen profile, Mima is soon coerced by both the show's producers and her talent agency to move further away from her original squeaky-clean image. She reluctantly agrees to play a graphic rape scene set in a strip club.

As Cham continue without her, Mima's attempts at maintaining her media profile (encouraged by Tadokoro) by partaking in a steamy nude photo session for photographer Murano turns off her former fans in droves. Meanwhile someone is charting her inner thoughts in diary form on the 'Mima's Room' internet fan site with obsessive attention to detail. Haunted by the skulking presence of former fan, Me-Mania, and with no one but her chaperone at the talent agency Rumi (herself a former pop idol) to turn to, Mima finds herself caught in the middle of a harrowing emotional tug-of-war between duty to her fans and the demands of her talent agency.

As her image becomes increasingly manipulated by those guiding her career, Mima begins to be tormented by the imaginary manifestation of her former pop persona, ('You're tarnished … filthy!'); a hallucinatory spirit dressed up in full pink-frilled, mini-skirted Cham regalia. The divisions between her personal, public and imaginary identity become increasingly confused as events in 'Double Bind' begin to echo that of her waking life. As various characters involved in the production are violently murdered, Mima finds herself plunged into a world in which the delineation between fantasy and reality becomes blurred to the point of incoherence.

With the unforgettable image that forms the centrepiece of its publicity material – that of our blood-spattered, wide-eyed heroine driving home a sharpened implement into an unseen victim against the pixelated backdrop of her own face – it perhaps goes without saying that Kon's idiosyncratic debut is hardly the stuff Disney's dreams are made of; but then again, the same could be said for a great deal of Japanese animation. Whether intended for television, cinema or the video market, with the percentage it comprises out of the entire national cinematic output ranking the highest in the world, the diversity of Japanese animation in terms of both subject matter and target audience stretches far beyond that of other nations, running the entire gamut between *Pokemon* to the bizarre phenomenon of erotic *anime* and the vicariously hyped '*anime* nasties' such as *Urotsukidoji* (*Legend of the Overfiend*, 1989), which created more waves on their widespread video releases abroad than they ever did in Japan.

The far more idiosyncratic animated offerings that have appeared overseas to some extent give a slightly skewed perception as to the true nature of the domestic marketplace, and it is worth stating that a good proportion of Japanese animation is actually pretty banal, both in terms of content and execution, aimed squarely at the teen or pre-teen market and finding its home either on late-night television or the OAV (Original Animation Video) series for the sell-through market. Nevertheless, at its best, from mainstream family favourites such as the work of Ghibli Studios' Hayao Miyazaki and Isao Takahata – such as *Tonari no Totoro* (*My Neighbour Totoro*, 1988), *Hotaru No Haka* (*Grave of the Fireflies*, 1988) and *Sen To Chihiro To Kamikakushi* (*Spirited Away*, 2001) – through to meditative and intelligent sci-fi parables in the vein of Mamoru Oshii's *Kokaku Kidotai* (*Ghost in the Shell*, 1995), it can be safely said that the boundaries marked out by animation cover a broader territory than elsewhere.

Despite examples of the more family-oriented of these playing on television in dubbed versions in a number of different territories (Osamu Tezuka's series *Tetsuwan Atomu* (*Astro Boy*) was the first *anime* to be broadcast abroad when it began showing on US television in 1963), *Akira* (Katsuhiro Otomo, 1988) is widely credited as the first full-length animated feature to play widely in cinemas outside of Japan; opening up the eyes of foreign audiences, long accustomed to thinking that cartoons were exclusively the domain of children, to the joys of what is sometimes referred to as 'Japanimation'. A dazzling tale of a young teenager with psychic powers run amok in a Tokyo of the future who unearths a government-sponsored terrorist conspiracy, *Akira* almost single-handedly set in motion the *otaku* craze in the West in the early 1990s. Otomo's name rapidly became synonymous with Japanese animation abroad – though ironically his work in the field has actually proven sparse and rather atypical, possibly because his background lies not in animation, but as a *manga* comic-book artist.

Manga's role in Japanese pop culture is undeniably a crucial one. In 1984, comics accounted for 27 per cent of Japan's publishing output, with a mind-staggering 1.38 billion volumes produced (though this figure appears to have decreased in recent years). Its influence on Japanese cinema has therefore been considerable, perhaps unsurprisingly so given that *Astro Boy* creator Osamu Tezuka, often cited as the founding father of the modern *manga* form, himself found his inspiration not in the existing comic publications of the time, in which the action was framed in a series of tableaux drawn from the perspective of an audience as if looking at the stage, but in the French and German films he saw as a child and the animated works of Walt Disney and Max Fleischer. In 1947, at the age of twenty, he published his first work, the groundbreaking 200-page *Shintakarajima* (*New Treasure Island*), setting in motion a multi-million yen industry in the process. As Frederick Schodt points out in *Manga! Manga! The World of Japanese Comics*, 'It's creative page layout, clever use of sound effects and lavish spread of frames to depict a single action made reading *Shintakarajima* almost like watching a movie.' Understandably therefore, the leap from the printed page to the moving image was not such a large one for Tezuka, setting up his own production house, Mushi Productions, in 1962 to develop a healthy sideline in animation for both television and cinema.

Like Tezuka and Otomo, *Perfect Blue* director Kon also started out in *manga*. As he points out in his interview with Tom Mes of *Midnight Eye*: 'When you make *manga* you need the talent to create a story and to direct, in the visual sense', all essential skills of the film director. As noted in *Manga Max*: 'The biggest difference is time. The speed of reading comics depends on the reader. You can read 200 pages in 30 minutes, 15 minutes, or you can even take two hours to finish it. In films, though, especially cinema, the audience sit down in the dark, and the creator can tell the story with his own rhythm. You can control time for the audience in films.'

Kon's relationship with Otomo goes far further than their shared background as comic artists. Having began his career in animation as background designer on Hiroyuki Kitakubo's *Rojin Z* (1991), which Otomo scripted, and Masaaki Osumi's *Run Melos*, a 1992 television animation adapted from a 1940 short story by one of Japan's most notable literary figures, Osamu Dazai, Kon's next major assignment came with Otomo's *Warudo Apaatoment Hora* (*World Apartment Horror*, 1991). An energetic live-action feature concerning the plight of a building full of Asian immigrants living in Tokyo harassed by an ineffectual *yakuza* eager to evict them (played by Hiroyuki Tanaka, who would later move on to feature directing himself under the pseudonym Sabu, with the cult favourites *Dangan Ranna* (*Dangan Runner*, 1996) and *Posutoman Burusu* (*Postman Blues*, 1997), Kon was responsible for drawing the *manga* adaptation.

But Kon's most remarkable work for the *Akira* director came with the script for *Magnetic Rose*, the first segment of the 1995 animated portmanteau feature, *Kanojo No Omoide* (*Memories*). Produced by Otomo, who also directed the film's third and final story, the intriguing and technically innovative 15-minute *Cannon Fodder*, set in a dystopian no-mans-land of the future where a young boy dreams of taking his father's role as one of the legions of operators of the huge cannons that encase the city walls firing shells off at a distant, unnamed foe, *Memories* has been described as one of the best anime of the 1990s.

Kon's screenplay for the *Magnetic Rose* segment, directed by Koji Morimoto, in many ways foreshadows the approach utilised in *Perfect Blue*, playing with the same themes of memory, fantasy and phantasm (not to mention female performers) and prompting the eternal question, 'What is reality?' A ragtag team of deep-space salvage operators stray into the 'Sargasso Zone' and are drawn towards a huge rose-shaped hunk of matter floating through the ether. Entering, they find themselves in a baroque opera house dominated by a huge chandelier and flanked by marble pillars. This setting turns out to be the floating tomb of a long-dead female opera singer named Eva, whose presence soon manifests itself by means of an array of projections and holographic images. The unwanted visitors soon find themselves overwhelmed by the singer's memories and active participants in a drama where the ghosts of Eva's past, including her deceased lover, act out their roles within this illusionary stage.

For publicity reasons, Otomo received a prominent billing on Kon's feature debut, under the catchall credit of 'Project Advisor'. In fact, Otomo played little part in the production of *Perfect Blue*; its genesis as a film was instigated by the author of the original novel, Takeuchi, who drafted a script that was originally intended for production as a live-action straight-to-video release. According to Kon, a number of directors were approached, including Shimako Sato, the female director of the highly regarded 1995 high-school horror, *Eko Eko Azaraku* (*Wizard of Darkness*), before it was finally settled that the film be made as animation. Kon himself confesses to being less than impressed with Takeuchi's script, which was substantially rewritten by screenwriter Murai Sadayuki with the director's (uncredited) input.

Now, given that the most remarkable aspects of the film – the 'Double Bind' film-within-a-film sequences, the Mima's Room internet fan site, the innovative narrative structure and the string of bloody corpses that pop up at various points in the proceedings – were all conceptions of the scriptwriter and director, it would appear that, beyond the bare bones of its premise, in its animated incarnation *Perfect Blue* bears scant similarity to its source material. The extent of Kon's departure becomes even clearer when viewed alongside a live-action adaptation of Takeuchi's novel filmed in 2002.

Perfect Blue: Yume Nara Samete was directed by Toshiki Sato, one of the four directors lumped together by Japanese critics under the collective banner of the 'Four Devils' (*Shitenno*) of the *pinku* – 'pink film' – a term used in Japan to denote the genre of softcore sex films which proliferated rapidly from the 1960s. Sato resolutely hammered away throughout the 1990s against the prevailing climate of straight-to-video sleaze (AVs, or Adult Videos) with a drove of large-screen erotic features which have been widely praised for attempting to deliver a degree of artistry and social comment amongst the acres of bare flesh. The other three *Shitenno* directors are Hisayasu Sato, Kazuhiro Sano and Takahisa Zeze.

Sato's film, one of several recent attempts by the director to branch out from erotica to mainstream film-making, sports the odd atmospheric shot, but as a whole comes across as a catalogue of wasted opportunities compounded by a noticeably low budget, insipid performances and a script that seems crude and prosaically linear when laid alongside the devious trickery of Murai's. In fact, were it not for Takeuchi's name attached to both versions, the films are sufficiently different in both content and style to make a comparison almost redundant.

The more recent release does, however, highlight the liberties Kon and Murai took with the original story, most notably with the character of Uchida (or Me-Mania). Kon admits in a number of interviews to having considerably played down the role of the stalker, stripping his role from the original script to that of a grotesque and mostly silent apparition who sinisterly loiters in the shadows with a knowingly sly smirk on his pockmarked face. In fact, Kon's amendments went a good deal further: 'We couldn't expect the audience to get interested in a character who merely "acted" suspiciously. So we actually changed him into a genuine murderer.'

No gruesome murders occur in Sato's rendition, which sees Uchida, played by Nao Omori (seen to more dynamic effect in Takashi Miike's *Ichi the Killer* (*Koroshiya 1*, 2001), as the morose convenience store clerk whose personal history with his idol (played by Ayaka Maeda, and in this instance named Ai rather than Mima) stretches back to her childhood, and who seems to spend the majority of his time on-screen gazing wistfully, in a shameless piece of product placement, at her image on a poster advertising Calpis soft drinks. With the two coming into contact fairly early on in the proceedings, the story is as much about Uchida as it is about Ai/Mima, with the slow mental collapse of both characters running parallel to one another.

If Takeuchi's book is indeed about this relationship between idol and fan and the warped artificial expectations and desires that exists between them, then on the basis of Sato's adaptation, it is a relationship that existed more successfully on the printed page where it is possible to detail such internal confusion more explicitly than on the screen. Sato singularly fails to achieve any insight necessary to draw the viewer into the drama as the two characters skirt around each maintaining a safe distance in a series of lengthy, wide-angle shots. The weakness is compounded by the fact that Ai's idol status is rather taken as read, evoked merely by means of modelling assignments, lengthy sessions in the recording studio (crooning the theme song of the film's title in its entirety no less than three times), or being ferried around in the isolated bubble of her manager's Volvo. There is little impression of a broader world beyond the limiting vacuum of the two main characters' day-to-day existence.

We can probably attribute this latter problem to budget limitations as much as anything else, and actually one of the strengths behind the decision to make *Perfect Blue* as an animation is that conjuring up images of crowded auditoriums and television studios is obviously more readily realisable in this format than staging them 'live' on film. Kon's opening up of the scope of the drama by portraying, in some considerable detail, the milieu of the big-budget entertainment industry, populated by greying cynical record company execs, scriptwriters, television production managers and obsequious publicity agents, all making decisions about Mima's career path behind her back, thus lends the forces that contribute to her hallucinatory fantasies a far greater credibility.

It also serves to emphasise the artificially constructed image that both fan and idol have of one another, a media collage of record sales charts, newspaper interviews and glossy photo shoots, building a bond based upon a spurious intimacy whilst reinforcing the barriers of fame to ensure that Mima and Me-Mania never actually meet until the time is right. Compare this with *Yume Nara Samete*, where Uchida comes face to face with his fantasy in an early scene when she pops into his store to pick up a pint of milk. Kon meanwhile fleshes out Mima's context by punctuating his film with the idle banter of a group of her original fans from the early Cham days, first seen jostling in the crowd at the trio's farewell concert, who turn up sporadically to perform the function of a Greek Chorus as they pass comment on her subsequent acting career.

Meanwhile, on Mima's side, as the excessive turns in her career find her increasingly isolated from both her original audience and her two former Cham-mates, the only means of defining her own identity comes from either the duplicitous companionship of her studio mentors, or by way of the feedback provided from the cannily-named Mima's Room internet site, a place where even her private thoughts may not be her own. But who exactly is behind this site? Who is able to document her thoughts and actions with such unerring accuracy as to be able to recount the exact contents of her shopping basket and which foot she puts down on the platform first as she gets off the morning train? And when, after the initial appearance of her floating disembodied simulacrum, these accounts begin to present an alternate fiction from what the viewer has witnessed ('Did I really go shopping in Harajuku today?'), which side of the fence are we sitting on in terms of the observer and the observed, when we have clearly been led to identify with Mima? *Perfect Blue* plays with such concepts of subjectivity and spectatorship in such a devious and tricksy manner that many viewers have dismissed the film as confusing and needlessly complicated. However, what some have seen as a compromised ending may be considered on subsequent viewings as having been implied from early on, when one realises that many key scenes are not only seen from Mima's perspective, but those of the subsidiary characters. Even though in the majority of shots Mima is clearly the focus of the image, she is not necessarily always intended as the focus of audience identification.

Kon also tries to induce the same feeling of paranoid delusion in the viewer by a disorienting use of a mixture of narrative tenses. From the moment we are thrust into the heart of Cham's final concert, we are not entirely sure whether we are witnessing the present, a flashback, or a memory and if so, whose memory? Is it that of Mima herself on stage in the next shot, humming one of Cham's songs on the train back to her apartment; Rumi, nervously twitching behind the backstage curtain; or Uchida, stood in the audience, holding up his hand to the stage to frame Mima's sprightly image dancing like a marionette in the palm of his hand?

Throughout the film, Kon provides nothing in the way of traditional cinematic cues such as cross-fades or dissolves to link changes in time, location or perspective. Instead he uses a seamless editing style that transforms us from scene to scene as if Mima's story was nothing more than fragments of a half-remembered dream, occasionally revelling in his trickery in such scenes as when Mima's voicing of her internal confusion to an unseen off-screen confidante is immediately shown to be a sequence being filmed for 'Double Bind'.

This experimentation with the themes of voyeurism has led many viewers outside of Japan to read into *Perfect Blue* aspects which are not there, accusing Kon of using the film to critique the exploitative nature of Japan's idol system whilst ultimately falling back upon the very same tropes he purports to condemn. If *Yume Nara Samete* is anything to go by, no such element existed in Takeuchi's novel, and Kon himself waives aside any such intention, claiming little more than entertainment status for his work. Indeed, such criticism does great disservice to what Kon has achieved here in terms of *Perfect Blue*'s power as a piece of shock cinema.

In fact *Perfect Blue* is so effective and self-contained, it almost seems like a metaphysical treatise on the psycho-thriller format, a technical *tour de force* that, whilst not ringing true in any non-filmic sense of 'realism', is so completely robust in its internal logic as to deflect any alternative readings. The animated format merely heightens this artificiality in form, allowing the director's complete control of the flow of images to hypnotically beautiful effect. When seen in this light, Kon's film is situated entirely within the tradition pioneered by the Italian director Dario Argento, whose work in *giallo* cinema (an Italian genre of violent psychological thrillers, in which showy cinematic technique is kept firmly in the foreground over characterisation) is best typified by the brutal *Tenebrae* (1982), the story of an American novelist on a promotional tour in Rome hounded by a murderously fanatical Catholic crusader against the moral 'corruption' manifested in his work.

Argento's influence on the thriller genre may have been overlooked elsewhere, but in Japan it cannot be understated. A long-running horror *manga* in the 1980s was named *Suspiria*, after Argento's 1977 classic occult horror, and direct references to the Italian director abound in Toshiharu Ikeda's body-count movie *reducto ad absurdam*, *Shiryo No Wana* (*Evil Dead Trap*, 1988) – notably a score more than a tad reminiscent of that of *Deep Red* (Dario Argento, 1975) and a predilection for menaced females gorily dispatched beneath expressionistic-coloured lighting and camera angles. *Perfect Blue*'s stylistic approach is similar enough to Argento's work to make such a comparison inevitable in terms of the sheer verve of the bloodletting scenes, the undeniably Goblin-esque soundtrack, and the disorienting approach of multiple perspectives that force the viewer outside of the scene to a more objective standpoint at crucial moments. Certain shots look like they could almost have been lifted directly from Argento's oeuvre. Similarly, when asked about his preference for female protagonists, Kon's response, 'I like women', intentionally or not, echoed Argento's infamous comment: 'I like women, especially beautiful ones. If they have a good face and figure, I would much prefer to watch them being murdered than an ugly girl or a man. I certainly don't have to justify myself to anyone about this.'

For his next project, Kon would again utilise a female protagonist to explore the concepts of subjectivity, objectivity and the fallibility of memory, though in every other respect *Sennen Joyu* (*Millennium Actress*, 2001) is an entirely different film. Charting the life story of a retired actress against the backdrop of fifty years of Japan's cinematic history, Kon uses a similarly elliptical approach to completely different yet equally potent effect in a film best described as romantic mystery drama. *Millennium Actress*'s global distribution rights were acquired by Steven Spielberg's DreamWorks SKG company in 2002 to be dubbed for the foreign market, further broadening Kon's international reputation.

With just two features under his belt, Kon has not only breathed fresh air into a field that was long seen as the domain of a fanatical few, but pointed to new directions in approaching otherwise generic material. It will remain to be seen how he builds on such impressive foundations. For the time being, far more than just cross-cultural curios, cartoons with adult themes and contents, *Perfect Blue* and *Millennium Actress* signal the arrival of one of the most exciting new talents to have emerged from Japan in the past decade.

Jasper Sharp

REFERENCES

Manga Max (1999) *Perfect Blue*. London: Titan.

Mes, T. (2002) *Midnight Eye*: Interview with Satoshi Kon. www.midnighteye.com/interviews/satoshi_kon.shtml.

Schodt, F. L. (1986) *Manga! Manga! The World of Japanese Comics*. New York: Kodansha America.

KANGWON-DO UI HIM THE POWER OF KANGWON PROVINCE 17

HONG SANG-SOO, KOREA, 1998

'I write for Koreans and my love of the Korean language', commented director Hong Sang-soo, underlining the fact that his films, though having attracted a wide international audience, are primarily for a Korean audience. His first film, *Doeji-ga Umure Bbajin Nal* (*The Day a Pig Fell Into the Well*, 1996), made while still holding down a day job at Seoul Broadcasting Station, was acclaimed at numerous international film festiavals, including Vancouver and Rotterdam, and was awarded Korea's Blue Dragon for Best New Director.

Born in Seoul in 1960, Hong studied filmmaking at Joongang University, finished his Bachelor of Fine Arts at the California College of Arts and Crafts and completed his Master of Fine Arts at the School of the Arts Institute in Chicago. His international success continued with his second film, *Kangwon-do Ui Him* (*The Power of Kangwon Province*, 1998). In addition to winning Best Director and Best Screenplay in Korea, he also received an *Un Certain Regard* Special Mention at the 1998 Cannes International Film Festival. The film confirmed Hong Sang-soo's position as a world-class filmmaker.

The Power of Kangwon Province consists of two separate stories whose endings eventually link together. The first story centres around a college student, Ji-sook (Oh Yoon-hong) and her two friends Mi-sun (Im Sun-young) and Eun-kyoung (Park Hyun-young) as they holiday in the mountains of Kangwon Province. On the trip, Ji-sook and her friends meet a policeman (Lim Yoo-suk) whom they all call 'Mister' and with whom Ji-sook establishes a relationship. She later returns to Kangwon Province alone to spend an evening with him, but their evening ends with her falling asleep in a chair and his passing out on the bed. The second narrative involves a married man, Sang-kwon (Baek Jong-hak), who is pursuing a full professorship. His friend Jae-woon (Chun Jae-hyun) invites him along for a brief sojourn to Kangwon Province. While there, Sang-kwon aimlessly pursues a relationship with a woman who ends up falling, or perhaps jumping, off a cliff to her death. Throughout Sang-kwon's story, hints are dropped he once had a relationship with Ji-sook, which is confirmed at the end of the film.

How Hong writes for Koreans is demonstrated in a scene where Sang-kwon visits a Professor Kim as protocol for obtaining a full professorship. Sang-kwon and Professor Kim's brief conversation revolves around the Professor's apartment. Professor Kim explains to Sang-kwon that the apartment was built according to the standards of the United States. The funding would have been taken away otherwise. Professor Kim's comments would resonate strongly with many Korean viewers with regard to the horrendous accident at the Sampoong Department Store in Seoul, when the store collapsed due to a faulty foundation killing 501 employees and customers and injuring over 900. *The Power of Kangwon Province* was released three years after that incident, so Professor Kim's comments would still resonate for many Koreans, prompting feelings of shame for some. This association of shame with Korean building standards versus United States standards appears to be utilised by Hong to represent the shame that Sang-kwon feels regarding his status in academia and amongst his friends. Sang-kwon does not feel he matches standards of the rest of his colleagues.

Sang-kwon's shame can also be found in the protocol process he must endure to obtain full professorship. The protocol itself is a further example of Hong writing explicitly for Koreans. Not only must Sang-kwon come to Professor Kim's house, but he must also bring a gift of whiskey. At no point, while talking with Professor Kim, does Sang-kwon specifically mention the professorship he seeks, but his appearance at Professor Kim's home and his presentation of a gift are all unspoken requests for Professor Kim's assistance. Upon leaving Professor Kim's apartment, Sang-kwon realises he left his umbrella, but decides not to go back, ashamed to ask for its return. The red umbrella becomes yet another gift given to Professor Kim, whom is last seen happily opening and closing the umbrella as if admiring his power over Sang-kwon. The protocol appears humbling for Sang-kwon, yet he plays his part with little resistance.

Although Hong writes for Koreans and his love of the Korean language, one need not *be* Korean nor knowledgeable of the Korean language to appreciate his films. Hong's attentiveness to everyday patterns heightens universal cycles many people find themselves in. In *The Power of Kangwon Province*, patterns are shared by Ji-sook and Sang-kwon to the point where they are sharing parallel moments in the same space at the same time, unbeknown to the other. The opening train scenes in each narrative exemplify this; both are on the same train with no knowledge that the other is there. The theme of shame that develops with the two central characters can be seen as a particular *within* a universal; we all experience shame. However, within Korea, as in other Asian countries, shame is a powerful force, as the way each person is judged affects how their family will be judged. Regardless, Hong disassociates shame upon the family from the shame he presents within his own characters. They are alone in their shame, and this 'disconnectedness' explains why they feel so alone.

Ji-sook's shame revolves around her relationships with older, married men. Both of Ji-sook's friends are aware of her pattern and do not approve. When everyone is drunk at dinner, Mi-sun confronts Ji-sook: 'You think you're so special, but you're no different. Everything about you is cliché.' Ji-sook responds, 'Can't you see what you can and cannot have in life! Unfortunately, I can. I try for what I can get and give up on the rest. Sometimes it hurts so much … It may sound corny, but I've been making sacrifices for my dreams.' Mi-sun's reply, 'You mean your relationship with the married man?' prompts Ji-sook to cry.

Eun-kyoung also feels strongly about Ji-sook's patterns, but voices her concern indirectly. When a drunken Ji-sook suggests to the married policeman that they head back to his place, Eun-kyoung's eyes widen and she asks the policeman how often he sees his wife. When he answers, 'Every day', Eun-kyoung leaves drunken Ji-sook with him as she goes off to see if Mi-sun, who has left the restaurant, is alright. Since the policeman has affirmed he sees his wife every day, Eun-kyoung leaves with some reassurance that he is trustworthy and will not take advantage of her. Unfortunately, Eun-kyoung's indirect assurance turns out to be wrong; the policeman takes Ji-sook to his room and attempts to have sex with her. Ji-sook's listless, drunken body flails around in the policeman's arms as he drags her to his bed. 'Eun-kyoung might misunderstand' are the only words of protest she is able to speak. Ji-sook rejects his more aggressive advances, yet thanks him for taking care of her and her friends. Hong cuts away from this scene early enough to leave an audiencee questioning whether they had sex. However, Ji-sook arranges another meeting with the policeman. 'He called me first', Ji-sook claims when asking Eun-kyoung to lie for her regarding her intended whereabouts. In a sense, Ji-sook also asks Eun-kyoung to accept her lie about what this relationship with another married man may hold. Eun-kyoung responds to Ji-sook's request with irritation and protest, but she still agrees to lie.

As previously noted, she and her friends call the policeman, 'Mister'. Although it is within cultural norms for younger Koreans to refer to older men in this manner, when Ji-sook begins a physical relationship with Mister, the protocol becomes discomforting – her trip to see him disappoints, if not disturbs, the audience as well as Ji-sook's friends.

Ji-sook never verbalises awareness of her patterns or her feelings of shame surrounding it, but her own internal protests do arise at times. When she reaches Kangwon Province for the second time, the policeman is late in meeting her. When he does finally arrive, Ji-sook is enraged with him. Calming down, she tells him that 'It was a hard trip. The bus was filled with scary-looking men.' When he asks if she is 'scared of people', she responds, 'It's not that

I'm scared of people. It's that those people were scary looking.' An interesting aspect of this exchange is how the policeman takes Ji-sook's words and filters them through his experience as a man. She mentions that there were scary-looking men on the train; he asks her if she is scared of people. He appears unable to empathise with the gender difference of their experiences. That is, what women often have to face travelling alone in any country. Staring men may be may have no malicious intent, but they are no less scary. Because of the policeman's reaction, she downplays her own gender-specific experience. The policeman's inability to appreciate Ji-sook's experience presents an unsafe space for Ji-sook to look further into her fear; of spending time in the isolated mountains with a strange man who desires her. Equally unacknowledged is her shame about taking this trip with yet another older, married man.

Eventually, the romantic encounter is undermined by the ambivalence that has been present since their first encounter. When he asks Ji-sook what kind of feeling she thinks he has for her, she replies 'Mister, I am very tired'. As they stumble through their drunkenness in the hotel room and Ji-sook refuses his advances, the policeman considers jumping off the balcony. He goes so far as to hang by his bare hands on the other side of the railing. Although this parallels the woman who fell/jumped off the cliff, which happened when Ji-sook first visited Kangwon Province, the scene also implies that Ji-sook almost jumped off an existential cliff herself, by taking her second trip. On her bus ride home, she breaks down crying; an acknowledgement of her pattern and her shame. They also suggest that she interrupted her pattern. She did not allow the relationship with another older, married man to continue. As much as she cries from the pain of whatever drives her to take dangerous risks, she has broken the cycle.

Whether or not Sang-kwon learns from his pattern, his shame is less determinable. Our first introduction to Sang-kwon's patterns is when he takes possession of two goldfish a colleague has left outside his office. He asks his young secretary, 'Aren't they cute?' She responds, 'You think everything's cute.' Married with a child, Sang-kwon is encouraged by a friend to pursue a position at Choonchun University and he meets with Professor Kim, as discussed earlier. However he is lackadaisical in his pursuit of the position. His wife admonishes him with a heavy sigh, 'Do what you want.' He almost misses the train that will take him to the Professor's and has his portrait taken for the application just prior to boarding. Later, getting off the train, he takes another photo because he is dissatisfied with the previous one, or, more truthfully, is dissatisfied with his career and his life. The protocol rituals he has to perform do not help matters, but Sang-kwon still idles his way through the process. Perhaps his apathy is a response to his shame. He will face consequences in his family and finances if he does not secure a certain position of standing. The protocol set up to obtain his professorship can be demeaning and difficult so his attitude may relate to his fear that he might fail. One way to avoid that fear, and the shame of it, is to refuse to fail by refusing to try, hence Sang-kwon's ambivalence.

Walking through the mountains of Kangwon Province with Jae-woon, they pass a woman (the woman who would eventually 'fall' off the cliff). Sang-kwon and Jae-woon turn to gaze at her walking over the bridge. Coming upon her later, Sang-kwon tells Jae-woon to follow her. Jae-woon returns to tell Sang-kwon that she wishes to meet up with them, adding that she specifically asked about Sang-kwon. With the same hesitant direction Sang-kwon pursues everything else, Jae-woon and Sang-kwon arrive at the meeting place late, only to find the woman gone. Shame may play a part here as well; shame regarding *his* pattern of extra-marital affairs: he wants this woman while at the same time not wanting her.

Sang-kwon's final encounter with the woman is somewhat odd. He shouts at her for lying to him for promising to meet them, even though she is with another male suitor. The woman tells Sang-kwon she did wait for him. On hearing this, Sang-kwon apologises. This interaction parallels Ji-sook's yelling at the policeman for making her wait. Sang-kwon, however, yells at the stranger for *not* waiting. She is merely a replacement for his anger at the opportunities he has missed, which are no-one's fault but his own.

The death of the woman can be seen as an omen for Ji-sook and Sang-kwon, if they bothered to pay attention to it, which only Ji-sook does. Hong surrounds the woman's death with ambiguity. The police report her death as a suicide, yet it is equally plausible that her male suitor had a hand in her demise. Later in the film, having read about her death in the newspaper, he telephones the police to provide them with the name of the male suitor he last saw her with. The woman could have either been pushed off the cliff or she could have jumped – we cannot know for sure. But we do know that Ji-sook and Sang-kwon are walking along an edge of their own existential abyss.

At one point in Sang-kwon's story, he notices a husband and wife walking along in the mountains. Jae-woon wonders why such people are 'so blind to the danger'. Sang-kwon disagrees with Jae-woon's interpretation, 'It's probably not that they're stupid. There must be a physical difference giving them the confidence to do that.' Ironically, Sang-kwon continually puts his family in danger of dissolution with his affairs, whilst placing his career in jeopardy with his reluctance to pursue advancement. Jae-woon knows Sang-kwon is a risk-taker. Like Mi-sun, Jae-woon confronts Sang-kwon about his patterns at a restaurant table, 'You should be trying harder for the position in Choonchun. That's your best bet. And don't waste your time.'

He knows Sang-kwon's propensity for wasting time and opportunities, risking everything. 'You have to make your move this time. Do it as if this is your last chance.'

Wandering through the town after dinner, Sang-kwon and Jae-woon find themselves bored and are drawn to a strip club. Wanting to procure Russian prostitutes for his friend, Sang-kwon asks how much they are. He is not told; instead the host merely retorts that they are very expensive. He saves face by saying he prefers Korean girls and retreats to the steps outside the club, where he extinguishes a cigarette in the centre of his palm, grinding the butt in deeper, causing further pain. The scene demonstrates the existence of the shameful pain within Sang-kwon, externalised through the self-inflicted wound.

This section of the film identifies how Sang-kwon's shame is not associated with his extra-martial affairs, but is connected to his inferiority complex in terms of his status to other men. Before going to the club, Sang-kwon paid for their meal even though he earns less than Jae-woon, a full professor. Jae-woon mentions at dinner that he has talked about Sang-kwon to the Choonchun professors. Sang-kwon's paying for dinner follows protocol; the presenting of a gift, saying thank you without saying thank you. However, it is also a way of competing with Jae-woon. As Jae-woon resides in a higher place in the professorship hierarchy, Sang-kwon struggles with insecurity about where he stands in relationship to Jae-woon. Being denied the Russian prostitutes prompts his masochistic act. It is also his shame that sparks his drunken argument with Jae-woon. In this scene, Sang-kwon reveals what he believes others think of him and, in turn, what he really thinks of himself. He sees himself as 'lesser' and this discourages him from pursuing anything better. He is not angry with Jae-woon but what Jae-woon stands for.

While waiting on standby for a flight home, Sang-kwon looks at the mountains they are about to leave and tells Jae-woon, 'I came here with her before. We stayed at the resort we passed on our way. We walked on the beach in the rain. We even had a secret wedding ceremony here like young lovers. Come to think of it, we did all sorts of things.' The unnamed 'her' is Ji-sook. Sang-kwon had previously looked at the mountains and talked about those who put themselves at risk. The people he spoke of possessed the confidence that allowed them to take risks. We now know of the risks he once took up in those mountains and what Ji-sook was trying to recreate with the policeman. Arriving home, he returns to Ji-sook's apartment to write a message by her door.

Before they meet up, Sang-kwon's is awarded the full professorship at Choonchun University. He flirts with danger and is faced with no consequences. Hence his confidence in taking risks is further reinforced. Meeting with his new colleagues over drinks they talk about how drinking affects sex. A past student of Sang-kwon's comes by and tells him how much she and the other students miss him. Sang-kwon's colleague comments on how he must have been popular with his students because he 'drank' with them so often – implying impropriety with his students, and acceptance of such impropriety amongst his peers.

We are introduced to Ji-sook, a student with whom he 'drank' often. Initially, she expresses frustration towards his advances. Yet she still goes to a motel with him. She tells him of an abortion she had, but his own pleasure is all that concerns him and he asks her to fellate him. Sadly, Ji-sook obliges without hesitation. This scene hints that their cycles will, inevitably, continue. A long list of parallels between these two characters exist, from their drunken verbal spats with friends over dinner and the ease with which they find new suitors, to the way they view themselves and their feelings of shame. Ji-sook and Sang-kwon have similar experiences, thoughts, actions and philosophies regarding their individual selves and their worldview.

What is even more poignant about the parallels is that Ji-sook and Sang-kwon engage in these parallel lives oblivious of the other's trajectory. They are drawn to the same place, perform similar acts and share the same experiences at nearly the same time. This further underscores their limited awareness of their patterns and how they are trapped in their cycles.

At the same time these parallels underscore the differences these characters experience due to gender privilege. The anger Ji-sook directs at the policeman is partly from a real fear of encountering strange men while travelling alone, whereas Sang-kwon hides anger about himself underneath a sense of entitlement to the woman stranger, Russian prostitutes and the professorship. Ji-sook is angry about having to wait for the policeman, while conversely, Sang-kwon is angry with the woman not waiting for him. These differences are no more prominent than in the different consequences Ji-sook and Sang-kwon face. Ji-sook becomes pregnant from the risks she took whereas Sang-kwon still obtains his professorship for his family. Judging from Hong's responses to questions regarding his awareness of such issues, he would probably say that his views on gender are not special and any such statements were unintentional. Still, the differing outcome for Ji-sook and Sang-kwon show how men and women can be left with different 'baggage' at the end of the same trip.

Although the fellatio scene appears to show they will both continue in their patterns, Ji-sook, having faced consequences, still appears to be the one who resists. She does make a conscious choice to behave differently when refusing the policeman. Even though she fellates Sang-kwon without hesitation, this could be more out of appeasement to the immediate situation in an effort to eventually escape. Ji-sook could have chosen to simply leave in response to Sang-kwon's insensitivity, which would have made her a more strong-willed person. However, Hong's films are more concerned with the decisions his characters are most likely to take. Instead of standing up in that moment, Ji-sook takes one last gasp before separating from Sang-kwon for good. Hong appears to leave us with a sign that the cycle has broken for Ji-sook. When Sang-kwon returns to retrieve his two goldfish, his secretary informs him: 'By the way, there's only one fish left.'

Ji-sook, it appears, has gone forward too. She is aware that Sang-kwon and other married men will not take care of her. She has realised that her actions are her responsibility alone. She does not possess the privileges Sang-kwon has, but she does chose to take control wherever she can. Perhaps she has stopped waiting and will now ask others to wait for her.

It is not clear whether Sang-kwon has learned any lessons. With his privilege, he could easily buy another 'goldfish' or have one given to him. The final shot is of him contemplating the lone fish; even though he may see his reflection in the water, it is unclear if Sang-kwon has become as enlightened as Ji-sook.

The Taiwanese director Tsai Ming-Liang is often mentioned when discussing Hong. Although there are similarities, such as their minimalism and infrequent use of close-ups, Hong's characters are too talkative and he employs fewer of the long silent takes to provide a solid comparison between the two. As for Hong's place in Korean cinema, he occupies a unique position at the forefront of the industry. There is something refreshing about Hong's characters stumbling through awkward moments and choices. With his less than exemplary characters, he could be seen to offer a window into the world around him and his audience, asking why we make the choices we make, and challenge ourselves to do better next time.

Adam Hartzell

INJONG SAJONG BOLGEOT EOBDA NOWHERE TO HIDE 18

LEE MYEONG-SE, KOREA, 1999

One does not have to look far today to see the influence that the Hong Kong film industry has had on moviemaking around the world. Hong Kong film stars, such as Jackie Chan, Chow Yun-fat and Jet Li have become household names, and in recent years have headlined Hollywood blockbusters. So too have numerous Hong Kong directors, who are developing huge international followings. Western filmmakers are even employing the visual dynamic of Hong Kong movies, bringing hyperkinetic martial arts action, 'wire-fu' and graceful gun battles to mainstream audiences in films such as *The Matrix* (Wachowski Brothers, 1999) and *Charlie's Angels* (McG, 2000).

Despite achieving such recognition abroad, the lustre of Hong Kong's home-grown film industry has faded considerably over the past decade. Challenged by a 'brain drain' of talent (with the best and brightest players pulling up roots and heading for the bright lights of Hollywood), successive recessions that have rocked the economy since the Handover in 1997, rampant piracy and the industry practice of 'shooting it fast, shooting it cheap', the magic of the golden era – the so-called Hong Kong New Wave – is all but gone.

But for those Hong Kong cinema aficionados who passionately followed the rise of the Hong Kong New Wave during the 1980s and early 1990s, only to become increasingly disenchanted since, there is a new destination for exciting and innovative cinema: South Korea. Since 1997, South Korea's local film industry has undergone a remarkable transformation. The staples of Korean cinema (staid melodramas and graphic exploitation movies) have given way to a new generation of filmmakers. Schooled abroad and influenced by their contemporaries around the world, this new generation of Korean moviemakers is revitalising the industry with bold arthouse productions, big-budget actioners, thought-provoking dramas and subversive satires. With its home-grown film industry gradually moving onto the world stage, South Korea is now increasingly referred to as 'the new Hong Kong'. Already a number of Korean films have found success in the North American market through limited release; an example being 1999's groundbreaking *Swiri* (*Shiri*) from director Kang Je-gyu. Meanwhile, Korean directors are being courted by major Hollywood studios for lucrative US remake rights, a trend started with Miramax snapping up Jo Jin-gyu's *Jopog Manura* (*My Wife is a Gangster*) in the autumn of 2001.

Of the many memorable films released since the start of the Korean New Wave, writer/director Lee Myeong-se's *Injong Sajong Bolgeot Eobda* (*Nowhere to Hide*, 1999) serves as a shining example of South Korean cinema's bold new direction and take-no-prisoners attitude – appropriately the film's original Korean title translates approximately as: 'I Don't Give a Shit About Anything'. Taking as its starting point a relatively simple story about two maverick cops tracking down an elusive killer, *Nowhere to Hide* breathed new life into the well-worn buddy-cop genre. Though the narrative occasionally feels disjointed as a result of its furious pace and experimentation with visual styles, there is no doubt that the film is a defining work of the latest Korean New Wave.

The film's story is loosely based on a real-life crime case involving a fugitive named Shin Chong-won. Events are set in motion by a murder committed at the '40 Steps' in downtown Inchon during a torrential downpour. Renegade Detective Woo (Park Joong-hoon) and his clean-cut partner Kim (Jang Dong-gun) are put on the case. Using their traditional investigative methods, which include roughing up informants and beating up potential accomplices, their search for the killer hones in on criminal Chang Sung-min (Ahn Sung-ki). But his capture turns into an extended game of cat-and-mouse that stretches from autumn into winter.

At first glance, the film's most obvious weakness is its plot. Essentially one big chase from beginning to end, very few details are given about its characters, particularly Chang, whose motives and background are never revealed. Fundamentally, the plot serves only as a platform from which to stage the numerous action sequences and explore various visual techniques. However, despite these issues of narrative weakness, *Nowhere to Hide* bears many of the qualities that make contemporary South Korean cinema so compelling. This perhaps then begs the questions: What makes the films of this latest Korean New Wave so special and why are they developing such an impressive global following?

The New Wave arguably began sometime around 1997, when the industry began to reap benefits from significant investments in its infrastructures, accompanied by a new entrepreneurial spirit. It was then that Chang Yoon-hyun's internet-romance *Cheob-sok* (*The Contact*) became a domestic hit, its success helping to create greater interest among Korean moviegoers for home-grown fare. However, it was not until 1999, a watershed year for South Korean cinema, that the New Wave became a creative force to be reckoned with. After spending many years taking a backseat to big-budget Hollywood imports, Korean filmmakers reclaimed the country's movie screens as nine home-grown productions earned a place in the box-office top 20. These included *Shiri*, Kim Sang-jin's *Chuyuso Supgyuk Sa Keun* (*Attack the Gas Station!*), Chang Yoon-hyun's *Tell Me Something* and *Nowhere to Hide*. Until this point South Korea's film industry had been able to remain competitive only through the country's quota system, in which the national theatres were mandated to show Korean films, while limits were placed on the number of foreign films that could be imported and how many days of the year that they could be shown (Korean theatres are still obliged to screen home-grown fare at least 106 days of the year). However, as this New Wave of filmmakers, trained in Europe and the United States, returned home to create commercially viable films that appealed to domestic audiences, the home-grown film industry no longer needed to rely solely on the quota system for its financial viability.

Upon closer examination, many of the films to emerge since the start of the New Wave possessed similar qualities: creativity, technical sophistication and a unique cultural perspective. Aficionados of Asian cinema will note that these were the same qualities ascribed to Hong Kong films of the late 1970s and early 1980s which helped Hong Kong gain international recognition as a source of innovative cinema and encouraged Hollywood studios to adopt its distinctive style.

Though filmmakers of the Korean New Wave have grown up with the films of Hollywood, Hong Kong and other countries, they do not constrain themselves to telling the same tired stories, or relying on cliché. Whenever possible, a number of these filmmakers deliberately break these rules. For example, Korean filmmakers are largely content mixing elements from different genres to create unconventional takes on standard formulas, or as Darcy Paquet, the English-language editor for the Korean Film Commission, calls it, 'genre-bending'. One does not need to look very far to find numerous examples of genre-bending throughout contemporary Korean cinema. Kim Ji-woon's *Choyonghan Kajok* (*The Quiet Family*, 1988) mixes black comedy with straight horror, Kang's *Shiri* blended traditional Korean romantic melodrama with Jerry Bruckheimer-style pyrotechnics, while *My Wife is a Gangster*, *Shinlaui Dalbam* (*Kick the Moon*, 2001) and other gangster comedies combined 'fish out of water' humour with the old standard of Asian cinema: the gangland saga.

Nowhere to Hide is an excellent example of Korean-style genre-bending, employing multiple genres to present an exhilarating entertainment. Though the story is essentially a standard police procedural plot, it quickly becomes apparent that Lee refuses to be constrained by the rules of the genre. Whilst the inclusion of martial artistry, Japanese *anime*-inspired cinematography and John Woo-style action choreography are staple elements, many of the film's other features play against audience expectations. Such is the case with Lee's use of humour. Viewers find sympathy with Woo and his colleagues difficult, especially given their habit of beating up suspects and the ineptness they display as they go about their work. However it is through this chaotic approach to police procedure that most of the comedy arises – echoes of *The Three Stooges* are evident while Woo and the gang are staking out the house of Chang's girlfriend, when an unexpected knock at the door leaves Woo's team in disarray as they madly scramble for a suitable hiding place.

Lee pulled few punches with the film, risking many things – including pacing, narrative cohesiveness and audience sympathy for the protagonists – in order to create an iconoclastic 'art-house actioner'. This is evident in the film's off-kilter set pieces that threaten to distract or even lose an audience's attention: fighting between Woo and a henchmen that transforms into shadow puppetry and ultimately a tango between the two combatants (complete with music), or an interlude during a stakeout in which thought bubbles appear over the heads of Woo and Kim, who are dreaming about bowls of piping hot noodles.

Another striking aspect of the Korean New Wave is the level of technical virtuosity. A combination of substantial investment and a fresh crop of visually oriented filmmakers, contemporary Korean films are visually stunning. From the urban sheen of Chang Yoon-hyun's chiller *Tell Me Something* to the MTV-school-of-filmmaking exuberance of Kwak Kyung-Taek's gangland saga *Chingu* (*Friend*, 2001) and the *wu-shu*-meets-CGI gloss of Kim Tae-gyun's *Whasango* (*Volcano High*, 2001), South Korean cinema has achieved the technical sophistication of Hollywood and Hong Kong. Nowhere is this more evident than in the iconic, rain-drenched '40 Steps' murder framed by the orange and golden hues of autumn and set to the tune of the Bee Gees' *Holiday* – which would later be parodied in Jang Gyu-seong's cine-parody, *Jaemitneun Yeonghwa* (*Funny Movie*, 2002).

During the latter half of the 1980s, following the signing of the Sino-British Joint Declaration Agreement in 1984, a heavy cloud of uncertainty hung over Hong Kong. The British colony was to be handed back to the People's Republic of China in 1997, and Hong Kong residents had mixed feelings as to how well the Chinese government might administer the promised 'one country, two systems' policy. Unsurprisingly this unease had a profound effect on Hong Kong cinema; a number of films preferred to bathe in the nostalgia of simpler times, triggering a resurgence in period dramas, such as Wong Kar-wai's *A Fei Jing Juen* (*Days of Being Wild*, 1991). By contrast, forward-looking films viewed the future with mistrust and cynicism

– John Woo's *Ying huang boon sik* (*A Better Tomorrow*, 1986), where Chow Yun-fat's character looks down at the neon-lit Hong Kong skyline and remarks, 'I never realised Hong Kong looked so good at night. Like most things, it won't last. That's for sure.' Inevitably, the visions of doom-and-gloom were heightened following the events of Tiananmen Square in 1989.

Like the filmmakers of Hong Kong's New Wave, South Korean filmmakers have not been immune to the social, cultural and political forces that have shaped their lives. The last century of South Korean history has been filled with turmoil: the fall of the long-standing Chosun Dynasty, the occupation by Japan, the post-war partition and the Korean War, successive military dictatorships, democratic reforms during the late 1980s and of course the emergence of South Korean democracy at the start of the new millennium. Indeed the South Korean people have made the painful transition from one political extreme to the other within the span of a single generation. It is not surprising therefore that the social and political traumas of the Korean people are played out on the nation's movie screens, such as in the politically savvy blockbusters *Shiri* and Pak Chan-wook's blockbuster *Kongdong Kongbi Guyok* (*Joint Security Area*, 2000), the controversial films of acclaimed director Kim Ki-duk, or any one of the many romantic melodramas in which two lovers find themselves separated by seemingly insurmountable obstacles, a metaphor for the divided nature of modern Korea.

Nowhere to Hide may not be as politically minded as some other entries in the Korean New Wave, but the imprint of the Korean cultural perspective is unmistakable. Like many of his contemporaries, spurred in part by the increased freedom of political expression since the mid-1990s, Lee was not afraid to show some of the more unflattering aspects of Korean society, particularly his black humour-laced portrayal of police brutality (torture has been a regular, though unofficial, practice of the Korean police and intelligence agencies in the past). Furthermore, the on-screen pugilism of *Nowhere to Hide* is representative of the pervasiveness of violence in modern South Korea, where the country's Constitutional Court condones corporal punishment of students in schools, where police occasionally ignore or fail to intervene in cases of domestic violence and physical abuse of employees by their managers in the workplace is not uncommon. While Lee's perspective may not be as uncompromisingly harsh as Lee Chang-dong's *Bakha Sating* (*Peppermint Candy*, 2000) or Kim Ki-duk's *Seom* (*The Isle*, 2000), his cynicism and acknowledgement of South Korea's violent underbelly is refreshing in what could otherwise have been dismissed as mere populist entertainment.

Nowhere to Hide brings together a number of established and rising stars from Korean cinema, both in front and behind the camera. Lee studied filmmaking at the Seoul Institute of the Arts. He worked as a writer and assistant director under the tutelage of Bae Chang-ho, finally making his feature-film debut in 1988 with *Gagman* and scoring a major box-office hit in 1990 with the romantic comedy *Na ui Sarang, na ui Shinbu* (*My Love, My Bride*). He quickly became one of the rising stars of Korean cinema, with a unique approach to imagery and composition his calling card. Unfortunately his three subsequent features of the early 1990s *Chut Sarang* (*First Love*, 1993), *Bitter and Sweet* (1995) and *Jidokahn Sarang* (*Their Last Love Affair*, 1996) – fared less well. He regained his popularity with *Nowhere to Hide*, introducing his unconventional perspective on filmmaking to a new generation of moviegoers.

In front of the camera are a number of familiar faces from the Korean New Wave and, despite the limitations of the script, the performances in *Nowhere to Hide* are impressive, particularly the leads, Park Joong-hoon, Jang Dong-gun and Ahn Sung-ki. With his distinctive looks it is not surprising that much of Park Joong-hoon's filmography prior to the Korean New Wave is made up of comedies. *Nowhere to Hide* was Park's comeback feature and inevitably a heavy hint of comedy permeated the proceedings, with his brutish and dishevelled looks put to good use as the dim-witted but determined Woo. Since *Nowhere to Hide*, Park, who learned his trade both in South Korea and New York, has diversified, appearing as the psychotic killer who harasses a vacationing couple in Him Sung-hong's harrowing *Say Yes* (2001). The next year marked his first appearance in a major Hollywood production with a supporting role alongside Thandie Newton and Mark Wahlberg in Jonathan Demme's *The Truth About Charlie*; a role he was offered shortly after Demme saw a screening of *Nowhere to Hide* at the 2000 Sundance Film Festival.

Heartthrob Jang Dong-gun, with his magazine-cover good looks, is one of the most popular actors in South Korea. Similar to Hong Kong stars Andy Lau, Jacky Cheung and Leon Lai, Jang's successful career spans both films and music. During the early 1990s he became a household name, starring in a number of popular television series and recording several best-selling albums that have made him a pan-Asian singing sensation. In 1997, Jang branched out into film with roles in Lee Kwang-hoon's romance *Paejabuhwaljeon* and Kim Yui-seok's homage to Wong Kar-wai, *Seoului Hyuil* (*Holiday in Seoul*). However, it was not until 1999 that Jang's film career took off, thanks to *Nowhere to Hide* and his portrayal of the fiercely loyal sidekick.

Ahn Sung-ki is one of South Korea's most prolific actors, having starred in over fifty films since starting his career at the age of seven in *Shibdaeui Banhang* (*Defiance of a Teenager*, 1959), directed by Kim Ki-young. His has appeared in numerous films from the Korean New Wave: Park Kwang-choon's *Toemarok* (*The Soul Guardians*, 1998), Lee Jeong-hya's romantic comedy

Misuhlgwa Yup Dongmulgwon (*Art Museum by the Zoo*, 1998) and Kim Sung-su's historical epic *Musa* (1999).

Of the other cast members, Park Sang-myun, who plays one of Chang's pugilistic accomplices, would later find fame in a number of gangster comedies in 2001, including *My Wife is a Gangster* and Park Cheol-kwan's *Hi, Dharma*. Choi Ji-woo, the film's love interest, acted in the horror success *Zzikhimyeon Jukneunda* (*The Record*, 2000), which was co-directed by Kim Gi-hun and Kim Jong-seok.

In addition to finding critical and financial success domestically, the films of the Korean New Wave have tapped the key element that formerly catalysed the phenomenal growth of Hong Kong's film industry: international sales. Not limited to the 600 domestic screens, filmmakers are reaching out to international audiences with their readily exportable films, boasting pristine production values and mainstream narratives. As an example of the explosive growth being enjoyed in the international market, total film exports grew 60 per cent between 1999 and 2000 and 56 per cent between 2000 and 2001, with its current level sitting just over US$10 million. To date Japan, Hong Kong and France have been the most receptive markets, though important in-roads are being made into the lucrative North American market.

As with many of the acclaimed films to emerge from the Korean New Wave, *Nowhere to Hide* has found success both at home and abroad. It was the first Korean film to secure a general release in the United States (albeit in an edited version that was cut by twenty minutes), as well as a subsequent North American and UK DVD release. Like Lee, the new generation of filmmakers are increasingly exposed to a receptive and growing audience, and frequently broken box-office records, both at home and abroad. This in turn has created a favourable climate for investment in the film industry, generating levels of investor fervour and market liquidity not seen since the halcyon days of the dot-com boom. As a result this potent concoction of renewed creative vigour, enthusiastic audience reaction and readily available financing has created a film industry on the verge of breaking out and fashioning its own unique identity on the world stage. Though the hallmarks of the Korean New Wave lend themselves to the glory days of Hong Kong, today's South Korean cinema is carving out its own unique cinematic identity. South Korean filmmakers are advancing the art form with their own unique blend of daring and innovation, making contemporary Korean movies one of the most exciting recent developments in world cinema.

Anthony Leong

SUMGYOL MY OWN BREATHING

BYUN YONGJOO, KOREA, 1999

Sumgyol (*My Own Breathing*, 1999) completes Byun Yongjoo's trilogy on the so-called 'comfort women': women who were forced into sexual slavery for the Japanese military army during Japan's colonisation of Korea. It opens with the subtitle, 'During World War Two, the Japanese military forced 200,000 women into sexual slavery and most were young and from Japan's colonies.' This is followed by depictions of the memorial ceremony that took place in December 1998. The next subtitle informs the audience that the two major interviewees from the first documentary, *Nazen Moksori* (*The Murmuring*, 1995) – which won the Ogawa Shinsuke prize at Yamagata International Documentary Festival in 1995 – and Kang Duk-Kyung from the second documentary, *Habitual Sadness* (1997), have died. Kang is remembered in particular, as a memorable and moving character; her paintings shown in *Habitual Sadness* symbolically and painfully represent her days as a sex slave. As the film evokes names of comfort women who have passed away over the years, audiences are implicitly asked to participate in mourning as sympathetic witnesses. *My Own Breathing* then follows *Peace Boat Cruise* (1998), and a gathering of comfort women in Mapanike, Philippines. From Korea, Yi Yongsoo who also appears in *Habitual Sadness* joins Laura (a comfort woman in the Philippines) at a welcome party. Yi becomes the central interviewer, who interacts with other comfort women. She joins a painful mourning process of acting out and working through the trauma. The camera observes, at times intervenes and often dwells on characters and the place. The dynamic and sympathetic interaction between the filmmaker, camera and characters distinguishes *My Own Breathing* from 'direct cinema' that largely avoids the filmmaker's intervention. In 'direct cinema' style, the filmmaker is invisible and uninvolved whereas Byun even rushes to her subjects' side when they are in need of help – and the camera rolls as the filmmaker runs errands for her subjects.

One of the most distinctive aspects of *My Own Breathing* as a documentary is the employment of a victim of historical trauma as a main interviewer to approach other victims who share similar experiences. As is often noted, the most difficult and knotty problems of testimony of survivors of trauma resides in the often elusive encryption of their stories.

Speaking of unspeakable events in public often manifests itself either as disavowal and amnesia. The silence, body gestures, ellipses, pauses and unfinished sentences often provide a significant semiotic field. The shame, denial and melancholy attached to 'non-reconciled' past and present render writing on and filming of such trauma extremely challenging. The trajectory of trilogy on comfort women betrays this problem but simultaneously tries to find a way in which a process of coming to terms with that problem could be fore-grounded. When the first documentary started, the comfort woman's issue had yet to become an issue in South Korea. Indeed, the stigma was strongly attributed to comfort women as if they were sources of the problem. Hence, the process of making a documentary needed a strong and trustworthy tie between the filmmaker and other comfort women. Before actual shooting, Byun frequently visited the subjects without a camera or recorder and gradually became their supporter, friend and even substitute granddaughter. She became, in short, a member of their community. Ultimately, the presence of her camera and crew became a part of their daily life and environment. The trilogy often shows the crew interacting and conversing with groups of comfort women; Byun and crew help them move, take them to hospital, join the comfort women's weekly protest in front of the Japanese embassy in Seoul, and even go on picnics together.

As Byun continued with the second documentary, some of comfort women moved to a House of Sharing (*Nanumuijib*) and asked the filmmaker to document their daily lives in their new setting. The publicity poster of *Habitual Sadness* showed a group of comfort women holding filming equipment as if they were themselves members of the crew. The narrative image of the poster humorously suggests that control of filmmaking is given to the comfort women themselves. *My Own Breathing* finally enables comfort women to speak to one another in front of the camera.

In this way, Byun's mode of making a documentary bears comparison with the work of Ogawa Shinsuke, who pioneered East Asian modes of documentary film-making. Ogawa translated the French model of *cinema vérité* documentary of Jean Rouch and direct cinema of Fredrick Wiseman, to fit into the social structures and working conditions of his society and culture. His approach involved political commitment and living a communal life with people who would become subjects for his films. Ogawa gave Byun his 16mm camera – itself a gift from Jean-Luc Godard – before he passed away. With the spirit of Ogawa, Byun has made a significant contribution to the way what women's cinema could and should be presented in South Korea. Thus, we can locate Byun's work in the context of a specific history of woman's film in Korea.

Woman's film, *yosong yonghwa*, is a relatively recent term, invented category or sub-genre, which dates back only to the early 1990s. The *yosong* of *yosong yonghwa* is a translation for woman in woman's film. In fact, the generic 'women' in English can be translated both as *yoja* and *yosong* in Korean. In the Korean dictionary, *yoja* is defined as a person who is born as *yosong*, which in turn, is defined as *yoja*, with an emphasis on sexual difference. The re-appropriation of *yosong* in 1990s feminist discourse among many female-related identities – *yoja*, *yoryu*, feminist and *yosong undongga* (feminist activist), for instance – may well be related to the growing interest in the politics of sexual difference derived from the feminist and gay movements in South Korea.

Before the recognition/emergence of *yosong yonghwa*, films intended for a predominantly female audience were simply labelled as 'weepies' (*ch'oeryumul*) or other similar derogatory terms. Indebted to Anglophone cine-feminists' pioneering work and the proliferation of feminist discourse in an area of cultural production and consumption, a few local film critics have (re)invented ways of reading popular films since the early 1990s. Well-known 'weepies' such as *Miwodo Dasihanbon* (*Bitter, But Once Again*, Chong So-Yong, 1968) were brought back under feminist scrutiny. A discussion ensued, with contemporary films that featured *yoja* explicitly in their titles which focused on women characters caught between their families and their careers. These were viewed as examples of women's film. At the time, lack of availability of feminist cinema encouraged feminist film critics to engage in the films for female audiences, which is not unlike Mary Ann Doane's reading of 1940s classical Hollywood texts: 'Because female identity in the cinema is constructed in relation to object-hood rather than subject-hood, an investigation of the contradictions resulting from an attempt to engage female subjectivity in a textual process such as the "woman's film" can be particularly productive.'

In 1993 Korean feminist cultural workers made an attempt to introduce a different kind of women's cinema. More precisely, these were the feminist films that had not yet reached the local audience. Detailed information and reviews of films by Chantal Akerman, Helke Sander, Michelle Citron and Sally Porter were disseminated in film magazines, public lectures and books. In addition, the women's video festival under the title of *Riddles of the Sphinx* programmed Euro-American feminist avant-garde works.

The appropriation of the specific term *yosong* to designate different kinds of cinematic practices, encouraged active reading of *yosong* films rather than simply conflating the female-audience-targeted film with feminist films. That the linguistic use of *yosong* is marked with sexual difference but oscillates between *yoja* and feminist (no equivalent term in Korean exist and the English term is currently in use) indicates the negotiated space and moment at which the emerging feminism in the cultural arena was grafted. The choice of a *yosong* among many female-related identities appeared less threatening not only to women of diverse positions but also to the mainstream media. For instance, women's magazines and the newly installed culture and women sections in the newspapers attempted to appeal to women readers who emerged as powerful consumers with a new identity. The outcome was to categorise the locally produced films of the period by Pak Chol-su and Yi Hyon-sung as *yosong* film. The exemplary text, preceding two directors' works, was even convincingly entitled *Tanji Gudaega Yojaranun Iyumanuro* (*Only Because You Are a Woman*, Kim Yu-jin, 1990) – it was praised as the breakthrough *yosong* film of this period. To put it another way, critics were/are re-categorising the *yoja* film as the *yosong* film. Similarly, Pak's films – which explicitly employ *yoja* in their titles, such as *Onul Yoja* (*Today's Yoja*, 1989) and *Murwirul Kotnun Yoja* (*Yoja Who Walks on the Water*, 1990) – are particularly notable with regard to these concerns.

Around the same time, there surfaced a series of issue-oriented films and videos in the newly-formed independent film and video-making scene: *Urine Aidul* (*Our Children*, Parito Women Filmmakers Collective, 1990) on the problem of daycare, *Chagun Puledo Irum Itsuni* (*Even Little Grass Has its Name*, Parito Women Filmmakers Collective, 1990) on the labour union movement of women workers in the late 1980s and *Asiaeso Yosonguro Sandanun Got* (*Living in Asia as Women*, Purun Yongsang Collective, 1991) on sex tourism. Even a brief look at the trajectory of the emergence of *yosong* film, both in the critical and filmmaking terrain in the early 1990s, reveals a quite condensed situation where the legacy of Anglophone cine-feminism intersects with two kinds of local filmmaking practices. Due to the fact that there has been a conscious reservation in not using the term 'feminist film' for locally produced works, the focus here on woman's film necessarily entails two modes of filmmaking. One is the result of market-strategies – that is geared toward female audience – while the other features works that are more consciously oriented towards women's issues. As a consequence, the popular film and the alternative film would inhabit the same ground known simply as women's film. As demonstrated by the two earlier films on the 'comfort women' issue, *The Murmuring* and *Habitual Sadness*, the *yosong* film in post-colonial South Korea inevitably dealt with the colonial past, which provided a matrix of unresolved anxiety that spilled over into the present. Between *The Widow* and *Habitual Sadness* lay a wide spectrum of film designed to draw female audiences that do not overlap with the ideal audience constructed by feminist film critics in the 1990s.

From the mid-1950s to the late 1960s, films targeting a female audience were known as rubber shoes (a signifier of common or underclass women), handkerchief army, and tear-jerkers (*choeryusong*), which might be equated to women's film. Instead of the generic term women, the metonymy was employed to indicate the desired but simultaneously degraded presence of female audience. The group of female spectators the film industry favoured were *ajumma* (a derogatory term for married women) in rubber shoes and armed with handkerchiefs. The melodrama genre was projected as an outlet for the women's repressive experience under the transforming neo-Confucian patriarchy; the kind that would help women release their *han* (pent-up grief).

In addition, the colonial past under the Japanese occupation has been one of the most under-represented (if not completely silenced) subjects in post-colonial South Korean cinema. Shying away from exploring the influence of Japanese colonial modernity, South Korean cinema has focused on the materials of the pre-colonial past and the present. Frequently visiting scenes of underdeveloped simulacrum of American modernity (the vicinity of US military bases such as Itaewon) and hinterland outside the attention of state-governed modernisation (forlorn countryside), it has seldom confronted the legacy of Japanese colonialism. Or perhaps, it has hardly considered colonial legacy as a marketable subject. The de-colonisation process is displaced with a nationalistic narrative, which glosses over 'Korean hyper-masculinity and vigilance about female chastity'. Then, it should not surprise anyone that the comfort woman issue has never been properly documented and even less, represented on the screen, until 1991, when three former comfort women publicly came forward. The South Korean military government's complicity with Japan also contributed to the silencing of the comfort women issue. In spite of political silence, the notion of feminine sexuality and body in post-colonial Korea has been associated with the shame attached to comfort women, which in turn demanded to construct the nationalistic narrative as it is poignantly pointed out by Park You-me: 'I do not remember the exact plot. It was one of the numerous stories in Korea in the 1970s that used the metaphor of women's bodies being violated and raped to narrate the story of Japanese occupation and the U.S. presence after the Korean War. Korea as a nation was compared to a virginal body that was trampled upon and violated by aggressive outsiders. Again and again, these (almost exclusively male-authored) texts deplored the lost virginity and the shame inflicted upon their mother country by foreign forces.'

In addition to this kind of literary imagination, the history of comfort women was appropriated either as a backdrop of gang-rape fantasy in 'sexploitation' films or a leverage to promote a nationalistic rescue fantasy in the television documentary. Indeed, these two kinds of representational practice fluctuate between over-sexualisation and de-sexualisation of Comfort Women. Byun, a feminist and independent filmmaker, made possible an alternative approach to Comfort Women. She has launched her film-making career toward the end of the 80s, when the independent film movement finally joined the populist *minjung* movement. The trajectory of her film-making itself is fascinating. The first documentary, entitled as *Living as Women in Asia* (1993), traced sex tourism from the Cheju Island in South Korea to Thailand. During filming, a sex worker for Japanese tourists in the Cheju Island, confessed that her mother was, in fact, a Comfort Woman: *The Murmuring* came out of this confession. Unlike women's film of Chungmuro, which tends to bypass the shared history of women, *The Murmuring* and *Habitual Sadness* recognised that the post-colonial genealogy of womanhood stemmed from the colonial history that had not been reconciled. The two films showed how the present notion of feminine sexuality and body is deeply entangled with the comfort women as if it were a historical transference. As such, the comfort women provided a way in which the identity of 'woman' can be historicised during the post-colonial period. When the comfort women speak in *The Murmuring*, after an astonishing 50 years of silence, the female spectator is invited not only to partake in their grief but also to understand her own involvement in this history. The film-maker explicitly declared that her films should address female spectators, who in turn responded to the film with enthusiasm. Many of them left their words of support on a board after the screening – others related their own experience of sexual violence to that of comfort women's.

The revision of women's bodies is most clearly present in the final scene of *The Murmuring*, when the camera dwells on a naked body of a comfort woman, who was forced to remain in China after having been released from the 'Blood-Sucking House' (the Comfort Women station). The camera gently reveals her sapped and wrinkled body. In general, *The Murmuring* is removed from the emasculated narrative of nationalism, which has subjugated the comfort women to a fossilised realm of a nationalist trope. In fact, this new 'yosong' film is a collaborated product of women's movement (in particular with the Korean Council for the Women Drafted for Military Sexual Slavery by Japan) and the independent film movement.

Whereas *The Murmuring* depended on a confessional mode of utterance to process the overdue mourning documented, *Habitual Sadness* mobilised songs and jokes as a vehicle to articulate the comfort women's long repressed desires and needs. In the film, a group of comfort women live together in a shelter at the outskirts of Seoul. Growing vegetables on a small farm and sharing everyday life, these women slowly move into a direction of self-healing by exchanging their painful memories. The fact that the making of *Habitual Sadness* was requested by one of the former comfort women also indicated this direction. Upon learning of her terminal cancer, Kang Duk-Kyung asked Byun to film her while she was still alive. The other members of the Sharing House also agreed to participate. Thus, instead of remaining a passive informant, they actively involved themselves in the filming process. Kim Sun-Dok wanted to be remembered as a hard working person and requested the film-maker to shoot her working on the pumpkin patch. Sim Mi-Ja Sim and Park Du-Ri took this occasion to reveal their wishes. Park Du-Ri who was reluctant to be filmed in *The Murmuring*, told jokes and sang songs to the film crew. As it was Kang Duk-Kyung who originallly asked Byun to film her and her friends, the members of the Sharing House seem to articulate their own experience more voluntarily, instead of remaining passive victims caught between the nationalistic trope and the Japanese economic reparation.

Notwithstanding the fact that these two films didn't reach a large audience, the discursive effect the films created was significant. The films toured college campuses across the nation; the story of the films and the film-maker was covered by the mass media – including the major newspapers, television, and women's magazines. The two films contributed, to a great extent, to inscribing the issues in the popular consciousness. In addition, Byun was to some length to link the case of Comfort Women to the ever-increasing sexual violence in the present-day South Korea. In the last scene of *Habitual Sadness*, she compares the statistics of today's rape cases with those of comfort women. Although it is not certain if the filmmaker's last minute attempt to make a connection is effective or persuasive, it clearly points to the historical burden imposed on today's women. In many ways, *The Murmuring* and *Habitual Sadness* distinguish themselves from the preceding women's film of *Chungmuro* not only in terms of their mode of production, distribution and exhibition but also in their approaches to women as a relevant part of history.

My Own Breathing, in its attempt to embellish on the issues raised in the previous films, asks Yi (a comfort woman) to be the main interviewer. Rather, the story goes that Yi volunteered to do so when she finished shooting *Habitual Sadness*. As interviewer, she not only listens but elucidates post-traumatic testimonies. In *Habitual Sadness*, Yi told the story of her modest financial success. She explained that she wanted to make money by all means, thinking that she thought Japan rampaged Korea and women like her because Korea was poor by then. As a self-made woman, yet with haunting traumatic past, Yi questions, listens and illuminates confessions. She also does this with humour, especially in a sequence where she accompanies Kim Boon Sun, in a visit to her hometown. Kim is 78 years old comfort woman who was sent to Taiwan. Arriving in her hometown, Kim recollects upon her past in the village where many Japanese took the lane to the gold mine. Yi asks when she was taken by Japanese soldiers. Kim answers that she was 17 years old when she was taken away in a truck. Talking about her friends, who were also spirited away, Kim sighs that no one returned except herself. Then Kim and Yi play hide and seek, just like little girls. The hide and seek game ambivalently conveys their mixed feeling of pleasure and fear as they chant, 'Hide well. Hide properly. So I can't see your hair. Come and find us … he saw us, right?' The playing tellingly captures their innocent days, soon to be irreparably damaged by sex slavery. The expression 'he saw us' chillingly visualises and expresses the advancing threat of a perpetrator. Finally the exchange between two comfort women ends with a dialogue, 'Yes, and I used to hide here, too. How do you feel? It's been 61 years.'

To deal with the experience of people who barely survived and suffered devastating losses, *My Own Breathing* carefully juxtaposes treasured moments of the pre-catastrophic with the aftermath. The looks and disjunctive articulations in Kim and Yi's exchange bring forth affect and empathy from the viewer. The unsaid throws their silent suffering into a relief. The elaboration and articulation are displaced upon non-linguistic signifiers such as body gestures and ellipses.

A comfort woman interviewing another would not resolve every one of the labyrinthine problems of a survivors' testimony. On one hand, it could create as La Capra has noted, 'the compulsive repetition of traumatic scene-scenes in which the past returns and the future is blocked or fatalistically caught up in a melancholic feedback loop'. The interviewer and the interviewee who share the traumatic event may be entrapped in that feedback loop. On the other hand, there could be moments that the viewers may feel like hearing what they are expected to hear. As a self-made and confident comfort woman, Yi is willing to encourage other women to speak out. But because of her strong will and commitment to the well-being of comfort women, she might unwittingly extract the statements from comfort women that would fit into her mode of testimony. This presumption proves overarching if it were not totally misplaced. There is a moment Yi speaks for other woman but she basically relates what she heard before from them. The feedback loop effect also diminishes as the comfort women's issues have gradually gained socio-cultural, political and historical understanding, as the trilogy moves on from 1995 to 1999. The support groups have been formed, and a partial reparation has been also made. The Women's International War Crimes Tribunal held in Tokyo in 2000 further rendered the issue as an international one.

In my view, the most captivating moment in *My Own Breathing* occurs when Kim Yoon-Shim (71 years old) appears with her handicapped daughter. Kim was sent to Harbin, China when she was 14 years old. For the last 26 years she has made her living by sewing. She is a soft-spoken and adoring character whose room is full of flowers. The camera shows the room as she sits on her balcony. Her face beams as flowers and sunlight gently surround her. In contrast to the setting, what she recounts is frightening. She speaks of her torn skin and bladder at the comfort women's camp. When she came back to Korea, she was forced to marry twice. From her second marriage, she had a baby who was born spastic due to her mother's syphilis. Kim ran away from her husband and raised her child alone. When Kim, accompanied by her daughter, is interviewed by Byun, she says that her daughter does not know of her past as a comfort woman. But during the interview, it turns out that the daughter has read her mother's biography and as a result is fully aware of her mother's history. Kim is greatly shocked by her daughter's confession and the camera responds to her shock. It makes sudden and faltering panning shots between mother and daughter. It is this moment that the intimacy and affection between them, as well as the filmmaker and the subjects, are fully revealed. Kim and her daughter interact with each other as if no-one were present. All the conversations of the mother and daughter are conducted in sign language, as Kim's daughter cannot speak. As their sign-language conversation is verbally translated by a woman present in the scene, this confession gains further layers and nuances. In between the time of the sign language and the verbal translation, the audience comes to realise the magnitude of the historical trauma and its effects on mother and daughter.

The reconciliation of mother and daughter symbolically marks an ending of the trilogy. The daughter's understanding of her mother would not resolve all the issues surrounding the comfort women. Nonetheless, it encourages one to look at the issues of comfort women from a perspective that is markedly different from the official, nationalistic discourse. And in the this discourse, the personal trauma of a comfort woman is often displaced upon the grand narrative of national pride, its loss and a will to recover it. *My Own Breathing* takes a different trajectory. As such, the film re-writes the history of both comfort women and woman's film in Korea.

Kim Soyoung

REFERENCES

Doane, M. A. (1984) 'The Woman's Film', in M. Doane, P. Mellencamp and L. Williams (eds) *Re-Vision: Essays in Feminist Film Criticism*. Frederick: American Film Institute.

ÔDISHON AUDITION

TAKASHI MIIKE, JAPAN, 2000

To the vast majority of Western filmgoers, *Ôdishon* (*Audition*, 2000) was their first introduction to the work of director Takashi Miike. After winning numerous prizes at film festivals, most notably a pair of critics' prizes in Rotterdam, it went on to enjoy theatrical distribution and almost universal critical acclaim. 'Director Takashi Miike has devised a modern-day Jacobean revenge nightmare', wrote *The Guardian*, while American entertainment industry bible *Variety* called it: 'A truly shocking horror film about obsession gone evil, *Audition* is made even more disturbing by its haunting beauty.'

However, what many regarded as a newcomer to cinema was, in actual fact, more of a seasoned veteran: a film director for nearly a decade with an impressive 34 films to his name prior to *Audition*. Starting out in the early 1990s as a director of straight-to-video films (collectively known as OV/Original Video or simply V-cinema), he specialised in that stalwart genre of the Japanese video industry: the *yakuza* or gangster film. Miike continues to work almost exclusively as a 'director-for-hire', making films on demand rather than originating personal projects. He is not a filmmaker who goes searching for a budget with a script in hand; instead producers approach him and ask him to direct projects – which in many cases already have a completed script, cast, budget and, sometimes, even a shooting schedule attached. *Audition* is one such film, as indeed are all of his better-known works: *Hanzaisha* (*Dead or Alive*, 1999), *Koroshiya 1* (*Ichi the Killer*, 2001) and *Hyôryuu-gai* (*The City of Lost Souls, 2000*).

Although this working methodology seemingly excludes the possibility of individual artistic expression, Miike's films nevertheless demonstrate very consistent themes, concerns and styles. This is thanks largely to the creative freedom given to Japanese filmmakers, particularly those working in the low budget sector of the industry. Even in V-cinema, which is notable for its assembly-line production mentality, directors are, to a large extent, free to do as they wish with the script, cast, budget and time they are given. This is why directors such as Miike, Kiyoshi Kurosawa, Shinji Aoyama, Takashi Ishii and Rokuro Mochizuki are considered to be among contemporary Japanese cinema's leading lights, even though the majority of their work was made within the constraints of the V-cinema industrial process.

Since the average budget for a straight-to-video production is roughly equivalent to US$500,000, financiers run few risks in terms of a return on their investment. The paradox that results from this is that even though V-cinema is inherently formulaic through its dependence on numerous archetypal genres and sub-genres, there is less need for directors to adhere rigidly to a formula within this. Provided the end result features the requisite elements that make the film marketable to an audience as a genre film, directors are free to do as they please with the material.

Ironically, *Audition* fell into Miike's lap when the attached production company, Omega Project, went looking for a director who could veer from the path of formula and genre expectations. The genre in this case was the horror film, which Miike at that point had not worked in. (Shortly after the completion of the film, however, he did direct two horror-themed television series, the *Buffy the Vampire Slayer*-esque schoolgirls-versus-vampires miniseries *Tennen Shojo Mann Next (N-Girls Vs Vampire*, 1999) and *Tajuu Jinkaku Tantei Saiko – Amamiya Kazuhiko no Kikan (MPD Psycho, 2000)*, about a schizophrenic police detective on the trail of a ghostly serial killer.)

Based on a novel by Ryu Murakami (who as a director adapted several of his own books for the screen, most notably *Almost Transparent Blue, Love & Pop* and *Tokyo Decadence*), *Audition* was intended to be both a cash-in on and a departure from the horror boom that had swept Japanese cinemas after the success of Hideo Nakata's *Ringu (Ring*, 1998, also co-produced by Omega Project.) Naturally, for what was envisioned to be an unconventional horror film the producers wanted an unconventional filmmaker. Miike is certainly that; a *yakuza*-genre film director who has ventured into whimsical fantasy with *Chuugoku no Chogin (The Bird People in China*, 1998) retro nostalgia (two entries in the *Kishiwada Shonen Gurentai* (1997) series) and vehicles for all-girl pop combos (*Andromedia,* 1998).

The end result is a wonderful example of Miike's ambivalent rapport with genre. Such ambivalence is of course inherently present in the V-cinema situation, but while he is often credited for his conscious attempts at undermining or bending genre rules and genre-based audience expectations, such acts are never an end unto themselves. 'I don't think about genre at all', the director has been quoted as saying. 'My films are categorised as being in a certain type of genre. But myself, I don't make the movie thinking about which category the film belongs in.'

Deviation from genre patterns is always a tool for Miike to get his message across, and the message more often than not lies in the characters and their personalities. When at the end of *Dead or Alive* the two protagonists engage each other in an increasingly outlandish final shoot-out that results in the destruction of planet Earth, this is not simply done to intentionally deviate from the standard pattern of the crime film. Rather, it expresses the protagonists' states of mind and the fact that all these two men have left in the world is their desire to destroy each other at any cost.

Miike has stated in numerous interviews that, as far as he is concerned, *Audition* is not a horror film. However, his formal approach to the film does tend to have a disconcerting effect on the audience. Much of this is the result of the pacing, playing up as it does the contrast between the relaxed, mostly un-suspenseful majority of the film and its gruesome finale. This deliberate pacing and the abrupt change for the finale leave the audience in a state of shock during the closing scenes. There is no safety net to catch the audience as they reel in horror at the unfolding scenes of torture, intensified by the film's formal, almost clinical, structure.

The final reel of *Audition* is a protracted torture scene, carried out by Asami (Eihi Shiina) upon the body of her fellow protagonist Aoyama (Ryo Ishibashi). What makes the scene so effective is Miike's use of sound (which suggests that which is not shown) and Eihi Shiina's performance. The actress smiles as she performs the tortures and talks in a hushed, almost comforting voice; the sounds she utters ('kiri-kiri-kiri') are a devastatingly stark contrast with the acts she is performing, makes them infinitely more disturbing. It is this contrast between the acts and the person who commits them (Shiina's frail beauty certainly adds to this) that make the scene so powerful, causing numerous audience walkouts wherever the film has been shown. *Audition* is unsettling, but does not have the deliberate intention of scaring the audience. Miike's intent was something very different and lies in Miike's approach to the source material. The novel started life as author Ryu Murakami's reaction to a failed affair, a love letter of sorts to an ex-lover. Miike's approach in adapting the novel to film was to imagine what that woman's reply would be.

That the response *Audition* received outside Japan had little to do with its merits as a pure horror film seems a recognition and an understanding of the director's objectives and methods. But the source for much of its critical acclaim was a wide misinterpretation of the film's message: *Audition* was perceived as a feminist statement. The story of a lonely widower looking for a new bride by duplicitous means was interpreted as an indictment of sexual politics, due in no small part to the film's finale, in which the victim of these manipulations strikes back at her supposed tormentor and subjects him to the aforementioned gruelling tortures, leaving him a human pin cushion and with one foot missing.

The feminist intent seems obvious from the synopsis alone. Any veiled misogyny in the vein of *Fatal Attraction* (1987), in which the scorned woman is turned into a caricatured harpy and the adulterous man is pardoned his missteps as a result, is firmly undone by the finale, in which the man lies helpless at the woman's feet. The attitude of the (Japanese) male towards women was attacked with a vengeance. The film sets up a series of incidents that could be regarded as sexist and which incriminate Aoyama, making Asami's revenge at the very least understandable and perhaps, perversely, justifiable.

This begins when Aoyama draws up a list of criteria to which his new bride must conform: she must be pretty, young, obedient, be able to cook and preferably have some kind of artistic skill such as playing the piano or dancing. The way he goes about finding his candidate is through an audition for a movie that will never be made and which only serves to supply him with several dozen pretty, seemingly subservient, girls to select from. Thirty women are tricked into bearing their breasts *and* their innermost feelings to two complete strangers all because of one man, who does not have the patience to meet women on equal terms. The way Miike films the audition scene emphasises the impersonal, and certainly mechanical nature of the proceedings. It starts with a shot of a single chair in an empty space, while behind it metal shutters are drawn over the windows, blocking much of the daylight from the room. Aoyama and his friend and co-conspirator Yoshikawa (Jun Kunimura) sit opposite it behind a desk and nearly every shot in the scene emphasises the position of the chair in relation to the room or to the desk. Aoyama confesses he feels like a criminal, but Yoshikawa enters into it with relish, firing off impertinent questions to the applicants about sensitive subjects such as family, sexual habits, drug use and prostitution. When Aoyama makes his choice, the 'winner' is half his age, beautiful and demure enough to pass as potentially obedient. He asks her out for a date, and in so doing abuses the power he has over her *and* the situation. To her he is, after all, the producer with the power to decide whether she gets the (nonexistent) role for which she has auditioned. She cannot say no to his request for fear of endangering her chances of success.

The case may seem clear, but Miike himself has always denied any feminist intent in *Audition*. Indeed upon closer inspection the film is revealed to be full of nuances that put the elements of sexism in a different light. Asami is not an immaculate, victimised foil. She too has lied to and deceived Aoyama. During her torture, she calls Aoyama a liar and blames him for deceiving her and the women at the audition. She is right, but self-righteously so. From the moment they met, everything she told Aoyama about herself during their dates was a lie; her feelings for him were true, without doubt, but even they came dressed in lies.

This is most clearly revealed in the jumps in time the film makes as it leads up to the finale. After he drinks the whiskey that Asami has poisoned, Aoyama falls over and the film cuts to a series of hallucinations that fulfil several functions. All are expressions of Aoyama's confused and drugged subconscious, divided between guilt and desire. These explain the scene where he imagines Asami dropping to her knees to perform oral sex on him. As she does, she changes into the secretary he once had a fleeting, failed affair with and then into the high-school girl his son has been dating. The hallucinations also set in motion Aoyama's imagination, which starts to fill in the blanks in an attempt to figure out what could have caused the demure Asami to turn so violently on him. Several revelations are made about her character, including her capacity for lies. At one point he imagines them reliving one of their dates, but this time around their conversation is completely honest and devoid of lies or evasion. Asami even offers: 'I want to tell you everything', – which naturally implies that before that moment she did not.

The other source for Asami's wrath is the discovery that he does not love just her. Learning about his late wife and the fact that he has a son makes her feel betrayed, but her demand of exclusive rights to Aoyama's love is unrealistic. Additionally, the function of Asami as a feminist symbol is undermined by the fact that one of her previous victims is revealed to have been a woman.

There are also too many nuances to the character of Aoyama for him to be dismissed as a mere male chauvinist. He recognises the impersonal nature of the audition and feels ashamed for going through with it. Further, despite the deception he employed to initially attract her, Aoyama's feelings for Asami are undeniably true; he is very much in love with this young woman. When she shows him her mutilated thighs, the result of years of systematic childhood abuse by her stepfather, he does not flinch, instead displaying concern and caring.

Feminist intent requires a film to display two factors: an ideological agenda and a sense of judgment, both of which are missing from *Audition*. The element of sexism is certainly present, but is never a basis for judgment. Aoyama is not portrayed as evil or intentionally sexist and even his colleague Yoshikawa, definitely the more sexist of the two men, shows glimpses of being no more or less than a lonely soul for whom the lack of human contact has resulted in bitterness. His disillusionment with love and relationships facilitate his gravitation towards sexist behaviour, but in a childish mode.

The element of sexism and the way Miike employs it is the key to *Audition*. Sexism here functions as a tool: one example of the ways human beings misunderstand each other. *Audition* is not about men's mistreatment of women or women's position in relation to men. Neither is it about providing an audience with pure entertainment (and certainly not about giving them a 'good time') through fear. At its most basic *Audition* is about two people who misunderstand *each other*; and this (often unconscious) mistreatment works both ways. This is brought fully to light in the film's final moments. Near the end of the torture scene, at a point when Asami attacks Aoyama's son, Shigehiko, after he unexpectedly returns home, the film cuts back again to Aoyama's hallucinations. Once more it is the re-enactment of an earlier scene, played out in a different way and filtered through his semiconscious state. We see Aoyama waking up in a hotel room after making love to Asami. Earlier in the film this same scene introduced the disappearance of Asami (and the start of her change from demure to vengeful). This time, coming at the tail end of the torture scene, the first thing he does after waking up is to pull back the sheets to see if his feet are still attached. He is relieved to find that they are, when Asami, still lying beside him, wakes up and asks him what's wrong. He replies 'Nothing', which suggests to the viewer that the torture scene was, after all, only a vivid anxiety dream/nightmare. But then she tells him she accepts his proposal of marriage. Far from merely being a jab of jet-black humour, this remark coaxes from Aoyama (in the shape of the hesitation that can clearly be seen on his face) the acknowledgement that he does not, and never will be able to, know Asami as an individual. It is the recognition of his misunderstanding.

Although the impact of the torture sequence is such that it is seen as the ending of the film, the actual final scene of *Audition* sees both Aoyama and Asami lying helpless on the floor, after she has broken her neck from a fall down the stairs. There is no woman standing triumphantly over the pitiful remnants of masculinity. There is neither triumph nor pity in those final shots. Aoyama and Asami lie there staring at each other, unable to move or look away. It is the most honest moment they share in the entire film, the moment when there is no more room for lies or deception. This moment gives sense to everything that has happened. We could consider it *Audition*'s central scene, the summation of its true intentions. Within it lies the film's entire truth.

Tom Mes

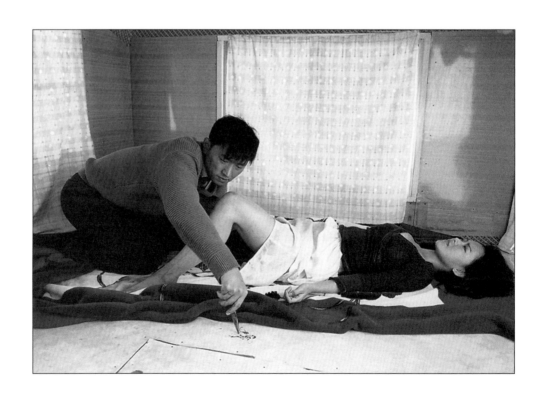

SEOM THE ISLE

21

KIM KI-DUK, KOREA, 2000

Since the early 1990s, Jang Sun-Woo, director of the daring and socially provocative *Na Pun Young Hwa* (*Timeless Bottomless Bad Movie*, 1997) and *Geojitmal* (*Lies*, 1999), has been Korean cinema's reigning *enfant terrible*. With the notorious international success of Kim Ki-duk's *Seom* (*The Isle*, 2000), followed by the extremely violent worlds depicted in his subsequent three films, *Suchwiin Bulmyeong* (*Address Unknown*, 2001), *Nabbeun Namja* (*Bad Guy*, 2001) and *Haeanseon* (*The Coast Guard*, 2002), Kim Ki-duk had successfully replaced him. Known to critics and a sizeable cult audience for a number of years, it was only with his seventh film, *Nabbeun Namja* (*Bad Guy*, 2001), that he scored a popular hit. Regardless, *The Isle* remains Kim Ki-duk's signature film. It attracted controversy and acclaim wherever it screened and was a hit at numerous festivals, winning awards at Venice, Sundance, Rotterdam, Moscow, Oporto and the Brussels International Fantastic Film Festival.

The Isle is a formally austere, meditative parable of a sadomasochistic, co-dependent relationship between two social outcasts; a mute, feral woman named Hee-jin (Suh Jung) and a morose man on the run from a violent past, Hyun-shik (Kim Yoo-suk). Set entirely in and around a picturesque lakeside setting, Hee-jin lives in a cabin by the lake and operates a taxi-boat service that ferries customers across to a small village of floating house-rafts, as well as providing inhabitants of the rafts with coffee, fishing bait and, when needed, sexual favours. The film opens peacefully, with shots of the tranquil lakeside location, as mist rises from the water. Hyun-shik arrives with only a small amount of baggage and Hee-jin takes him to one of the house floats. A bloody flashback/nightmare inter-cuts this first meeting, which not only implies the violent past of the new arrival, but suggests a similar fate lays in store for the boat's occupants. The flashback is comprised of three shots: a red-lit room, in which a couple are having sex; a dead, naked woman being dragged along a bloodied floor; and the same dead woman, her corpse thrown on to the top of her dead lover. A crime of passion, perpetrated by Hyun-shik. Hyun-shik has rented the float with the intention of comitting suicide. Hee-jin stops Hyun-shik from shooting himself by swimming under his float and stabbing a knife into his leg from a crack in the floorboard. Her act sets in motion a relationship where the infliction of pain is an essential factor.

It seems Hee-jin has become attracted to Hyun-shik. Hyun-shik tries to force himself on her, but she instinctively and aggressively rejects his advances. In an attempt to make her jealous, Hyun-shik employs a young prostitute who had arrived a few days earlier, at the request of another man. Hee-jin acts on her jealousy by taking the prostitute to an abandoned float, handcuffing her and locking her in the cabin. Tragedy strikes when the prostitute forces the cabin door open and accidentally rolls off the float and drowns in the lake. A second death occurs when a pimp comes looking for the prostitute, falls into the lake in the course of a fist fight with Hyun-shik, and appears to be pulled down into the water by an unseen force, revealed as Hee-jin.

As the film progresses and the relationship becomes more complex, Hee-jin and Hyun-shik both save each other from killing themselves from severe acts of self-mutilation (which are notorious for the shocked responses they have elicited from audiences). The scenes occur approximately twenty minutes apart, and are intended to mirror each other. The first occurs when a group of police officers come to search each float as part of a murder investigation (possibly the one alluded to in the flashback). Hyun-shik, seeing the police, decides to circumvent the confrontation with the authorities by performing a desperate act. He takes a throng of fishhooks he has made, swallows them and tries to eviscerate himself by pulling them back up his throat. Hee-jin arrives moments before the police and clears the place of evidence. After the police leave she opens the outhouse trapdoor where Hyun-shik has been hidden underwater. Pulling him up with a fishing line, she proceeds to clear his throat of the fishhooks with the aid of pliers. The second scene takes place after Hyun-shik has decided to leave Hee-jin and has set off rowing the boat. After Hee-jin realises that Hyun-shik has gone she takes a second throng of fishhooks and forces them into her vagina; pulling them outwards. The sound of her screams carries across the edit to a long shot of Hyun-shik who reacts to the cry of help by turning his boat and retracing his path back to Hee-jin. There he performs the same 'curative' duty with fishing line and pliers. By this point the two have become completely co-dependent, leading to the film's enigmatic and breathtaking concluding sequence where they appear to fuse into one, within their surrounding landscape.

Given that the film is set on and around the lakeside, one might expect the film to draw on the freedom of the open landscape. Yet Kim manages to project a sense of entrapment in the spacious exteriors by filming much of the action from a distance, through heavy mist, and by the visual motif of framing characters through various frames, such as windows, doors and cabin portals. Kim also counterpoints the harshness of his characters with gentle, rhythmic camera movements, and serene images of the undulating mist, gentle flowing waters and the soft patter of light rain showers.

The Isle has the timeless feel of a fairytale. Any sense of temporal spatiality is undermined as day, night, dusk and dawn blend into each other. There is no indication of timeframe the story unfolds over. The images shift from harshly naturalistic (a brusque businessman cuts the flank of a live fish, Hee-jin hits a frog against a rock and then skins it by hand) and contemplative (a high-angle shot of Hee-Jun and Hyun-shik lying in a boat moored in a grassy islet, interspersed with long, mist-filled shots of the lake populated with a number of colourful floats), to the surreal and nightmarish (the 'mute' Hee-jin making a telephone call behind a closed window, the final image of a nude Hee-jin lying submerged underwater, in the boat).

Many critics have condemned the film for being overly violent and brutal, yet this violence plays more of a symbolic than realistic role. Yet it can be argued that Kim does not use brutality or cruelty as an exploitative or shocking aesthetic gesture, as many have accused him of, but as a metaphorical replacement for something other than physical pain. Violence may conventionally be the enactment of physical pain, but this is not what Kim is interested in. Instead, he sees violence as a direct outgrowth, if not reflection, of emotional pain. He has stated as much in numerous interviews, commenting on the walking wounded that populate his films: 'These scenes of self-mutilation are all about sadomasochism. They are the only type of immediate responses that my characters are capable of showing. At the same time, the physical wounds are symbols, expressing how the characters are struggling in society.'

The use of physical pain/violence as a metaphor for emotional pain runs through the majority of Kim's films. It is expressed most overtly in *Suchwiin Bulmyeong* (*Address Unknown*, 2001). The film was set in 1970, in the small Korean town of Pyongtaek, where the central characters, all living on the fringe of society (invariably Kim's favourite characters), exist in the shadow – both literally and symbolically – of the Korean War and US military presence. The traumatic and far-reaching effects of the Korean War on the local body politic is expressed figuratively by Kim. Every character suffers to some extent from the effects of the war – be it directly or indirectly – and expresses their own pain by physically inflicting pain and violence on others. One of the central characters, a son born of a black US soldier (a 'cross breed' as people call him), regularly beats his mother and is in turn beaten by his mother's lover. In what might be the film's most emotionally harrowing moment, the son takes a knife to his mother's breast to cut away the tattoo bearing his absent father's name. Kim defended such scenes in response to mounting criticism:

The characters in *Address Unknown* are all lacking something, which I believe is a symbol for the problems of modern Korean society. Our fathers brought us up in a society that had a lot of problems. The concept of *han*, a Korean feeling of deep sadness that cannot be forgotten, has not been washed away from my father's generation. For example, my father still uses the name 'red communist' in a contemptuous way. He gets angry when he sees the South Korean government giving rice to North Korea. You see, he was shot and tortured by Northern troops. The Korean War was the most extreme and intense experience in our modern history. These memories are difficult for him to forget. Although his physical wounds have healed, his psychological wounds will never heal. My father's mental anguish has become my own. These feelings are projected into my films.

As in any arena where nerves are frayed, there is a pecking order to the violence, with the strong invariably preying on the weak. *The Isle* may present its pain more opaquely, surreally or metaphysically, but it is remains a pain that cannot easily be healed.

Hee-jin's mute is not dissimilar to Han-gi, the mute in *Bad Guy*. In both cases, their affliction – muteness – is employed as an external projection of internal pain. But whereas in *Bad Guy* Han-gi's silence is a gesture which allows his violence to 'speak' for his emotional pain, in *The Isle* the muteness also allows Kim to bring us back to a primitive, pre-symbolic (with language as entry into the social order) natural existence. Hee-jin's seemingly inhumane treatment of animals, the moments of anger meted out to her dog, the way she nonchalantly turns a frog into feed for Hyun-shik's birds, are not there for exploitative shock value (as a number if Western critics have argued), but to underscore her primitive, feral nature. Kim explained that 'the religious elements in my stories offer a return to Mother Nature and innocence. These days, our lives are full of artificiality. We have to try much harder to regain our innocence.'

The two notorious fishhook scenes, though brutal, are filmed to avoid being excessively gratuitous. Nothing is shown explicitly; everything remains implied, though still shocking. Their visceral impact is a testament to Kim's directorial skills and the power of the audiences' own imagination. They demonstrate how, even in a media-saturated world of so-called 'desensitised' spectators, a well-crafted combination of 'show and hide' can still move and shock.

Kim is not the only contemporary director to showcase negative aspects of contemporary Korean society. Korea is a nation that suffered through 35 years of a brutal Japanese occupation (1910–45), followed by five decades of US military presence, a psychologically devastating civil war (1950–53), and three successive military governments, until its first civilian-elected government in 1993, headed by the former opposition leader, Kim Young-Sam. Add to this unsettling mix a modern capitalist economy co-existing with an ingrained Confucian-based morality that sees female chastity as a national virtue and women as second-class citizens, and one can begin to understand how Korea has the potential to suffer from a somewhat problematic national identity. Further, it can explain the issues surrounding paternalism, authoritarianism and gender. One of the ways this troubled political history (colonialism, occupation, etc.) is filtered through Korean cinema is in the use of physical violence as a form of intimidation and a vessel for authoritarianism. Aggression and physical abuse has often been represented through acts of humiliation in recent Korean films, including *Jidokhan Sarang* (*Their Last Love Affair*, Lee Myung-sae, 1996), *Yeo-go-goedam* (*Whispering Corridors*, Park Ki-hyung, 1998), *Chang* (*Downfall*, Im Kwan-taek, 1998), *Juyuso Seup Gyeok Sageoni* (*Attack the Gas Station!*, Kim Sang-jin 1999) and *Geojitmal* (*Lies*, 1999) by Jang Sun-woo. And Kim's own *Address Unknown*, features an orgy of physical beatings, ritualistically meted out in a 'survival of the fittest' pecking order (once again, with the stronger preying on the weaker).

Within this larger issue of physical violence and aggression rests the depiction of rape, prostitution and physical violence toward women, which feature prominently in *Paran Daemun* (*Birdcage Inn*, 1998), *The Isle*, *Address Unknown* and *Bad Guy*. *The Isle* has attracted a significant degree of outrage from feminist groups; there are clearly scenes that could be construed as misogynistic, at least on a superficial level. However, this issue is anything but straightforward, particularly for a non-Korean (and male) critic. Given the film's highly metaphoric (almost fairytale) quality, it is difficult to assign political meaning to the film with such direct social import, largely because the film is not intended as a realistic depiction of the social world. For example, the misogyny the film is accused of is perpetrated against one woman, Hee-jin, yet she cannot be seen as a representation of womanhood, or even as any woman taken from the 'real' world. A mermaid, a feral, wild beast, an avenging angel, a female 'creature from the black lagoon', perhaps, but not a what might be considered a realistic representation of a 'woman'. *The Isle* is, if anything, an adult fairytale: Adam and Eve becoming one again. Man and Woman reverting to their primitive, primal origins. Even much of the their behaviour does not accord with natural law or common sense. For example, how do Hee-jin and Hyun-shik manage to stay under water as long as they are able to? How can they recover so quickly from their physical ordeal? Although these non-realist elements do not completely exonerate the film from the accusations levelled against it, or even the general level of violence directed towards all humans, or the moments of animal cruelty, they do help underscore the film's thematic-metaphoric intentions. It is thus problematic to read the gender dynamics between Hee-jin and Hyun-shik as if they represented those of a couple from the real world.

Alongside the violence against Hee-jin, there is also considerable violence perpetrated against men in the film: the fish hooks in Hyun-shik's throat, the fight between Hyun-shik and the pimp (and who is subsequently beaten and drowned), the man murdered in the flashback, the guilty customer who tries to elude the police by diving into the water and is shot dead. Together, the violence inflicted throughout the film (to humans and animals alike) suggests other possible metaphors: life is like a fish on a hook, or humanity has lost its way and has become like a 'fish out of water'. And of course, there is the enticing conclusion, where the man is literally 'lost' in the tiny reed islet, which then transforms into a female pubis. When not sparring with Hee-jin or contemplating suicide, Hyun-shik spends his time carefully crafting wire figurines. With the 'man becoming woman' ending, it is possible that the film is a reflection on the symbiotic nature of art, and the need for art and artists to succeed in the synthesis of their male and female qualities. The title, the claustrophobic use of the setting, coupled with the transmigrational ending, also suggests that each person is an island unto themselves.

Continuing with the question of gender, one sympathetic reviewer interpreted the film as a tale of how women must continually help men: 'This is a parable for male-female relationships in general. So often, women have to help the men in their lives finish growing up ... This is that kind of story about how women change men, but it's a parable set in a mythical waterworld, not an American living room.' In fact, Hee-jin does save Hyun-shik from death on three occasions (his first suicide attempt, removing the fish-hooks and hiding him from the authorities, and rescuing him from drowning). However, the consensus among Korean feminists has been that the film represents a male fantasy on male-female relationships. Indeed, it appears to be just men who rent the tiny floats, and women only go to them to service them – sexually or otherwise.

Although it is problematic to recognise how a positive male fantasy can be extracted from *The Isle*, the notion of the film as a male fantasy is questionable if seen in light of the film's characterisations. There is little doubt that Hee-jin is the strongest and most fascinating character in the film. Although mute throughout, Hee-jin expresses everything we need to know through her baleful gaze, body language and sense of being at ease with the natural environment. She also shows no fear of the men in the film and chooses to have sex when she wants and always on her own terms. For example, she refuses Hyun-shik's first sexual advances, instead taking control in their first sexual encounter.

In terms of characterisation and gender politics, it is interesting to see Hee-jin within the context of the Korean horror and fantastic film where, as professor Kim So-young notes, 'The Korean horror films with female ghosts (almost all ghosts are female in Korean cinema) and dangerous women such as films by Kim Ki-young employ sexual motifs connected to desire for social mobility and question the female sexuality in the male fantasy.' Like a ghost, Hee-jin is omnipotent in her ability to suddenly appear in the most unexpected places; under the floorboard at the moment of Hyun-shik's suicide attempt, under the water precisely where the pimp falls, peering up through his outhouse trapdoor while Hyun-shik is engaged in sex with the prostitute, or emerging from the moon-lit waters like a sea creature. If *The Isle* is a male fantasy, Hee-jin's apparent dominance throughout the film at the very least makes such claims less clear, leaving a greater sense of unease and perhaps asking more questions than either it or its audience may be able to answer.

In Kim's defence, two of the film's most contentious moments in terms of gender politics, Hyun-shik's attempted rape of Hee-jin and the later scene where Hyun-shik kicks Hee-jin in the groin and then procedes to have sex with him, are filmed in such a way as to de-dramaticise and de-sexualise the events. Both occur in the same physical space, the front landing of Hyun-shik's float, and are shot from a distance, with a static camera, and employing extremely long takes (one minute and twenty-eight seconds for the first, fifty-eight seconds for the second). In both cases, Kim's aesthetic distanciation makes it difficult, if not impossible, for a viewer to gain any sense of excitement or pleasure from the moment (sexual or cinematic). Kim also shows the same ethical concern in several politically delicate scenes in *Bad Guy*. When asked by interviewer Jung Seong-il about the harrowing scene in which student-turned prostitute Sun-Hwa loses her virginity to a paying customer Kim responded:

> I am very conscious about the chastity issue in Korea. But my primary aim was to avoid a melodramatic scene. There was no room in my film for cheap sympathy. I feel uncomfortable when films use gratuitous nudity as a symbol of sexual desire. The sex scene in *Bad Guy* was cruel and very real. Women all over the world are often forced to have unwanted sex. I didn't even look at the actors during the shooting of the sex scene. I just heard the girl scream. I couldn't bear to watch it. The critics who watched this scene and criticised me for it are definitely crueller than I am because they did not turn away. I worked with a female script editor on *Bad Guy*. I saw her turn completely pale when she watched the sex scene. Many Korean

women will feel the same way. They will feel humiliated by this scene because the sanctity of chastity is ignored.

I will conclude with a closer analysis of the film's final scene, which has confounded viewers and critics alike. It is reminiscent, with its receding aerial shot of the lake and isle, and over-determined symbolism, of the ending of Andrei Tarkovsky's *Solaris* (1972). The central characters leave the area where the film has taken place on their float-turned-boat. Subsequent images of the float moving along the blue waters ends on a fade to white. In the next shot, Hyun-shik is stood waist high in a small reedy islet. The camera tracks right until he is lost among the heavy foliage. It then cranes back and away, portraying the islet as a near circular island thatch. The image dissolves to a more distant aerial view of the thatch, then once again to an aerial shot of Hee-jin lying nude, submerged in the low water that has leaked into the boat. The slow dissolve between these final shots makes a strong graphic parallel between the islet and Hee-jin's pubic hair. Hyun-shik, last seen lost in the islet, has in effect become 'lost' in Hee-jin's sexuality; their increasingly strong co-dependency meets its final stage: they merge and become one within the landscape. However, this is perhaps just one reading of what is obviously intended to be vague, poetic and open-ended.

The penultimate scene between Hee-jin and Hyun-shik casts an interesting light on this particular reading of the conclusion. The scene begins on the morning after Hee-jin's fishhook ordeal. Things appear paradisiacal, with Hee-Jin lying between Hyun-shik's legs as he caresses her hair under the warm sunlight. They both appear as never before in the film; content, at peace with each other and with themselves. A few moments later, they are seen painting the float together. Their co-dependency, now complete, is playfully represented in the close-up of their two yellow-soaked paint brushes pressed against the side of the float, caressing and painting over each other, like two young animals in the wild. The colour is significant and could be read through teachings on Buddhist art, which offer an insight into the synthesis between the characters, in the film's final scenes: 'Yellow previously worn by criminals, was chosen by Gautama Buddha as a symbol of his humility and separation from materialist society. It thus signifies renunciation, desirelessness and humility. It is the colour of earth, thus a symbol of rootedness and the equanimity of the earth.'

Donato Totaro

REFERENCE

Jung, S. (2002) *Korean Post New Wave Film Director Series: Kim Ki-duk. Screening the Past.* Translated by Aegyung Shim Yecies and edited by Brian Yecies. Available on-line: http://www.latrobe.edu.au/screeningthepast/firstrelease/fr0902/byfr14a.html.

DAEHAKNO-YESEO MAECHOON-HADAKA TOMAKSALHAE DANGHAN YEOGOSAENG AJIK DAEHAKNO-YE ISSDA

TEENAGE HOOKER BECAME KILLING MACHINE IN DAEHAKNO

NAM GEE-WOONG, KOREA, 2000

22

Daehakno-yeseo Maechoon-hadaka Tomaksalhae Danghan Yeogosaeng Ajik Daehakno-ye Issda (*Teenage Hooker Became Killing Machine in Daehakno*, 2000) has the kudos of being the first South Korean digital video production to receive a theatrical release in that country and is a potent example of the Korean independent cinema underground. It is important to view this in the context of the new revolution in digital/experimental cinema and the freedom to experiment within this medium. The analysis of the film here will serve as an introduction to its wider context, not least contemporary Korean cinema and the renaissance in the country's output.

Paradoxically, the mid-1990s Korean cinema 'new wave' emerged from a threat to banish it altogether. The Korean Government was under international pressure to lift the quota system of homegrown films that had to be produced and released each year. The decision was misjudged and the government faced defiant protests from the local film community. However, as Kim Myong-sik, Director of the Korean Information Service, noted in *Korean Cinema Today*, a curious thing also began to take place: 'Unfolding to their great advantage was a new atmosphere of liberalism and openness in the Korean art world coming after long years of rigidity under the influence of successive authoritarian administrations. Creativity bloomed and a long-awaited "renaissance" came.' At weekends, long queues started forming outside cinemas, and on the most celebrated public Korean holiday, *Chusok* (also known as the Harvest Moon Festival), Korean films did something that had been inconceivable for some twenty years: they began to outdo Hollywood imports. Moreover, several films did this by a considerable margin. As a result, new directors found it much easier to find willing investors. Three films played a large part in this. *Swiri* (*Shiri*, 1999), a contentious political thriller based upon the North-South rivalry in Korea, defeated *Titanic* (1997) at the South Korean box office. Also catching this momentum, *Kongdong Kongbi Guyok* (*Joint Security Area*, aka *JSA*, 2000), broke *Shiri's* box-office record and then *Chingu* (*Friend*, 2000), a film seen by over eight million people in Korea, grossed more than its predecessors.

Director Nam Gee-woong was therefore well placed, in both time and location, to begin his directorial career. Born in Kyungbook, South Korea in 1968, he spent his teenage years acting, but never realised his dream of attending film school. He began his career as an assistant director in opera, an experience that would prove to have a profound effect on him, and started working in film in 1992 as an assistant director role on Kwak Jae-yong's *Autumn Journey* (also known as *A Sketch of a Rainy Day 2*). It was during this period that he experimented with a camcorder. His first film was *The Festival of Walpurgis* (1994), although it was six years before he found recognition, with the video short *Kangchul*, which won the Best Video award at the Pusan Asian Short Film Festival 2000.

Daehakno-yeseo Maechoon-hadaka Tomaksalhae Danghan Yeogosaeng Ajik Daehakno-ye Issda (literally translated as *The High-School Student Who Got Chopped Up While Selling Herself in Daehakno is Still in Daehakno*) was shot while *Kangchul* was being edited, underlining the immediacy and momentum gathered after Nam's breakthrough short. As well as being director, he also wrote the screenplay, operated the cameras, composed the music and co-edited, with Lee Chang-man. The film was financed with the support of the first Digital Feature Film Distribution Support Fund, which was part of the Korean Film Commission. Using 6mm digital video stock, Nam created much of the film's original look through the use of a wide-angle lens. However, the angle of the lens seen in this film is the combination of a different spectrum of angles than those used in most other films. A fascination with such lenses and a willingness to experiment led Nam to buy three thick lenses from a market optician, at a cost of just 10,000 won (approximately GB£5.00) each. He then cut the sides of the lenses so that they would fit the aperture of the camera, thus constructing a distorted lens that would create a 'new look' and mood for his film.

Teenage Hooker Became Killing Machine in Daehakno tells the story of a young girl who is impregnated by her teacher, killed and dismembered only to be reconstructed by a mysterious organisation, transforming her into the ultimate cyborg assassin. The title already conjures up the notion of sci-fi trash-horror with perhaps a little camp humour. During the opening credit sequence, the heroine schoolgirl (Lee So-Woon) is seen walking in slow-motion through a wooded area. What begins as dream-like mood in a rural location immediately cuts to an urban environment. Once away from the rural setting, with its classical music as transient indicator of narrative progression and into the city (Seoul) the mood becomes more akin to what the title implies. Her image is frozen, and a contemporary soundtrack with lyrics sung in English begins. The background changes to a busy shopping arcade. It is over seven minutes into what is a relatively short feature when the credits finally end – already hinting at style taking precedent over narrative. The girl emerges from the freeze-frame and walks down a dark, seedy alleyway and is eventually confronted by a strange-looking man. The music changes yet again as she works her last trick of the night. The stylised lighting, with its exaggerated *chiaroscuro*, is reminiscent of German Expressionism and American *film noir* (albeit rendered in colour). Aside of the opening scene, the film was shot entirely at night – a brave decision for those working in digital video – which gives the film a unique look. Nam also re-created a cartoon effect by using primal colours for video, as the vividness of colour falls short of the quality one gets in film stock. Here the colour becomes smudged at times and delineation between colours unclear. This has a positive effect in digital video as it creates 'new' colours. This is seen in the opening moments, when the screen is flooded with greens and in the scenes of violence, when red dominates. This use of 'new' colours colliding with primary colours is what the director calls 'digital colour', akin to painting a picture on screen.

As for narrative progression, the first implausibility occurs when we see the girl being chased by what looks to be a monster-like phallus (accompanied by the echo of a man's manic laughter over the music). The music continues as the girl has sex in a doorway. We cut to a candle-lit room and an old woman (Yoo Joon-za) who is becoming hysterical because of the noise outside. The girl and client stop when she sees a deranged-looking man: her teacher and illicit lover (Kim Dae-tong). He screams at her, 'Bitch, consider yourself expelled', complaining that she has woken his grandmother. He than dances with a file in his hand as though dancing to the non-digetic music.

Few films since *Eraserhead* (David Lynch, 1976) create such a bizarre atmosphere. Tony Rayns has described it as 'A riot of bizarre, fevered images set to a Saint-Saens-meets-acid-techno soundtrack, Nam's film stands in relation to Korean indie cinema exactly as Tsukamoto's *Tetsuo* once stood in relation to Japan's.' Nam himself has referred to his camera as having wings and the shooting style as, 'Fly(ing) like a bee, shoot(ing) like a butterfly.' In order to create the style, he employed an electric motor and a gear wheel to create a device that would allow the camera to turn 360 degrees with zoom and crane shots. As a result, the camera mounted on the device was able to shoot scenes moving freely up and down, and in an arc. Additionally, a device made from a tripod intended for stills cameras made it possible to have a stable hand-held camera similar to a steadycam, which created the sense of speed in the chase scenes through the small alleyways. Again this was devised by Nam's production team, who came up with these new inventions to achieve the director's aim of creating a revolutionary look, whilst at the same time maintaining a low budget.

The frequently jarring soundtrack helps give the film its bizarre mood. The use of operatic arias, Primal Scream and Sun Ra's light jazz, creates an overall effect that has been attempted rarely since Jean Jacques-Beineix combined classical and rock music for the soundtrack of his first feature film, *Diva* (1982). In fact, many scenes, with their lack of dialogue, resemble a music video; the songs are almost always played in their entirety, so that the soundtrack practically dictates the pace and rhythm of the film. Two scenes in particular, highlight this feature.

At the teacher's house, the girl is watched by her lover as she plays on a swing (a vivid representation of child-like innocence). They then make passionate love on the bed. A high-angle static shot of the empty swing now symbolises absence but also underlines the fate of the girl. Framed in soft light and using the words, 'Hey Sweetie' and 'The Moon was right for me to have a baby', she tells him she is pregnant, determining the events that follow. Classical music becomes quieter as the scene fades, followed by the image of three men in white coats entering the room. The mood changes suddenly as a bang is heard and the girl runs into another room and attempts to open a locked door. The teacher appears with a gun and fires two shots at her as the camera zooms in on him. Again, classical music plays, but the visuals are in stark contrast to the previous scenes. The music is juxtaposed with echoes of her screaming as the camera moves up her bloodstained body, to her shocked face. Her torso has been eviscerated.

In another scene, the three brothers (Bae Soo-baek, Kim Ho-kyum and Yang Hyuk-joon) appear. One asks, 'You wanna try chatting?' to which the girl replies, 'Who is it?' Again, classical music accompanies her beating at their hands. Implausibly she appears to be watching them as they take a hacksaw and begin cutting up her body. She now appears to be 'undead'. This scene of mutilation is inter-cut with what appears to be the girl on a stage. On closer inspection we see that she is on the roof of a building at night; the darkness and the city lights making it appear as though she is performing for an audience. It shows that in death she is free. The sequence perfectly suits the music, and can be seen to refer to Nam's background in opera. A mysterious man with dark glasses enters dragging a bag with the girl's body in it. In a large room, he stops near a seated woman; both look like 'human machines'. They glance at each other but say nothing. A third person stands between them. A sewing machine is in the foreground, suggesting that they are sewing the girl back together. Again comparisons can be drawn with *Eraserhead*. Framed alone, the tall man says, 'That killing machine is going to go to work at SDH.' Asked by the small man which assignment is she to be delivered to, the tall man replies, 'Division 6.'

Classical music and arias are used for the scenes immediately preceding the murder, the murder itself, and the re-birth of the girl as the killing machine. The camera pans over the girl's suspended torso, now full of wires. She steps down naked and (via a match-cut) steps into the street fully clothed, wearing the navy dress she wore at the beginning of the film. The resurrection is complete. She re-enters society in the next scene, when she walks into a bar. A slow pan along the bar representing the girl's point-of-view. This scene resembles the first assassination sequence in *Nikita* (Luc Besson, 1990). Now sat at a table the girl/killing machine is joined by the man with dark glasses who presents her with a gun. In slow-motion and hiding the gun under her dress, she gets up and walks to another part of the bar, pulls out her gun and fires, killing the three men infront of her. She tries to escape via the washroom but finds the door locked and realises she has been set-up. As she attempts an escape two men fire at her; she falls down but gets up again, exposing wires from her left breast. A flashback to her previous life and her murder transform her from assassin to avenging angel.

The remainder of the film moves at a fast pace, as she searches for those responsible for her death. The only conspicuous departure in terms of pace in is a point-of-view shot from the inside of a van, although the identity of the driver is not immediately revealed. We cut to a close-up of a butterfly in the road and reverse to the point-of-view of the butterfly as we see the van's headlights up ahead. The van stops as the girl appears and she starts towards the van, stopping before she reaches it. Music plays on the van's radio as it is revealed that it is the three brothers who are in the van.

Finally, the girl confronts her teacher/killer at his house. His comment, 'I programmed you. Your only function is to shoot and die', creates an ambiguity as to whether he was responsible for her being rebuilt as a killing machine. Regardless, he certainly would not have expected her to malfunction and still less to remember him. The girl lifts her navy dress up to reveal a gun barrel protruding from her crotch. The mechanical crotch-gun – seen in close-up – both underlines Nam's use of humour and pays tribute to films such as David Cronenberg's *Videodrome* (1983), with its literal 'hand-gun', and the *Tetsuo* (1988; 1992) films of Shinya Tsukamoto. Overtly phallic and with deliberate connotations of penis envy, there are echoes of *Ms. 45* (Abel Ferrara, 1981) and Czech filmmaker Václav Švankmajer (son of surrealist Jan Švankmajer) and his animated film, *Test* (2000), which also featured a mechanical penis-gun.

Since *Teenage Hooker Became Killing Machine in Daehakno*'s completion, JoPok films (the term derived from 'Jo Jik Pok Ryug Bae', which translates as 'Organised Gangsters' and reflecting the underbelly of a society in films in the same way as American Mafia, Japanese *yakuza* and Hong Kong Triad) have proven increasingly popular in Korean Cinema. Though there were 15 horror films produced/released in 2000, compared to eight JoPok films in 2001, it is the

DAEHAKNO-YESEO MAECHOON-HADAKA TOMAKSALHAE DANGHAN YEOGOSAENG AJIK DAEHAKNO-YE ISSDA latter that have proven most commercially viable. Horror films may now be less in vogue than they once were, or just that Korean audiences simply fail to accept them as readily as the more culturally established gangster film.

When a renaissance or revolution takes place in a country's national cinema, directors often gain the confidence to create experimental, daring, challenging and sometimes 'off-the-wall' films. Many countries have embraced digital film because, for the new directors, it is a cheaper as well as challenging medium and an alternative route to getting films seen at festivals. For older directors (for example, Britain's Mike Figgis with *Timecode* (2000) and *Hotel* (2001), and America's Richard Linklater with *Tape* (2001)), it is a new direction and frees them from the industry bureaucracy that some have found disdainful. *Teenage Hooker Became Killing Machine in Daehakno* does not seek to do anything truly original, though paradoxically there has been no other film like it. Using low-budget digital stock as a platform for its homage to cinema, it makes Nam South Korea's answer to Quentin Tarantino and his postmodern oeuvre. It also proves that you can make a sci-fi film with special effects with little funding, which both reaffirms and celebrates the liberating 'anyone can do it' low-/no-budget ethos of digital cinema.

Teenage Hooker Became Killing Machine in Daehakno may be the only chance we get to see Nam Gee-woong working in such a raw and experimental manner, as his subsequent film (with the delicious working title *Chow Yun-Fat Boy Meets Brownie Girl*), was shot on 35mm – a move which often necessitates certain artistic restrictions and demands from financiers.

Steve Yates

BATORU ROWAIARU BATTLE ROYALE

KINJI FUKASAKU, JAPAN, 2000

When Batoru Rowaiaru (*Battle Royale* 2000) was first released internationally, film journalists in the west reached for the same handful of pop culture references as a comparison. Included were the reality TV show *Survivor*; two novellas written by Stephen King (*The Long Walk* and *The Running Man*, both written under the pseudonym Richard Bachman) in addition to the most obvious reference, William Golding's novel *The Lord of the Flies*.

That the comparisons are multitudinous says much about the 'high concept' of *Battle Royale*, based on Takami Koushun's successful 1999 novel of the same name. The Hollywood 'high concept' approach of pitching a story in less than thirty seconds, in a way that an audience can grasp without having to even think about it, was popularised by the powerhouse partnership of producers Don Simpson and Jerry Bruckheimer. But 'high concept' was an approach so simple – and, arguably, simplistic – that it was never destined to be restricted to the North American continent. The plot of *Battle Royale* can be pitched in a sentence: 'A class of junior-high school students are taken to a deserted island to take part in a game where they must kill one another until only one survivor remains.' Although this simple concept attracted cinemagoers with ease, it fails to encompass the various levels the film works on and Kinji Fukasaku's film is a far richer, deeper and more rewarding piece of work than those cultural predecessors listed above. In addition to being an exhilarating piece of action cinema in its own right, it works as a satire, political allegory, social comment, love story and paranoid thriller, whilst acting as a cautionary tale, with small personal tales of tragedy and friendship featured amidst the gore.

The opening scenes immediately introduce both the tone and the themes of the film. Following the brief image of raging waters crashing against rocks off the coast of an island, with a bombastic classical score thundering in the foreground, Fukasaku swiftly cuts to some expository text that informs the viewer that this story takes place in an alternate present. The text, music and imagery give the film the grand texture of much-loved epic series, like the *Star Wars* saga. The devoted and fanatical cult following that *Battle Royale* has gained since its release is not dissimilar to the adoration and devotion that has been dedicated to the worlds created by George Lucas and J. R. R. Tolkien.

At the dawn of the millennium, Japanese society has suffered a severe economic collapse, leading to widespread youth apathy and 800,000 students boycotting school. Adult society sought to reassert their authority by passing the Millennium Education Reform Act, otherwise known as the BR Act. The brief introduction gives way to manic shots of news crews and army troops converging at the end of the previous year's Battle Royale, before we see flash cuts of the game's winner: the demonic smile on the cherubic face of a sweaty and blood-spattered little girl hugging an equally bedraggled toy doll. The image is comic and horrific in equal measure; in much the same way as the action yet to come.

Next we see a school photograph of Class B of Zentsuji Middle School. The first face the camera focuses upon, significantly, is that of the class teacher Kitano, 'Beat' Takeshi Kitano. The Kitano character is the only major digression from Takami's source material. In the novel, the character is a stranger to the students of Class B, a government employee called Sakamochi; a hateful authority figure with no redeeming qualities. In Fukasaku's adaptation, Kitano is their embittered and cynical former class teacher, with a fully realised back story. His relationship with his daughter is rapidly deteriorating and he has suffered at the hands of the students, particularly Kuninobu Yoshitoki, who once stabbed him in the buttocks. By casting such a recognisable star in the crucial role of Kitano, all attention is on him when he delivers the expository information that will make sense of why the children are in captivity and what they need to do to survive. And in naming him Kitano, allusions are drawn with the iconic media polymath's own persona.

By fleshing out the personality of the Kitano character, Fukasaku improves on Takami's one-dimensional comic-book villain, and also extends the idea of father figures and the way they shape their children, either consciously or by their absence. The next character introduced in *Battle Royale* is Shuya Nanahara (Tatsuya Fujiwara), who discovers the corpse of his father after he has committed suicide. Scrawled on toilet paper, he reads the words: 'Go Shuya! You can make it Shuya!' Words that will carry greater significance once the game is underway. The words of Shuya's voice-over embody the underlying tension and fear between adults and children that runs throughout the film: 'I didn't have a clue what to do and no-one to show me either.' The students of Class B will have to deal with their own insecurities, egos and inexperience in the world of Battle Royale, as no-one, least of all an adult, is going to help them. The adults need the weakness and helplessness of children to give them the feeling of control and superiority, whilst the disillusioned children crave the guidance and protection of adults.

At other moments in the film, we hear hacker whiz-kid Mimura Shinji talk about his activist uncle who taught him how to make bombs and other explosives, tragic hero Shogo

Kawada frequently attributes skills he has learned to his father's experience, and there is Kitano, whose obsession with revenge on the children of Class B merely serves to perpetuate the idea of the failure of adults in their responsibilities, by neglecting his own daughter.

At times, the film feels strikingly original. Yet it can also be seen as a re-working of the themes and situations familiar throughout the history of Japanese (and international) film and popular culture, whilst simultaneously reflecting genuine concerns about issues afflicting modern society. With this in mind, it is easy to see the way in which *Battle Royale* acknowledges the past, crystallises the present and warns of the impending future. Consequently, it is no surprise that the original novel was the work of first-time author Koushun Takami, and the film was the sixtieth feature film of 70-year-old veteran Kinji Fukasaku, bridging the gap between the preoccupations of Japanese history, and the genuine fears (and hopes) for the nation's unwritten future.

Bearing in mind that Takami was a student who dropped out of Nihon University's liberal arts correspondence course programme, before spending five years between 1991 and 1996 working as a writer for the prefectural news company Shikoku Shinbun, it is interesting that his novel had such a significant impact on Fukasaku. The director was fifteen years old as World War Two drew to a close. His class was drafted into the war effort, and they found themselves working in a munitions factory. The carnage of the war was still something abstract, which the teenagers were only aware of from a distance, and via air raid shelters. However, in July 1945, the classmates were caught in a barrage of artillery fire. Just like the fictitious world Fukasaku would chronicle fifty-five years later, there was barely any chance of escape from violent and messy death. The survivors of the attack used the corpses of their friends as cover and, after the violence had passed, Fukasaku and his surviving friends were given the task of disposing of the body parts of their former classmates. Not surprisingly, this experience influenced both his worldview and the films he would make during the course of his career. Virtually overnight, Fukasaku developed a deep-rooted hostility and distrust towards adults and authority figures, and the lies they tell their children to control and mould them, as well as a sense of bonding towards his friends.

This bonding surfaces throughout *Battle Royale*. If the film was little more than a series of gruesome and inventive set pieces, it would function as acceptable entertainment and mindless spectacle, but the emotional journey of the characters gives the film another dimension. With the exception of the ruthlessly psychotic Kazuo Kiriyama, the pain, confusion and disappointment the students feel is evident throughout. Even the scythe-wielding Mitsuko Souma, who attacks the game with relish, has moments when she comes across as something more than just a heartless killer. As we hear in voice-over more than once, 'I didn't want to be a loser anymore', perhaps intimating earlier traumas.

Battle Royale is a savage indictment of a failed competitive education system, a nation's disaffected youth, and a proud but ailing martial civilisation punishing the next generation for its own failings. The children of Class B are initially presented as unreachable rebels. They write the words 'Taking the day off cause we want to' on the blackboard, and attack people, including their teacher, for no apparent reason. But as the game progresses, we see normal teenage behaviour surfacing (albeit magnified by the abnormal circumstances); they harbour secret crushes or petty grudges on classmates, and, in the case of Hiroki Sugimura, he constantly puts himself in peril to fulfil a naïve romantic whim, to find the girl he has a crush on, just so he can tell her how he feels. It costs him his life, as she riddles his body with bullets in a moment of blind panic.

The game becomes a microcosm of the behavioural traits of children in inhuman circumstances. Their humanity and emotions are raw and exposed. By turns, we feel their anger, fear, paranoia, regret, denial, panic, terror, helplessness and, occasionally, their malice. Tellingly, by removing the normal restrictions of civilised society, these emotions appear more dramatically. *Battle Royale* exposes not only the depths of genuine friendship (the unlikely alliance between Shuya, Noriko, and former winner of BR, Shogo), but also the limits of friendship when tested. Class representative Yukie Utsumi attempts to impose structure on the situation by hiding out in a lighthouse with a handful of girls. It starts like a perverse pyjama party, with guard shifts and cooking rosters, giggling and playfulness, but the smallest signs of jealousy and paranoia easily shatters the fragile tranquillity.

Battle Royale is far less stylised than many of Fukasaku's films. He attributed the controlled and mostly static directorial style of *Battle Royale* to necessity, borne out of his young cast's inexperience, and his frustration with their *manzai* (interaction). Nevertheless, it is the naturalism and slight awkwardness of the children that lends the film much of its authenticity, and the performances are uniformly strong and generally convincing. In particular, Tatsuya Fujiwara in the role of Shuya Nanahara has to carry most of the film's emotional weight, and he acquits himself well. There is a striking difference between Shuya's innocence and Shogo Kawada's experience. The man Shogo has become was forged in the crucible of his previous participation in Battle Royale. Shuya, however, is shaped by his feelings of responsibility for Noriko, and the lesson's about life's unfairness and its harsh realities as espoused by Shogo.

It is far too easy to fall into the trap of analysing the very real and important issues at the heart of *Battle Royale*, at the expense of acknowledging that Fukasaku's film is also an exceptionally entertaining and often hilarious action movie, with moments like the severed head with a hand grenade stuffed into its shocked mouth flying through the air; Kitano's dry announcements to the children ('It's tough when friends die on you, but hang in there!'); and the sight of a student with an axe buried deep in the centre of his forehead assuring Shuya that he is absolutely fine. Without the bursts of odd humour, *Battle Royale* could potentially be an unpleasant trudge to the finishing line; yet it has a dynamic energy to it, borne from the fact that Fukasaku clearly believes deeply in the subject matter, and the importance of communicating truthfully with Japan's youth.

The rules of the game (and the film) are simple, and seductively compelling. After a school class are picked randomly and taken to a secret and secluded location (in this particular instance, an island where all the inhabitants have been forcibly evacuated), the rules are explained in two complementary ways. There is the amusing training video with its flashy camerawork and garish colours, and, by contrast, Kitano's demonstration of the game, which results in the gruesome death of two students. The rules are: each student is fitted with a collar that will track their location, and can be automatically detonated if the wearer tries to remove it or escape from the island. The game will last for three days. If there is more than one person still alive at the end of three days, all the collars will detonate. Portions of the island will become 'forbidden zones' at announced intervals. Any contestant remaining in one of the zones after the allotted time will have their collar detonated. Each contestant is provided with food, water, a map, a compass, a flashlight and a weapon, which, as Fukasaku illustrates in one of the film's many moments of gallows humour, can turn out to be anything from Shuya's virtually useless kitchen pot lid, to the psychopathic Kiriyama's lethal automatic rifle. As the game commences, a title card flashes up. 'The Game Begins. Day One. 1.40am.'

In the tradition of countless stalk-and-slash horror movies, such as Ridley Scott's *Alien* (1979) and John Carpenter's *The Thing* (1982), *Battle Royale* works on the most basic level; its entertainment value lying in the many ways in which the students are despatched. And as a satire of the public's terrifying blood lust and appetite for the humiliation and suffering of complete strangers, as well as the way both the media and the government blur the lines between entertainment and propaganda, in order to keep the masses docile and distracted, the film is reminiscent of Norman Jewison's *Rollerball* (1975). *Battle Royale* shows the ways in which the public are complicit in the suffering of these children. Violence as entertainment is condemned, as we watch entertaining violence. As viewers of Fukasaku's film, we are complicit too. Just as in the novel, Fukasaku regularly puts the current score on the screen, so we can keep track of who is dead, and who is still out there fighting for survival. *Battle Royale* gives new meaning to the phrase 'extreme sports'.

There are other ways that *Battle Royale* signifies the way the past, present and future dovetail. Towards the turn of the century, a handful of notable filmmakers from the 1950s and 1960s caught their second wind in their twilight years, and returned to prominence after decades of relative anonymity: Seijun Suzuki with *Pistol Opera* in 2001, Imamura Shohei with 1997's Palme D'Or-winner *Unagi* (*The Eel*) and 2001's *Akai Hashi No Shitano Nurui Mizu* (*Warm Water under a Red Bridge*), and Nagisa Oshima's *Gohatto* in 1998.

Fukasaku's career was interesting, erratic and wildly successful, spanning five decades, including the ground-breaking *auteur* of the *Jingi Naki Tatakai* (*Battles Without Honour and Humanity*) series in the early 1970s and the big-budget sci-fi helmer of 1978's *Uchu Kara No Messeji* (*Message from Space*). With hindsight, Fukasaku's career almost looks like a rehearsal for *Battle Royale*, a distillation of his commercial savvy, his love of youthful and violent storytelling, and a virtually autobiographical representation of his experiences living in post-war Japan.

The political furore that erupted in Japan before the film had even been released ironically echoed many of the ideas bouncing around in Fukasaku's film. Education Minister Nobutaka Machimura tried to convince cinemas not to screen the film, whilst opposition politician Koki Ishii railed against *Battle Royale* in a House of Representatives committee meeting the day after its theatrical release, despite the fact that he had not seen the film; even going so far as to strongly advocate the introduction of new legislation to increase regional and national censorship laws. The politicians paraded the stock excuses for censorship. There were claims that the film could incite copycat incidents. In 2000, there had been a number of stories in the Japanese press about youth violence: an adolescent had hijacked a bus and killed a passenger; one boy beat his mother to death; another detonated a home-made bomb in a video store; and a 17-year-old stabbed and killed three neighbours. There were terrified adults, both inside and outside of the government, whose feelings were uncomfortably close to the paranoia of the adults trying to control their rebellious youngsters in the film unspooling across cinema screens all over the nation.

Despite a few moments where the government looked uncomfortably close to preventing the release of *Battle Royale*, Fukasaku's impressive fable was released in Japan on 16 December

2000, and was hugely successful. Youngsters camped outside cinemas overnight to get tickets. Fukasaku's target audience was turning up in droves, at least the ones who were permitted admission. Unfortunately, Japan's self-regulating censorship board and ethics committee, Eirin, chose to rate the film R-15, meaning that no one under the age of fifteen could be admitted.

Other countries were not so fortunate. The American public were still reeling from the massacre at Columbine High School that took place in Littleton, Colorado on 20 April 1999, which left 13 dead and 25 injured. In the real world, children were dying at the hands of other children, and the film was never widely available in the US. The advent of multi-region DVD players, however, ensured that the curious cineaste could effortlessly secure a copy of the film.

In the UK, *Battle Royale* was released theatrically just three days after the terrorist attacks on the World Trade Center and the Pentagon. In a week where carnage and bloodshed on such a huge scale was streaming 24 hours a day on news networks globally, here was a film that in many ways approved of retaliatory violence. The ways in which audiences responded to *Battle Royale* seemed to have a direct bearing on the prevailing mood of the general populace in any given corner of the world, in particular as the film raises questions about problems and solutions. The solutions in *Battle Royale* are massively disproportionate to the problems caused by juvenile delinquency.

The legacy and power of *Battle Royale* continued to attract new fans. In 2003, English translations of Takami's novel and the *manga* adaptation by Takami and Masayuki Taguchi were successfully published in the US for the first time. Quentin Tarantino's valentine to Japanese cinema, *Kill Bill* (2003), paid homage to both Fukasaku and *Battle Royale*. Tarantino even cast the striking Chiaki Kuriyama (the actress who played Takako Chigusa in *Battle Royale*) as Go Go Yubari, going so far as to clothe her in a school uniform.

Battle Royale II: Requiem, the film Fukasaku was working on at the time of his death, illustrates the never-ending cycle of the relationship between parents and children. Although he was aware he was dying of cancer, he defiantly threw himself into pre-production with energy and passion. When Fukasaku died on 13 January 2003, the completion of the film, and the continuing development and evolution of the *Battle Royale* saga, became the responsibility of his son Kenta, who had also scripted the first *Battle Royale*.

At the end of *Battle Royale*, Fukasaku appears to directly address his young audience, with words that form the true core of the story: 'No matter how far, run for all you are worth … RUN!' The words are neither a warning nor a call-to-arms, but rather a positive rallying cry to help guide his nation's youth. Although the film is filled with a plaintive yearning and sadness, the ending shows that faced with seemingly unbeatable obstacles, faith in the future can survive. Even at the grand old age of 70, after a lifetime witnessing anguish and despair, and a movie full of death and destruction, Fukasaku ends on a genuinely hopeful note, with a remarkably powerful, important and strangely optimistic film.

Anthony Antoniou

JOINT SECURITY AREA

PAK CHAN-WOOK, KOREA, 2000

In 1999, with the release of Kang Je-gyu's *Swiri* (*Shiri*), the concept of the 'Korean blockbuster' was realised. A major commercial event in Korean cinema history, it was the beginning of a new era for an industry that could begin targeting bigger audiences and investing larger budgets. One year later, Pak Chan-wook's *Kongdong Kongbi Guyok* (*Joint Security Area*, aka *JSA*) was released by CJ Entertainment. It cemented the popularity of a thriller sub-genre that employed impressive actions set-ups, a plot played out against the backdrop of the North-South divide, and an enormous marketing campaign to ensure its success.

The film opens as a car heads towards the barbwires, checkpoints and soldiers of one of the most heavily guarded locations in the world: the Joint Security Area of Panmunjon, better known as the DMZ (demilitarised zone). A radio announcer is heard reporting on recent events where, in a surveillance post on the edge of the demilitarised zone, two North Korean soldiers have been shot dead, with another wounded. A young South Korean soldier has confessed to the crime. In the car is Sophie Jean (Yi Young-ae), a Swiss observer sent by the Neutral Nations Supervisory Committee to investigate the crime. As she conducts her investigation she begins to understand that two South Korean soldiers had befriended two North Korean soldiers and met cordially whilst on duty, until one night, when one of them pulled a gun.

In investigating the incident, Sophie Jean gradually draws on her own history and experiences, which parallel the larger troubles around her. Before he abandoned her, her father served in the North Korean army, but moved away after the war. As her investigation deepens, her increasing lack of self-assurance becomes increasingly noticeable, transforming her into a symbol of the split identity of the country, both seemingly unable to control their own destiny. Her character is embedded in the picture that she carries with her, showing her as a child with her stepmother; and stood next to them, but hidden from view, her father. The picture has been folded for so many years that it is permanently damaged; the line that separates daughter and father irremovable. Unity only stands in division, or, you must be two to be one. This idea is the central tenet of the film, of being in the middle or centre – caught between two sides (the word centre in Korean *chung* is derived from the Chinese character *Zhong*).

For centuries, Koreans believed they possessed no 'centre'. China was seen as the centre of the world, even by Koreans. In Korean, the word 'China' retained its Chinese definition: *Chung guk* or 'the country of the centre'. Korea called itself *Dongguk* – 'the country of the east'. There is a telling letter by King Sonjo of Korea, responding in 1590 to a message from Japanese emperor Hideyoshi, who was planning to attack China: 'What are you thinking about? Every country from the inside and the outside are the subject of *Chung guk*.' To King Sonjo, attacking China was impossible, not because it was too big or too strong, but because by attacking it, the countries would destroy their own centre. Korea's existence was based on a balance where China was the centre, therefore the collapse of China equated to self-destruction. Over 300 years later, the centre did fall when the summer palace of Beijing was destroyed by Western countries led by Great Britain and France. The impact of this event was enormous for Koreans, who then had to find a new centre against which to balance. This new balance was a line drawn within its own borders and the area of land that lay upon it: the Joint Security Area.

Of course, any represented space possesses a centre. Most of the time it is implicit, but in *Joint Security Area* Pak Chan-wook's camera stove to remind us where this centre lay. The use of static shots, accentuating the placement of objects, characters and scenery within the frame can draw the eye to a specific point in an image, or underline the importance of a certain area. Moreover, certain objects – a tree, an electric pole, a wall, a fence – within a frame can physically divide the image, and in this, Pak Chan-wook succeeded in being both subtle and creative. Some shots take the form of geometrical compositions, where the characters appear like figures on a chessboard. This is most evident in the scene when Sophie Jean is reconstructing the murder using figurines made out paper.

The character of Sophie Jean represents the centre of the film, accentuated by her playing darts; she can be seen as the dart aiming for the centre of the board. Again, at the end of the film there is an aerial shot over Sophie as she stands, under an umbrella, on the point where two lines meet.

Rudolf Arnheim has theorised on the notion of the centre, most significantly in his book, *Power of the Centre*. To him, the centre is an ambiguous position as it is both a place of division and unification: 'When a composition is built on two segregated halves, the weight of a central axis, be it vertical or horizontal, divides the two parties effectively. More than separation is needed, however. If those parties did not interact, there would be no good reason for them to be united in the same composition. Therefore, the dividing axis commonly carries a bridging element as well.' This is equally true in Asia, where the term 'centre' not only refers to the spatial but also to the dynamic. Angela Zito of Columbia University studied the role of the centre in imperial sacrifice rituals. In her essay *Silk and Skin: Significant Boundaries*, she claims that the word *zhong* is not only a name, but a verb in classical Chinese: '*Zhong* has no proper opposite term. As a noun it means middle but an empty one, found between the inner and the outer, where the upper and lower meet and where there is no movement in the four directions. As a verb *zhong* means to hit the centre. "Centering" thus constantly creates itself through the correct separation of upper and lower, the correct bounding of inner and outer … When people "make the triad with heaven and earth" they *zhong*, providing meaningful connection.'

The geographical paradox of *Joint Security Area* resides in what separates North and South Korea: a bridge. The film tells the story of 'zhonging people'. Believing that they are bridging the opposite poles, in the same act, they are creating the 'correct' separation. Sophie Jean is sent to Panmunjon to play the role of the neutral centre in order to unify the pieces of a broken story. As the story unfolds, she tries to unite facts and people, but realises it is beyond her control; she can only play the part of divider. The interrogation scene is pivotal in blurring the role she plays. The scene takes place in one of the cabins on the border. Sophie Jean, sat at a table with a South Korean soldier (Yi Pyongh-on) to her left and a North Korean (Song Kang-ho) to her right, has her back to the camera. The composition is perfectly symmetrical, with Sophie Jean's physical presence dividing the screen. The rest of the frame is similarly symmetrical. On the left a video camera is facing Song while on the right a video camera is shooting Yi. In front of Sophie Jean is a large television screen. Suddenly, the sequence cuts 180 degrees, to face Sophie Jean, who remains centre screen. However the rest of the composition has reversed. The North Korean soldier is now on our left and the South Korean on our right. In two static shots, Pak demonstrates the simplest of truths: there is no right or left when there is no middle. The centre is geometrically unable to create unity. In other words, if there were no Swiss – or foreign – force in the middle, there would be no North or South Korea. The centre is, literally, metaphorically and, in this case, geographically, pivotal. The rest of the film highlights the political consequences of this reality.

This idea that a united Korea is a Korea without a centre is expressed when the young South Korean soldier crosses the border for the first time. We do not witness him crossing the line. He is shown walking to the bridge and then stopping. The camera movement begins from a close-up on his face and then moves around him. Then the camera moves in the opposite direction, only to revert to its original course, undermining any sense of geographical space. When the camera stops, the soldier has crossed the border and is in North Korea. This scene demonstrates why *Joint Security Area* is not a film about erasing the divide, not a film about unity. Instead, the film argues that as the centre divides, it simultaneously provides a fragile balance.

The first encounter between the North and South Korean soldiers occurs at night, in a deserted field in the DMZ. The South Korean soldier has isolated himself from the rest of his company to urinate in private. Suddenly, he walks into a wire and looks down to realise the horror of his situation – he has just stepped on a mine. If he walks back and releases the pressure, or steps forward, he will break the wire and detonate the mine. He can only stand still in the middle of this empty space and wait for someone to come to his rescue. Unfortunately, when he looks on his portable radar, he realises that he is out of reach. He has not walked very far, but he is beyond reach. He is in North Korea. Alone in the middle of nowhere, the thin wire becomes a border between life and death, and soon between North and South, as two soldiers approach him. Finally, the mine is diffused after the South Korean soldier is ridiculed for trying to act heroically at first, only to whimper and beg for help. Yi's clownish acting diffuses the dramatic situation. Indeed *Joint Security Area* is full of humour, albeit tinged with danger.

Because the story is told in flashbacks, we know from the beginning that this friendship is doomed; that unity between the soldiers can exist, if at all, only briefly. In this lies another fascinating aspect of the film: there is no real explanation as to the cause of the tragedy, just the knowledge that the victim and perpetrator were on opposing sides. This is why, when the young South Korean soldier shoots his North Korean friend, his eyes are closed. No one is responsible. Circumstance alone has made it tragic, yet inevitable. It is the flow of time, symbolised here by an audiotape, that prompts the vio;ent outburst. Before the shooting begins, the friends are listening to a tape playing a nostalgic Korean pop song. Suddenly, after a short silence, the tape reverses and the sound of a violent rock guitar bursts out of the speakers. At the sound of the music, both sides have unholstered their guns. Like the audiotape, there are two sides to history and life alternates between them. One for friendship and unity, the other for death and disparity; a time to love and a time to kill. They are less oppositional than interconnected, alternating in a regular and unbreakable rhythm. One cannot do anything about it. 'Once Yin, once Yang, this is the Tao', according to the Chinese proverb. In this way, although *Joint Security Area* is presented as a thriller, it is in truth a typical Korean melodrama where a tragic fate affects the characters – and through them, the country – without apparent reason.

I have argued that through its organisation of space, *Joint Security Area* describes a Korean political reality and also expresses the idea that Korea is not responsible for its division.

The commercial success of the film, as has often been noted while comparing *Joint Security Area* to *Shiri* (which features conventional 'red devil' clichés), is that it relies more on the action sequences than the portrayal of a 'human side' of North Korea. However, the North Korean aspect of the film does play an important part in the film and its relation to the audience.

It is common to neglect the existence of the spectator in the process of film-making. For instance, an actor looking into the camera is deemed unusual, unless performed within a specific context (Brechtian distanciation, parody, etc.). By looking directly at the camera – that is, its eyeline – the artifice of film can be shattered. This fear of 'the look' is constant in the history of Western art, and is related to the concept of aestheticism. In his trilogy on the origins of modernity in Western painting, Michael Fried has called 'absorption' the attitude of a subject who is absorbed by his thoughts or activity. To him, the character is, in fact, avoiding eye contact with the spectator. Fried describes the innovation (by Manet amongst others) of the face-to-face connection between spectator and subject as a violent confrontation. However, the subjects in Korean painting never seem to avoid eye contact with the viewer. On the contrary, it seems that they accept their role of represented subject, and an audience must accept their role of viewer. This is true also of cinema. In Shin Sang-ok's classic *Sarangbang Sonnim-Kwa Omoni* (*The Guest and My Mother*, 1961) a young girl opens the film by introducing herself directly to the audience. Audiences are invited into the action, to be observers and passive participants in the unfolding events.

Early in *Joint Security Area*, there is a scene featuring a young American tourist is visiting Panmunjon (a visit forbidden to South Koreans) with a group guided by an American soldier. A wind blows suddenly and her red cap flies over to the other side of the border. The American soldier walks to the famous line and North Korean soldiers approach him. A shot of a hand picking up the cap pulls back to reveal a North Korean soldier, at first appearing as the Western cinematic archetype of a communist soldier; unemotional, with a stony expression. He dusts off the red cap and suddenly breaks into a smile. Handing back the cap, he is not smiling at the American soldier in front of him, but to the South Korean audience looking at the movie from the other side of the screen/border. From his side of the screen, the North Korean soldier seems to tell us 'I saw you'. Thus, a border is created between the viewer and the fiction. This new screen creates an inter-subjective relation with the viewer. In other words, the screen 'zhongs', creating a union-separation relationship between inner and outer, between viewer and film.

Pak Chan-wook uses the screen to compose symmetrical filmic space where the screen represents a centre – *zhong* between the spectators and North Korea. Watching the less than realistic narrative of *Joint Security Area* unfold (it was noted in the South Korean press shortly after the film's release that any encounter between North and South soldiers is impossible), one may not be close to the political truth, but one is closer to the North than ever before. In his essay on Chinese screen painting, *The Double Screen*, Wu Hung points out that, 'The screen transforms space into places that are definable, manageable and obtainable. The concept of space is thus political.' What is said here about the traditional painted screen is equally true for the modern cinema screen. If *Joint Security Area* implies that separation is a fatality, it also shows that reunion is briefly possible, because of the very role of the centre: the base of a construction, but also a turning point, a pivot. For South Korean viewers, this was a unique experience.

It can be argued, therfore, that the success and singular quality of *Joint Security Area* resides in its very precise organisation of space. The director bases his compositions and direction on a simple architectural reality as described by Rudolf Arnheim; the place of division, the centre, is also a place of brief and yet possible encounter between two sides.

In 2002, when the great Korean director Im Kwon-taek received the Best Director award at the Cannes Film Festival for *Shiwaseom* (*Drunk on Women and Poetry*, 2002) he stated that his award was not only for South Korea, but for the 'two Koreas'. His act was a sign of reconciliation and peace through the image of cultural unity between North and South. However, by saying this, he also recognised the very *existence* of two Koreas and the concept of division. The tragic truth shown in Pak Chan-wook's film was thus demonstrated in Im's inability to orally express unity without talking about division. Indeed, this is the mathematical truth of *Joint Security Area*: to become one (to unite), the precondition is to be two divided entities. There is no unity if no division existed – therefore, division is always the promise of unity.

Adrien Gombeaud

REFERENCES

Arnheim, R. (1988) *The Power of the Centre. A Study of Composition in the Visual Arts.* Los Angeles and London. University of California Press Berkeley.

Wu, H. (1996) *The Double Screen. Medium and Representation in Chinese Painting.* London. Reaktion Books.

FILMOGRAPHY

KURUTTA IPPEJI A PAGE OF MADENESS 1926
Director: Kinugasa Teinosuke
Production: Kinugasa Teinosuke, Shin Kankaru-Ha
Screenplay: Kinugasa Teinosuke, Kawabata Yasunari
Photography: Sugiyama Kohei, Tsuburaya Eiichi
Cast: Inoue Masao (custodian), Nakagawa Yoshie (wife), Iijima Ayako (daughter), Nemoto Hiroshi (young man), Seki Misao (doctor)
Running Time: 58'

SAYON NO KANE SAYON'S BELL 1943
Director: Hiroshi Shimizu
Screenplay: Yoshitomo Nagase, Torashiro Saito, Hiroshi Ushida
Photography: Suketaro Inokai
Cast: Ri Koran, Hatsu Shimazaki
Running Time: 74'

JAYU MANSE HURRAH! FOR FREEDOM 1946
Director: Choe In-gyu
Production: Choe Hwan-kyu
Screenplay: Jeon Chang-keun
Photography: Han Hyeong-mok
Editing: Yang Ju-nam
Music: Park Tae-young
Cast: Hwang Yeo-heui (Hyeja), Jon Jang-gun (Hanjung), Yoo Kye-seon, Jeon Taek-yi, Ha Yeon-nam, Kim Seung-ho
Running Time: 60' (estimated)

NORA INU STRAY DOG 1949
Director: Akira Kurosawa
Production: Motoki Sojiro
Screenplay: Kikushima Ryuzo, Kurosawa Akira
Photography: Nakai Asakazu
Editing: Goto Toshio, Sugihara Yoshi
Music: Hayasaka Fumio
Cast: Mifune Toshiro (Detective Murakami), Shimura Takashi (Chief Detective Sato), Kimura 'Ko' Isao (Shinjuro 'Yuro' Yusa), Awaji Keiko (Harumi Namaki), Yamamoto Resiaburo (Honda), Sengoku Noriko (girl), Kawamura Reikichi (Ichikawa), Miyoshi Eiko (Madame Namiki)
Running Time: 122'

SAIKAKU ICHIDAI ONNA THE LIKE OF OHARU 1952
Director: Kenji Mizoguchi
Production: Hideyo Koi, Kenji Mizoguchi
Screenplay: Saikaku Hiharu, Kenji Mizoguchi, Yoshikata Yoda
Photography: Yoshimi Hirano, Yoshimi Kono
Editing: Toshio Goto
Music: Ichirô Saitô
Cast: Kinuyo Tanaka (Oharu), Tsukie Matsura (Tomo), Ichirô Sugai (Shinzaemon), Toshirô Mifune (Katsunosuke), Toshiaki Konoe (Lord Harutaka Matsudaira)
Running Time: 148'

GOJIRA GODZILLA 1954
Director: Honda Inoshiro
Production: Tanaka Tomoyuki
Screenplay: Honda Inoshiro
Photography: Tamai Masao
Editing: Taira Yasunobu
Music: Ifukube Akira
Cast: Shimura Takashi (Professor Yamane), Takarada Akira (Ogata), Kochi Momoko (Emiko)
Running Time: 98'

OBALTAN AIMLESS BULLET 1961
Director: Yu Hyun-mok
Production: Kim Seong-chun
Screenplay: Yi Jong-gi and Na So-un, based on a short novel by Yi Beom-seon
Photography: Kim Hak-seong
Editing: Kim Hui-su
Music: Kim Seong-tae
Cast: Choi Mu-ryong (Young-ho), Kim Jin-gyu (Chul-ho), Seo Ae-ja, Kim Hye-jeong, Noh Jae-shin, Moon Jeong-sook, Yoon Il-bong
Running Time: 106'

SARANGBANG SONNIM-KWA OMONI THE GUEST AND MY MOTHER 1961
Director: Shin Sang-ok
Production: Shin Sang-okk
Screenplay: Lim Hee-jae
Photography: Choi Su-young
Editing: Yang Seong-nam
Music: Jeong Yun-ju
Cast:: Kim Jin-kyu (Han), Choi Eun-hee (widow), Jeon Young-seon (daughter), Han Eun-jin (mother-in-law)
Running Time: 103'

KOROSHI NO RAKUIN BRANDED TO KILL 1967
Director: Suzuki Seijun
Production: Iwai Kaneo, Mizunoe Takiko
Screenplay: Hachiro Guru
Photography: Nagatsuka Kazue
Editing: Tanji Matsuo
Music: Yamamoto Naozumi
Cast: Shishido Jo (Hanada Goro), Ogawa Mariko (Hanada Mami), Annu Mari (Misako), Nambara Koji (Number One), Tamagawa Isao (Yabuhara Michihiko), Minami Hiroshi (Kasuga Gihei)
Running Time: 98'

AI NO CORRIDA IN THE REALM OF THE SENSES 1976
Director: Oshima Nagisa
Production: Anatole Dauman
Screenplay: Oshima Nagisa
Photography: Itoh Hideo
Editing: Uraoka Keiichi, Patrick Sauvion
Music: Miki Minoru
Cast: Eiko Matsuda (Sada), Tatsuya Fuji (Kichizo)
Running Time: 108'

SALINNABILEUL GGOTNEUN YEOJA KILLER BUTTERFLY 1978
Director: Kim Ki-young
Production: Jeong Jin-woo
Screenplay: Lee Mun-woong
Photography: Lee Sung-chun
Editing: Kim Hee-su
Music: Han Sang-ki
Cast: Kim Jung-chol, Kim Man, Kim Cha-ok
Running Time: 110'

HIMATSURI FIRE FESTIVAL 1984
Director: Yanagimachi Mitsuo
Production: Shimizu Kazuo
Screenplay: Nakagami Kenji
Photography: Tamura Masaki
Editing: Yamaji Sachiko
Music: Takemitsu Toru
Cast: Kitaoji Kinya (Tatsuo), Taichi Kiwako (Kimiko), Nakamoto Ryota (Ryota), Miki Norihei (Yamakawa), Yasuoka Rikiya (Toshio), Miyashita Junko (Sachiko, Tatsuo's wife), Sugai Kin (Tatsuo's mother), Matsushita Sachiko (Tatsuo's sister), Yagi Masako (Tatsuo's sister)
Running Time: 120'

SONO OTOKO, KYOBO NI TSUKI VIOLENT COP 1989
Director: Kitano Takeshi
Production: Nabeshima Hisao, Yoshida Takio, Ichiyama Shozo
Screenplay: Nozawa Hisashi
Photography: Sasakibara Yasushi
Editing: Kamiya Nobutake
Music: Kume Daisaku
Cast: Kitano Takeshi (Azuma), Hakuryu (Kiyohiro), Kawakami Maiko (Akari), Ashikawa Makoto (Kikuchi), Sano Shiro (Police Chief Yoshinari), Hiraizumi Shigeru (Iwaki), Otonashi Mikiko (Iwaki's Wife), Kishibe Ittoku (Nito)
Running Time: 103'

TETSUO THE IRON MAN 1988 / **TETSUO 2** TETSUO 2: BODY HAMMER 1992
Director: Tsukamoto Shinya
Production: Kurokawa Fumio, Takeuchi Nobuo
Screenplay: Tsukamoto Shinya
Photography: Tsukamoto Shinya
Editing: Tsukamoto Shinya
Music: Chu Ishikawa
Cast: Tsukamoto Shinya('The Salaryman'), Taguchi Tomorowo, Kim Sujin
Running Time: 83'

SOPYEONJE SOPYONJE 1993
Director: Im Kwon-taek
Production: Lee Tae-won
Screenplay: Kim Myung-gon, based on short stories by Lee Chung-joon
Photography: Jung Il-sung
Editing: Park Soon-duk
Music: Kim Soo-chul
Cast: Kim Myung-gon (Yu-bong), Oh Jung-hae (Song-hwa), Kim Kyu-chul (Dong-ho)

Running Time: 112'

PERFECT BLUE 1997
Director: Kon Satoshi
Production: Okamoto Koichi
Screenplay: Murai Sadayuki
Photography: Shirai Hisao
Editing: Ogata Harutoshi
Music: Ikumi Masahiro
Cast: Iwao Junko (Mima), Matsumoto Rica (Rumi)
Running Time: 81'

KANGWON-DO UI HIM THE POWER OF KANGWON PROVINCE 1998
Director: Hong Sang-soo
Production: Ahn Byeong-ju
Screenplay: Hong Sang-soo
Photography: Kim Young-cheol
Editing: Ham Seong-won
Music: Won Il
Cast: Oh Yoon-hong (Ji-sook), Baek Jong-hak (Sang-kwon), Im Sun-young (Mi-sun), Park Hyun-young (Eun-kyoung), Chun Jae-hyun (Jae-woon), Kim Yoo-suk (The Policeman)
Running Time: 109'

INJONG SAJONG BOLGEOT EOBDA NOWHERE TO HIDE 1999
Director: Lee Myeong-se
Production: Chung Tae-won
Screenplay: Lee Myeong-se
Photography: Jeong Kwang-seok, Song Haeng-ki
Editing: Go Im Pyo
Music: Cho Sung-woo
Cast: Park Joong-hoon (Woo), Jang Dong-gun (Kim), Ahn Sung-ki (Sung-min Chang), Choi Ji-woo (Juyon)
Running Time: 112'

SUMGYOL MY OWN BREATHING 1999
Director: Byun Yongjoo
Production: Shin Hyeeun
Screenplay: Byun Yongjoo
Photography: Byun Yongjoo
Editing: Park uokji
Cast: Lee Yongsu
Running Time: 78'

ÔDITION AUDITION 2000
Director: Miike Takashi
Production: Suyama Akemi, Fukushima Satoshi, Yokohama Toyoyuki
Screenplay: Tengan Daisuke
Photography: Yamamoto Hideo
Editing: Shimamura Yasushi
Music: Endô Kôji
Cast: Shiina Eihi (Asami), Ishibashi Ryo (Aoyama), Kunimura Jun (Yoshikawa), Sawaki Tetsu (Shigehiko), Matsuda Miyuki (Ryoko), Ishibashi Renji (Shimada)
Running Time: 115'

SEOM THE ISLE 2000
Director: Kim Ki-duk
Production: Lee Eun
Screenplay: Kim Ki-duk
Photography: Hwang Suh-shik
Editing: Kyoung Min-ho
Music: Jeon Sang-yoon
Cast: Suh Jung (Hee-jin), Kim Yoo-suk (Hyun-shik), Park Sung-hee (Eun-a), Cho Jae-hyung (Mang-chee), Jang Hang-sun (Middle-aged Man).
Running Time: 90'

DAEHAKNO-YESEO MAECHOON-HADAKA TOMAKSALHAE DANGHAN YEOGOSAENG AJIK DAEHAKNO-YE ISSDA TEENAGE HOOKER BECAME KILLING MACHINE IN DAEHAKNO 2000
Director: Nam Gee-woong
Production: Woon Ki-jin
Screenplay: Nam Gee-woong
Photography: Nam Gee-woong
Editing: Lee Chang-Man, Nam Ki-woong
Music: Nam Gee-woong
Cast: Lee So-woon (teenage girl), Kim Dae-tong (teacher), Bae Soo-baek ("spottie" brother 1), Kim Ho-kyum ("spottie" brother 2), Yang Hyuk-joon ("spottie" brother 3), Yoo Joon-za (old woman)
Running Time: 60'

BATORU ROWAIARU BATTLE ROYALE 2000
Director: Fukasaku Kinji
Production: Kayama Tetsu, Kamatani Akio, Sato Masao
Screenplay: Fukasaku Kenta
Photography: Yanagijima Katsumi
Editing: Abe Hirohide
Music: Amano Masamichi
Cast: Fujiwara Tatsuya (Nanahara Shuya), Maeda Aki (Nakagawa Noriko), Yamamoto Taro (Kawada Shogo), Ando Masanobu (Kiriyama Kazuo), Shibaski Kou (Souma Mitsuko) Kitano 'Beat' Takeshi (Kitano)
Running Time: 114'

KONGDONG KONGBI GUYOK JOINT SECURITY AREA 2000
Director: Pak Chan-wook
Production: Yi Un, Sim Chae-myong
Screenplay: Kim Hyun-sok, Yi Mu-yung, Chong Song-san, Pak Chan-wook
Photography: Kim Song-bok
Editing: Kim Sang-bom
Music: Cho Yung-wook, Bang Jun-sok
Cast: Yi Young-ae (Major Sophie Jean), Song Kang-ho (Sgt Oh Kyongpil), Yi Pyonh-on (Sgt Lee Soo-yeok), Sin Hag-yu (Jeong Woo-jin), Ulrich Herbert (Swedish officer), Christoph Hofrichter (Swiss officer)
Running Time: 110'

BIBLIOGRAPHY

GENERAL WORKS

50 ans d'Archives du Film/50 Years of Film Archives (1988). Brussels: FIAF.

Anderson, B. (1991) *Imagined Communities: Reflections on the Origin and Spread of Nationalism.* London: Verso.

Bhabba, H. (1990) 'Introduction: Narrating the Nation', in H. K. Bhabba (ed.) *Nation and Narration.* London: Routledge.

Cherchi Usai, P. (2000) *Silent Cinema: An Introduction.* London: British Film Institute.

Hjort, M. and S. Mckenzie (eds) *Cinema and Nation.* New York: Routledge.

Lau, J. (ed.) (2003) *Multiple Modernities: Cinemas and Popular Media in Transcultural East Asia.* Philadelphia: Temple University Press.

Lent, J. (1990) *The Asian Film Industry.* Austin: University of Austin Press.

McClintock, A. (1995) *Imperial Leather: Race, Gender and Sexuality in the Colonial Contest.* New York: Routledge.

Riotto, M. (1993) *Chronologie: Cinéma, Culture et Société. Le Cinéma corén, sous la direction d'Ariano Aprá.* Paris: Editions du Centre Pompidou.

Sato, T. (1995) *Encyclopedia of Asian Cinema.* Yamagata: Japan.

Shohat, E. (1997) 'Gender and the Culture of Emprire: Toward a Feminist Ethnography of the Cinema', in M. Bertstein and G. Studlar (eds) *Visions of the East: Orientalism in Film.* New Brunswick: Rutgers University Press.

Zito, A. (1994) 'Silk and Skin: Significant Boundaries in Body Subject and Power in China' in Zito, A and T. E. Barlow (eds) *Body, Subject and Power in China.* Chicago and London: University of Chicago Press.

JAPAN

Anderson, J. L. and D. Richie (1982) *The Japanese Film: Art and Industry* (expanded edition). Princeton: Princeton University Press.

Andrew, D. and P. Andrew (1981) *Kenji Mizoguchi: A Guide to References and Resources.* Boston: G. K. Hall.

Barrett, G. (1989) *Archetypes in Japanese Film: The Sociopolitical and Religious Significance of the Principal Heroes and Heroines.* Selingsgrove: Susquehanna University Press.

Bock, A. (1989) *Japanese Film Directors.* Tokyo: Kodansha.

Bordwell, D. (1988) *Ozu and the Poetics of Cinema.* Princeton: Princeton University Press.

Buehrer, B. B. (1990) *Japanese Films: A Bibliography and Commentary, 1921–1989.* Jefferson: McFarland.

Burch, N. (1979) *To the Distant Observer: Form and Meaning in the Japanese Cinema.* Berkeley:

University of California Press.

Buruma, I. (1984) *Behind the Mask: On Sexual Demons, Sacred Mothers, Transvestites, Gangsters, Drifters and Other Japanese Cultural Heroes*. New York: Pantheon.

Ching, L. (2001) *Becoming 'Japanese': Colonial Taiwan and the Politics of Identity Formation*. Berkeley: University of California Press.

Clements, J. and H. McCarthy (2001) *The Anime Encyclopedia: A Guide to Japanese Animation Since 1917*. Berkeley: Stone Bridge Press.

Desser, D. (1988) *Eros plus Massacre: An Introduction to the Japanese New Wave Cinema I*. Bloomington: Indiana University Press.

____ (1983) *The Samurai Films of Akira Kurosawa*. Ann Arbor: UMI Research Press.

Dissanayake, W. (ed.) (1988) *Cinema and Cultural Identity: Reflections on Films from Japan, India, and China*. Lanham, MD: University Presses of America.

____ (ed.) (1993) *Melodrama and Asian Cinema*. New York: Cambridge University Press.

____ (ed.) (1994) *Colonialism and Nationalism in Asian Cinema*. Bloomington: Indiana University Press.

Erens, P. (1979) *Akira Kurosawa: A Guide to References and Resources*. Boston: G. K. Hall.

Frieberg, F. (1997) '*China Nights*: The Sustaining Romance of Japan at War', in J. W. Chambers and D. Cuthbert (eds) *World War Two: Film and History*. Oxford: Oxford University Press.

Gailbraith, S. (2001) *The Emperor and the Wolf*. London: Faber.

Gillette, J. and D. Wilson (eds) (1976) *Yasujiro Ozu: A Critical Anthology*. London: British Film Institute.

Goodwin, J. (1994) *Akira Kurosawa and Intertextual Cinema*. Baltimore: Johns Hopkins University Press.

____ (1994) *Perspectives on Akira Kurosawa*. New York: G. K. Hall.

Hayashi, S. (2003) *Traveling Film History: Language and Landscape in the Japanese Cinema, 1931–1945*. Dissertation, University of Chicago.

High, P. (2003) *The Imperial Screen: Japanese Film Culture in the Fifteen Years' War, 1931–1945*. Madison: University of Wisconsin University Press.

McDonald, K. (1983) *Cinema East: A Critical Study of Major Japanese Films*. East Brunswick: Associated University Presses.

____ (1984) *Mizoguchi*. Boston: Twayne Publishers.

____ (2001) 'Saving the Children: Films by the Most "Casual" of Directors, Shimuzu Hiroshi' in D. Washburn and C. Cavanaugh (eds) *Word and Image in Japanese Cinema*. Cambridge University Press.

Mellen, Joan. (1975) *Voices from the Japanese Cinema*. New York: Liveright.

____ *The Waves at Genji's Door: Japan Through Its Cinema* (1974) New York: Pantheon.

Nolletti Jr, A. and D. David (1992) *Reframing Japanese Cinema*. Bloomington: Indiana University Press.

Novielli, M. F. Girola and B. Fornara (eds) (1999) *Yanagimachi Mitsuo*. Bergamo: Bergamo Film Meeting 99.

Oshima, N. (1992) *Cinema, Censorship and the State: the Writings of Nagisa Oshima, 1956–1978*.

Cambridge, MA: MIT Press.

Prince, S. (1999) *The Warrior's Cinema: The Cinema of Akira Kurosawa* (revised edition). Princeton: Princeton Univeersity Press.

Richie, Donald. (1971) *Japanese Cinema: Film Style and National Character.* Garden City: Anchor Press.

_____ (1974a) *The Japanese Movie* (revised edition). Tokyo: Kodansha, 1982.

_____ (1974b) *Ozu: His Life and Films.* Berkeley: University of California Press.

_____ (1984) *The Films of Akira Kurosawa* (revised edition). Berkeley: University of California Press.

_____ (1990) *Japanese Cinema: An Introduction.* New York: Oxford University Press.

Sato T. (1982) *Currents in Japanese Cinema*, trans. Gregory Barrett. Tokyo: Kodansha.

Svensson, A. (1971) *Japan: Screen Series.* New York: A.S. Barnes.

Tucker, R. (1973) *Japan: Film Image.* London: Studio Vista, 1973.

Vidal Estévez, M. (1992) *Akira Kurosawa.* Madrid: Ediciones Cáterdra.

Wada-Marciano, M. (2000) *The Production of Modernity in Japanese Cinema: Shochiku Kamata Style in the 1920s and 1930s.* Dissertation, Univeersity of Iowa.

Yomota, I. (ed.) (2001) *Ri Koran to Higashi Aga* (*Li Xianglan and East Asia*). Tokyo Daigaku Shuppankai.

Yoshimoto, M. (2000) *Japanese Cinema in Search of a Discipline: Kurosawa, Film Studies and Japanese Cinema.* Durham: Duke University Press.

KOREA

Ahn, B. (1987) 'Humour in Korean Cinema', *East-West Film Journal*, 2, 1.

An, J. 'The *Housemaid* and Troubled Masculinity in the 1960s', http://www.asianfilms.org/korea/kky/KKY/Window/AJS.htm

Ahn, M. 'Representing the Anxious Middle Class: Camera Movement, Sound, and Color in *The Housemaid* and *Women of Fire*', http://www.asianfilms.org/korea/kky/KKY/Stairway/AMH.htm

Armstrong, C.K. (2002) 'The Origins of North Korean Cinema: Art and Propaganda in the Democratic People's Republic', *Acta Koreana* 5, 1.

Bae, C. (1988) 'Seoul In Korean Cinema: A Brief Survey', *East-West Film Journal* 3, 1.

Berry, C. 'Genrebender: Kim Ki-young Mixes It Up', http://www.asianfilms.org/korea/kky/KKY/Stairway/CB2.htm

_____ 'Kim Ki-young and the Critical Economy of the Globalized Art-House Cinema', http://www.asianfilms.org/korea/kky/KKY/What-Saw/CB1.htm

_____ (1999) 'My Queer Korea: Identity, Space and the 1998 Seoul Queer Film and Video Festival', *Intersections*, 2.

_____ (2003) 'What's Big about the Big Film?: "De-Westernizing" the Blockbuster in Korea and China', in Julian Stringer (ed.) *Movie Blockbusters.* London: Routledge.

_____ 'When Too Much Is Never Enough: Analytic Excess in the Cinema of Kim Ki-young', www.asianfilms.org/korea/kky/KKY/Stairway/CB3.htm

Choi, C. (1998) *Nationalism and Construction of Gender in Korea* in E. H. Kim and C. Choi (eds) *Dangerous Women: Gender and Korean Nationalism*. New York: Routledge.

Choi, E. S. 'Forbidden Desire and the Fantastic: *Killer Butterfly*', http://www.asianfilms.org/korea/kky/KKY/Window/CES.htm

Choi, E. Y. 'A Feast of Opposing Colors: *Iodo*', http://www.asianfilms.org/korea/kky/KKY/Stairway/CEY.htm

Choi, H. C. 'Capitalist Controls on Mass Media in Korea', *Korea Studies in Media Arts*, http://www.mykima.com/docs/capitalist_controls_on_mass_media.pdf

Chung, H. S. (2001) 'From Saviors to Rapists: G.I.s, Women, and Children in Korean War Films', *Asian Cinema*, 12, 1.

Copola, A. (2002) *Korean Cinema: Story of a Revelation*, www.filmfestivals.com.

Curnette, R. (2002) 'Passages of Time: Motifs of Past, Present, Future in Contemporary Korean Films', *Film Journal*, 1, 2.

Diffrient, D. S. (2003) 'South Korean Film Genres and Art-House Anti-Poetics: Erasure and Negation in *The Power of Kangwon Province*', *CineAction*, 60.

Gateward, F. (2003) *Korean Cinema (Images of Asia)*. Oxford: Oxford University Press.

Huh, C. (1989) 'Anatomy of the Korean Film Industry', *Koreana* 3, 4.

Hummel, V. (2003) Interview with Kim Ki-Duk, *Senses of Cinema*. http://www.sensesofcinema.com/contents/01/19/kim_ki-duk.html.

Hyun, D. (2001) 'Renaissance of Korean Film Industry', *Asian Cinema*, 12, 2.

James, D. E. (2001) 'Im Kwon-Taek: Korean National Cinema and Buddhism', *Film Quarterly* 54, 2.

_____ (2002) 'Opening the Channels of Communication: An Interview with Film Director Park Kwang Su', *Korean Culture* 23, 2.

James, D. E. and H. K. Kyung (eds.) (2002) *Im Kwon-Taek: The Making of a Korean National Cinema*. Detroit: Wayne State University Press.

Kim, C. (1993) 'The Problems of describing the early Korean film history and a redefinition of the beginning of Korean Film', *Korean Cinema Critiques*, 5.

Kim, S. (2001) *Spectres of Modernity*. Korean Cinema Project, The Japan Foundation Forum: 22–8.

Kim, S. and C. Berry (2000) 'Suri suri masuri: The Magic of the Korean Horror Film – A Conversation', *Postcolonial Studies* 3, 1.

Knoll, C. (2003) 'Unlikely Direction: Kim Ki Duk's got a different direction for Korean Cinema', *Koream Journal* (October), 64–7.

Koh, H. H. (2001) '*Chunhyang*: Bringing a classic Korean art form to film', *Persimmon: Asian Literature, Arts, and Culture*, 2, 2.

Kwak, H. J. (2003) 'Discourse on Modernisation in 1990s Korean Cinema', in J. K. W. Lau (ed.) *Multiple Modernities: Cinemas and Popular Media in Transcultural East Asia*. Philadelphia: Temple University Press.

LaCapra, D. (2001) *Writing History, Writing Trauma*. Baltimore and London: John Hopkins University Press.

Lee, H. (1997) 'A Peculiar Sensation: A Personal Genealogy of Korean American Women's

Cinema (Race in Contemporary American Cinema, part 8)', *Cineaste*, 23, 1.

Lee, H. (2000a) 'Ch'unhyangjon: Gender, Class and the Past in Post-War Korean Cinema', *The Review of Korean Studies*, 3, 2.

____ (2000b) *Contemporary Korean Cinema: Culture, Identity and Politics*. Manchester: Manchester University Press.

____ (2000c) 'Cinema and Construction of Nationhood in Contemporary Korea', *The Journal of Asiatic Studies*, 43, 2.

____ (2000d) 'Conflicting Working Class Identities in North Korean Cinema', *Korea Journal*, 40, 3.

____ (2001) *Contemporary Korean Cinema: Identity, Culture, Politics*. Manchester: Manchester University Press.

Lee, Y. (1997) 'Mapping the Korean Film Industry', *Cinemaya*, 37.

____ (1998) *The History of Korean Cinema: Main Current of Korean Cinema* (Translated by Richard Lynn Greever). Seoul: Motion Picture Promotion Corporation.

____ (2000) 'Three Readings: One Text. Im Kwon-taek's *Chunhyang*', *Cinemaya: The Asian Film Quarterly*, 49, 17–19.

Lent, J. A. (1990) 'South Korea', in *The Asian Film Industry*. Austin: University of Texas Press.

Leong, A. C. Y. (2003)) *Korean Cinema: The New Hong Kong*. Victoria: Trafford Publishing.

Leong, T. H. (2000) 'Sex in Asian Cinema', *Kinema*, http://www.arts.uwaterloo.ca/FINE/juhde/kfall00.htm

McHugh, K. A. (2001) 'South Korean Film Melodrama and the Question of National Cinema', *Quarterly Review of Film and Video*, 18, 1.

Noh, K. W. (2001) 'Formation of Korean Film Industry under Japanese Occupation', *Asian Cinema*, 12, 2.

____ (2003) 'Transformation of Korean Film Industry During the U.S. Military Occupation Era (1945–1948)', *Asian Cinema*, 14, 2.

Pok, H. (1997) 'On Korean Documentary Film', *Documentary Box*, 10, http://www.city.yamagata.yamagata.jp/yidff/docbox/10/box10-3-e.html

Rayns, T. (1998) 'Cinephile Nation', *Sight and Sound* , 8, 1.

____ (1994) 'Korea's New Wavers', *Sight and Sound*, 4, 11.

____ (2000) 'Sexual Outlaws', *Sight and Sound*, 10, 2.

Rist, P. (1998) 'An Introduction to Korean Cinema', *Offscreen*, http://www.horschamp.qc.ca/offscreen

____ (2001) 'Neglected 'Classical' Periods: Hong Kong and Korean Cinemas of the 1960s', *Asian Cinema*, 12, 1.

Sato, T. (1991) 'Tradition and Transition: Im Kwon-Taek', *Cinemaya*, 12.

Shin, M. (2004) 'Block Bust of Boom? The Journey of the Korean Blockbuster', *Koream Journal*, 15, 2.